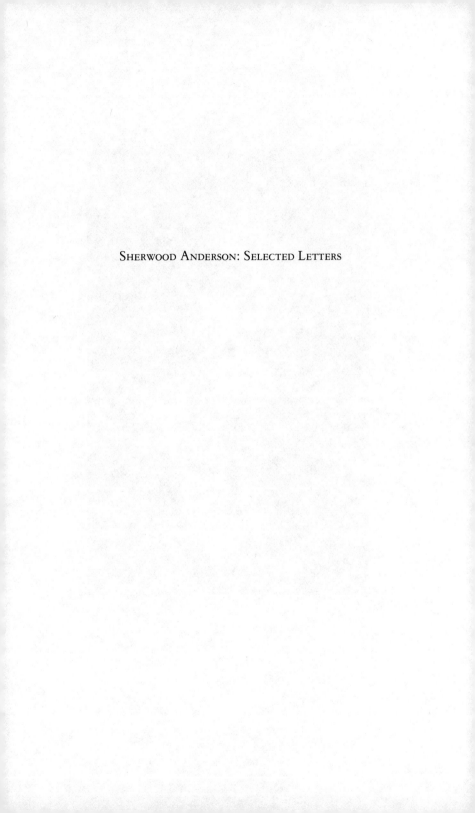

Sherwood Anderson: Selected Letters

Sherwood Anderson
Selected Letters

EDITED BY

CHARLES E. MODLIN

THE UNIVERSITY OF TENNESSEE PRESS

KNOXVILLE

Second printing, August 1984

The paper in this book meets the guidelines for permanence and durability
of the Committee on Production Guidelines for Book Longevity
of the Council on Library Resources.
Binding materials have been chosen for durability.

Frontispiece: Sherwood Anderson. COURTESY OF ELEANOR ANDERSON.

Library of Congress Cataloging in Publication Data

Anderson, Sherwood, 1876–1941.
Sherwood Anderson: selected letters.

1. Anderson, Sherwood, 1876–1941—Correspondence.
2. Authors, American—20th century—Correspondence.
I. Modlin, Charles E. II Title.
PS3501.N4Z48 1983 813′.52 [B] 83–6530
ISBN 0–87049–404–X

For my father, H. Eugene Modlin,
who, like Sherwood, loved life

Acknowledgments

I WISH TO THANK THE LIBRARIES which have given me access to their collections of Sherwood Anderson's letters and approved the publication of those included here. I am indebted to a great number of librarians who have generously provided me with their services.

I am grateful to the Newberry Library for a fellowship that enabled me to begin my work, and to the Department of English, Virginia Polytechnic Institute and State University, for many forms of aid along the way.

These persons have made important contributions to this book: Hilbert H. Campbell, Charles Haney, Diana Haskell, Carol Orr, Marjorie Pryse, Walter B. Rideout, Welford D. Taylor, and G. Leota Williams. I owe a special debt to Eleanor Copenhaver Anderson, whose help and friendship have made it all possible. The letters in this volume appear with her kind permission. Finally, I thank my wife, Marjorie, and children, Andrew and Margaret, for their support from the time this project began during a memorable Bicentennial summer in Chicago.

Contents

Illustrations

Introduction

SHERWOOD ANDERSON regularly wrote in the morning and spent the afternoon at other pursuits—a routine that led the young William Faulkner in New Orleans to exclaim, "If this is what it takes to be a novelist, then that's the life for me."[1] The principle behind Anderson's schedule was to maintain a balance between the worlds of the imagination and experience. The writer, he insisted, must stay close to life and absorb its "flow." Anderson's morning of work ordinarily began with the writing of letters, an activity that functioned partly as a limbering-up of his writing skills but more importantly as a medium of communication with the world beyond his study. In helping to overcome the isolation with which he often felt afflicted, his correspondence served, like his afternoon activities, as an important complement to his work. Letters provided him a flexible means of expression in which he could choose his reader and move freely through a wide range of both literary and personal topics. The letters in this volume have been selected on the basis of their unusual interest in revealing Anderson's literary and personal concerns during the quarter-century between his first emergence as a writer in 1916 to shortly before his death in 1941.

Of particular literary interest are those letters dealing with his career as a writer. This volume begins with Anderson's soliciting the help of Henry Mencken and Theodore Dreiser in publishing his first book and eventually reaches a point where he has become, as he puts it in 1939, "a kind of Papa" to younger writers like John Steinbeck. Over the years, Anderson provides frequent remarks on his own works in progress, past accomplishments, and plans for the future. The letters comment extensively on his impressions of and relations with a great many of his fellow writers—including Hart Crane, F. Scott Fitzgerald, Ernest Hemingway, Carl Sandburg, Jean Toomer, and Thomas Wolfe—as well as critics, editors, and publishers, such as V. F. Calverton, Henry S. Canby, Ben Huebsch, Horace Liveright,

1. "Sherwood Anderson: An Appreciation," *Atlantic Monthly* 191 (June 1953): 29.

Maxwell Perkins, and Burton Rascoe. In these letters Anderson also discusses many of his own ideas about writing, especially his firm commitment, even in periods of failure and discouragement, to artistic integrity and his aversion to literary tricks and "slick" appeals to popular taste. An additional literary value of the letters is to be found in occasional passages which share the virtues of some of his published writings—effective vignettes, for example, of a boat ride up the Ohio River, a foxhound-calling competition in the Virginia mountains, a tense courtroom scene, a charming semifictional visit to his mother-in-law's birthplace. As annotations will indicate, Anderson did, in fact, use some of the material from his letters in his publications.

Personal references in the letters trace the important developments of Anderson's life, including his frustration with and ultimate break from the advertising business, his career as a newspaper editor, his involvement in social and political causes, his rediscovery of the pleasures of rural and small-town life, and his loves and friendships through the years. The letters provide insight into Anderson's relationships with close friends, such as his brother Karl, Laura Copenhaver, Jasper Deeter, Charles H. ("Andy") Funk, Lewis Galantière, Ferdinand Schevill, and Roger Sergel. In a large group of letters, Anderson, frequently caught between financial insecurity and a need to be independent, reveals his difficulty with the patronage extended to him by his wealthy friends Burton and Mary Emmett. Anderson also makes candid observations on various family matters, including his touching renewal of ties with his dying brother Earl in 1926, his re-establishment of relations with his children as they matured (he became especially close to John), the breakup of his first three marriages, and the happy success of the fourth with Eleanor Copenhaver Anderson.

The personality that emerges from Anderson's letters is an engaging one that sometimes surprised even his friends, for he was usually able to convey his feelings and ideas more effectively in writing than in person. Maxwell Perkins, after reading Anderson's letters to Van Wyck Brooks published in 1943, observed that they were "fine and revealing" and "In some ways . . . make me think more highly of Sherwood than he himself did."[2] Burton Emmett, who collected a large number of Anderson's literary manuscripts, wrote to him in praise of his letter of 17 April 1930 and remarked, "I often feel as if your letters are the most wonderful of all my Sherwood Anderson things.

2. *Editor to Author,* ed. John Hall Wheelock (New York: Scribner's, 1979), 224. Perkins refers to "Sherwood Anderson: Letters to Van Wyck Brooks," in *The Shock of Recognition,* ed. Edmund Wilson (Garden City, N.Y.: Doubleday, 1943), 1254–90, originally published in *Story* 19 (Sept.–Oct. 1941): 42–62.

They are a part of Life in a way that no 'collector's item,' a first edition or a manuscript can be." Anderson himself wrote of his excitement with letters such as those of Vincent Van Gogh that were "so terribly close to all life." Because of their immediacy in capturing the spirit of the moment, Anderson's letters present him in a great variety of moods ranging from jocularity to deepest gloom; predominant, however, is a quality that Anderson himself aptly called a "poetic fervor for life." Writing to Miriam Phillips in November 1935, he characteristically marvels at "this damn fascinating thing . . . life": "Jesus, even at its worst, I wish sometimes I could have a thousand years of it." As his correspondence clearly shows, Anderson's fascination with the challenges of his work and the restless adventure of his life persisted to the end.

Most of the letters in this volume are here published for the first time. A few exceptions have appeared in works not principally concerned with Anderson.[3] None is duplicated in the principal publications of Anderson's letters.[4] The only previous major edition, *Letters of Sherwood Anderson,* published 401 letters of high quality, selected almost totally from the collection of the Newberry Library, which, as Howard Mumford Jones and Walter B. Rideout note, "is so rich that another equally interesting volume might have been assembled . . ." (p. xix). The present volume, however, includes not only some excellent letters from the Newberry for which there was no room in *Letters* but also many others that were not available earlier, including recent acquisitions, such as the Harry Hansen letters, and some "reserved" correspondence which, until its release in 1975, could not be published. While the Newberry's collection of over 5,000 of Anderson's letters is imposing and provides the nucleus of the present selection, many other libraries have significant smaller holdings. This volume, in fact, is greatly strengthened by the inclusion of important letters from twenty-three additional libraries. Access to private collections

3. For example, the letters to Upton Sinclair and F. Scott Fitzgerald have appeared, respectively, in *My Lifetime in Letters,* ed. Upton Sinclair (Columbia: Univ. of Missouri Press, 1960), 152–55, and *Correspondence of F. Scott Fitzgerald,* ed. Matthew J. Bruccoli and Margaret M. Duggan (New York: Random, 1980), 127–28.

4. "A Selection of Letters," *The Portable Sherwood Anderson,* ed. Horace Gregory (New York: Viking, 1949), 584–631; *Letters of Sherwood Anderson,* ed. Howard Mumford Jones in association with Walter B. Rideout (Boston: Little, Brown, 1953); "Letters to Van Wyck Brooks" and "Letters from Sherwood Anderson" in *Homage to Sherwood Anderson,* ed. Paul P. Appel (Mamaroneck, N.Y.: Appel, 1970), 63–97, 193–212; *Sherwood Anderson/Gertrude Stein: Correspondence and Personal Essays,* ed. Ray Lewis White (Chapel Hill: Univ. of North Carolina Press, 1972); *Sherwood Anderson: Centennial Studies,* ed. Hilbert H. Campbell and Charles E. Modlin (Troy, N.Y.: Whitston, 1976), 1–60.

has also made possible the inclusion of a few letters—an important series to Arthur Barton for example—which are here made public for the first time.

The editing of this volume is intended to provide a clear, readable text. Obvious slips of the pen, misspellings, and grossly aberrant punctuation have been silently corrected. A few additions of words omitted in the original text or alternate readings of problematic passages are supplied in brackets. Commas have occasionally been added for clarity. All letters are complete; where ellipsis periods occur, they are Anderson's, meant to provide pauses. All page references in footnotes to Anderson's published works are to the original editions, with the exception of the *Memoirs,* citations to which refer to the Ray L. White edition of 1969.

Letter headings include the date and location of each, with information not supplied by Anderson himself included in brackets. At the end of each letter is the abbreviation "MS" or "TS," signifying manuscript or typescript, followed by an abbreviation for the location of the original letter, and sometimes an additional designation in parentheses—"cc" for carbon copy or "ph" for photocopy. Abbreviations for letter collections are as follows:

AAA	Jerome Blum Papers, Archives of American Art, Smithsonian Institution, Washington, D.C.
Ark.	John Gould Fletcher Papers, University of Arkansas Library, Fayetteville
Boston	Hedgerow Theatre Collection, Boston University Libraries, Boston, Mass.
Cal.	The Bancroft Library, University of California, Berkeley
Camden	Eleanor I. Jones Archives, Camden Public Library, Camden, Ohio
Columbia	Lewis Galantière Papers and Granville Hicks Papers, Rare Book and Manuscript Library, Columbia University, New York.
Cornell	Cornell University Library, Ithaca, N.Y.
Fisk	Fisk University Library, Nashville, Tenn.
Harvard	Houghton Library, Harvard University, Cambridge, Mass.
Ill.	University of Illinois Library, Urbana-Champaign
Ind.	The Lilly Library, Indiana University, Bloomington
Kennedy	Hemingway Collection, John F. Kennedy Library, Boston, Mass.
LC	Library of Congress, Washington, D.C.

NC	Burton Emmett Papers, Southern Historical Collection, University of North Carolina Library, Chapel Hill
NL	Newberry Library, Chicago, Ill.
NYPL	Henry L. Mencken Papers and Victor F. Calverton Papers, Rare Books and Manuscripts Division, The New York Public Library, Astor, Lenox and Tilden Foundations, New York.
NYU	Fales Library, New York University, New York.
PC	private collection
Penn.	Rare Book Collection, Charles Patterson Van Pelt Library, University of Pennsylvania, Philadelphia
Princeton	John Peale Bishop Collection, F. Scott Fitzgerald Papers, and Charles Scribner's Sons Archive, Princeton University Library, Princeton, N.J.
Smith	The Sophia Smith Collection, Smith College, Northampton, Mass.
SHSW	August Derleth Papers, The State Historical Society of Wisconsin, Madison
Texas	Humanities Research Center, University of Texas, Austin
Va.	Sherwood Anderson Papers, Clifton Waller Barrett Library, University of Virginia, Charlottesville.
Yale	Beinecke Rare Book and Manuscript Library, Yale University, New Haven, Conn.

Chronology

1876	Born 13 Sept. in Camden, Ohio, third of six children of Irwin M. and Emma Smith Anderson.
1884	Family moves to Clyde, Ohio.
1895	His mother dies.
1896 or 1897	Moves to Chicago, works as laborer.
1898–1899	Serves in U.S. Army during Spanish-American War.
1899–1900	Attends Wittenberg Academy, Springfield, Ohio.
1900	Begins work for advertising firm in Chicago.
1904	Marries Cornelia Lane.
1906	Moves to Cleveland to become head of mail-order business.
1907	Moves to Elyria, Ohio, becomes head of paint company; birth of first son, Robert Lane Anderson.
1908	Birth of second son, John Sherwood Anderson.
1911	Birth of daughter, Marion Anderson.
1912	Has nervous breakdown, 28 Nov.
1913	Moves to Chicago in Feb., resumes advertising work.
1914	Begins publishing stories.
1916	Divorced from Cornelia Anderson; marries Tennessee Mitchell; *Windy McPherson's Son* (Lane).
1917	*Marching Men* (Lane).
1918	Lives in New York during fall; *Mid-American Chants* (Lane).
1919	*Winesburg, Ohio* (Huebsch).
1920	Lives in Mobile and Fairhope, Ala.; moves to Palos Park, Chicago suburb, in fall; *Poor White* (Huebsch).
1921	Visits Europe during summer; receives award from *Dial; The Triumph of the Egg* (Huebsch).
1922	Lives in New Orleans during winter; moves to New York in August.
1923	Moves to Reno, Nev., in February; *Many Marriages* and *Horses and Men* (Huebsch).

1924 Divorced from Tennessee Mitchell; marries Elizabeth Prall; moves to New Orleans in July; *A Story Teller's Story* (Huebsch).

1925 Quits Huebsch, joins Liveright publishers in April; spends part of summer in Troutdale, Va.; travels on lecture tour; *Dark Laughter* (Boni and Liveright).

1926 Travels on lecture tour; moves to Troutdale, builds house at Ripshin Farm; leaves for Europe in December; *Sherwood Anderson's Notebook* and *Tar: A Midwest Childhood* (Boni and Liveright).

1927 Returns from Europe in March; receives honorary doctorate at Wittenberg; buys two weekly newspapers at Marion, Va.; *A New Testament* (Boni and Liveright).

1929 Extensive travel; *Hello Towns!* (Liveright).

1931 Travel; *Perhaps Women* (Liveright).

1932 Travel; divorced from Elizabeth Prall Anderson; to Amsterdam in August to attend peace conference; *Beyond Desire* (Liveright).

1933 Spends winter in Kansas City; marries Eleanor Copenhaver; to New York in fall; *Death in the Woods* (Liveright).

1934 Travel for *Today* magazine; dramatic version of *Winesburg, Ohio* presented at Hedgerow Theatre; *No Swank* (Centaur).

1935 Visits Corpus Christi, Tex., in winter; *Puzzled America* (Scribner).

1936 Trip to Southwest during winter; *Kit Brandon* (Scribner).

1937 To Corpus Christi in winter, violently ill there; attends writers' conference in Boulder, Colo.; *Plays, Winesburg and Others* (Scribner).

1938 Trip to Southwest and Mexico in winter.

1939 In winter revisits Clyde, lectures at Olivet College in Michigan; to California in fall.

1940 Lives in New York much of year; *Home Town* (Alliance Book Corp.).

1941 Begins trip to South America 28 Feb.; death from peritonitis, 8 March, at Colón, Panama; buried at Marion, Va.

Letters of Sherwood Anderson

TO Henry Mencken[1]

4 January 1916, Chicago

Dear Mr. Mencken:

I have your letter of recent date and I was afraid the Elmer Cowley story[2] would not fit *Smart Set*.

I hadn't much sense of the magazine world and so have to offer the stories blind and have had no success with New York agents. Of course, it should not be true that *Smart Set* readers are limited in their outlook and if a story is close enough to life it should be good enough for any magazine. However, that opens a field of discussion into which I know you don't care to go.

I am today asking Mr. Dell[3] to send you the manuscript of the novel *Windy McPherson's Son*. I am going to ask you to read it and I am going to ask Dreiser to read it. My experience with my novels has been that the publishers say they like them themselves but are afraid the readers won't like them. If I could get you and Dreiser to read the novel it may be a big help to me. If you think it first-class work you might be able to say a word to the publisher that would help put it over and win my eternal gratitude.

I am going to send the novel to John Lane Co.[4]

You may be sure I will have *Smart Set* in mind. I have a bunch of short stories that are packed away and will get them out the first opportunity and see if there are not some of them in the mood of the one you published.

I am unable to express my gratitude for the interest you are taking in my stuff.

Yours very truly,
Sherwood Anderson

TS. NYPL

1. Then editor, with George Jean Nathan, of *Smart Set*, which published Anderson's "The Story Writers" in its Jan. 1916 issue, 243–48.

2. "Queer," published in *Seven Arts* 1 (Dec. 1916): 97–108, and later in *Winesburg, Ohio*.

3. Floyd Dell, an editor of *Masses* in New York and formerly the literary editor of the Chicago *Evening Post*.

4. An English firm, which published the book in September.

TO Theodore Dreiser

10 January 1916, Chicago

Dear Mr. Dreiser:

I am addressing you on a matter in which you might not be much interested but which is tremendously interesting to me.

Someone once told me of the difficulty you have had with publishers so perhaps you will sympathize with me.

I want to ask you to read one of my novels. There is one that I am sending to John Lane Company and I have asked Mr. Mencken of *Smart Set* to look it over. When he has done this I am going to ask you to take a look at this book also.

I know, of course, that you will not have to wade through the entire book in order to decide whether or not I have the merit that might warrant you throwing some of your established influence to helping to put this book over with John Lane.[1]

I have written four long novels and none of them have been published.

I am nearing forty years of age and the big load of doing a long novel each year also giving eight hours a day to business is beginning to tell on me. There is a lot of work ahead that I want to do and I want to begin getting publication.

I realize that when you read *Windy McPherson's Son* it may not seem to you to merit any support that you might be able to give it and if it does not seem worthwhile to you I shall not be annoyed. Surely we who write should under any circumstances reserve our privilege of judgment.

If all this seems an imposition on you don't do it, Dreiser. I only make bold to approach you on account of the indication of friendliness that you have already shown toward me on one or two occasions.

Yours very truly,
Sherwood Anderson

P. S. The book in question is in Mencken's hands and I am asking him to turn it over to you. 735 Cass St., Chicago.

TS. Penn.

1. Lane had published Dreiser's *The Titan* (1914) and *The "Genius"* (1915).

TO Upton Sinclair[1]

12 December 1916, Chicago

My dear Sinclair:

Your letter set me thinking. It was a cold snowy afternoon in Chicago. I left my office at four and started to walk home across the city. A man with a withered hand ran down a stairway out of a tenement. He had no overcoat and his clothes were thin. The blue veins on the back of the withered hand were ghastly blue. He saw me looking and stared into my eyes. His lips mumbled words.

A middle aged policeman came along the street. A young girl came out of an office. The cold made her cheeks glow. She was alive with life and something in the stolid figure of the policeman tempted her. Their eyes met and he stopped and stared. He perhaps had a wife and family at home but he was stirred by the sight of the young girl who was not unwilling to flirt with him. His lips also mumbled words.

And so I went along seeing things and thinking. I also muttered words. I kept thinking of you and what you had said to me about socialists.

Man, you seem to see and feel them as things apart. You ask me to pity and understand socialists as you might ask me to understand the Arabs or the Chinese.

Truth is, Sinclair, I'm married to a socialist[2] and when I vote I vote that ticket myself but if I thought the fact of my doing so set me apart in the way your letter suggests I'd quit in a hurry.

Really I'm tempted to go at you hard in this matter. There is something terrible to me in the thought of the art of writing being bent and twisted to serve the end of propaganda. Why should we as writers be primarily socialists or conservatives, or anarchists, or anything else.

Here is all America teeming with life that we haven't begun to really cut into or to understand. We aren't making our fellows understand it. It's wrong, man, terribly wrong.

Here is this man I shall go to lunch with tomorrow. He is rich, is piling up more riches daily. And he is becoming brutalized. Dimly he knows it. He wants to know about himself. God, he don't want me to preach at him.

I have a book coming next year called *Marching Men*. I hope you will read it and like it. But it also finds nothing of great value to the world in the socialists. My man McGregor meets and knows socialists. At one place he cries out to his marching men, "If men preach at you from a box knock them down and keep on marching."

Sinclair, your letter was something like a cry to me. Can I not get into this letter the beginning of a cry to you?

I do so want to see writers quit this drawing themselves apart, becoming socialists, or conservatives or whatnot. I want them to stay in life. I want them to be something of [a] brother to the poor brute who runs the sweatshop as well as to the equally unfortunate brutes who work for him.

Won't we serve better thus? We are so terribly young. We haven't even begun to understand our own American life. As writers can't we leave politics and economics to the more lusty throated ones and run away, one by one, into the streets, the offices and the houses—looking at things—trying to write them down.

Damn it, you have made me go on like a propagandist. You should be ashamed of yourself. Come see me won't you when a wind blows you this way.

Very truly yours,
Sherwood Anderson

TS. Ind.

1. Author of *The Jungle* (1906) and many other novels and essays. Sinclair explains in *Money Writes!* (1931) that he had read *Windy McPherson's Son* with enthusiasm and wrote Anderson "to make a Socialist out of him" (113).

2. Tennessee Mitchell, Anderson's second wife. They were married on 31 July 1916, following his divorce from Cornelia Lane Anderson.

TO Carl Sandburg
[April 1917, Chicago]

My dear Sandburg—

I think of course that no attempt should be made to express in the form of a poem what could possibly be expressed in prose. Am I right in this. Some time ago I wrote a paper in which I proposed that the title "poet" be abolished. My thought was that to put that label on a man was a piece of rank injustice. Imagine if you can a man compelled to go through the world bearing the name of lover. Could one possibly love such a man?

Is it not true that a poem should be like a flash of lightning revealing a piece of meadow land, a pair of lovers standing by a fence, a tree "drowsing and sleeping on the shoulders of the running waters"?[1]

Best of all I like "Loam." I like also "Adelaide Crapsey," "Fire-Logs," "Prairie Waters by Night," & "In Tall Grass."

I like, but not so well, "Early Moon."

I can't help thinking that things like "Alix" and "Street Window" belong to prose. Perhaps when I have read them over several times I will catch the music in them.

Oh I like "Loam" damn well.

Anderson

TS. Ill.

1. Anderson slightly alters a line from Sandburg's poem "Prairie Waters by Night": "And the long willows drowse on the shoulders of the running water. . . ." This and the other Sandburg poems that Anderson goes on to mention appeared in the Apr. 1917 issue of *Poetry*.

TO Carl Sandburg

17 April 1917, Chicago

Dear Carl:

I sure did enjoy the blow-out Saturday night.

In my own mind I felt profoundly the difficulty that is facing the radical people of America in the present situation.

It is significant that as Jim Larkin[1] said when Socialists had got through with their national meeting in St. Louis and wanted to sing, they were compelled to sing the Marseillaise.

I am very sorry, indeed, that we did not get more of a talk from the little Russian nihilist. I liked her childlike sincerity and earnestness and the absolute sincerity of the question she put to everyone and which no one answered.

The man across the room facing us who brought up the question in regard to your songs—whether or not they did not need to sing—did I believe ask a question, Sandburg, that you did not answer.

I myself believe that the old folk songs, about which you talked, have stayed in people's minds not because of any vivid picture, but because of their singing quality, and I do sincerely believe that your own songs are best where the singing quality is most in evidence. Again thanking you for a good evening, I am

Very truly yours,
Sherwood A.

Pipe on oh piper.

TS. Ill.

1. James Larkin, leader of labor movements in Ireland, who was raising funds in America to support the Irish rebellion against England.

TO Waldo Frank[1]

[5 September 1917, Chicago]

Dear Brother—

Now that I am back at my desk in the city and in the midst of all the clatter of things[2] I am having an experience that is always a delight to me. The thing is something that I am always being reminded of and always forgetting. It is this—that I always work better and most freely when conditions for working are the worst.

I don't know that I clearly understand the reason for this but believe I do. In a business office such as ours the mental conditions are at the very worst. Men are occupied with matters so trivial and so very unimportant that their minds run about in little crazy circles. In self defense one is compelled to create and sustain in his own mind a world of people who have significance. Day by day as he goes on, this created world becomes a thing more definite. It comes to have height, breadth and thickness.

I have on several occasions heard you curse your own education and I begin to understand why. I suppose, for the most part, education consists in gathering confusing facts. These facts divert and occupy the mind. They prevent a man's falling back on something buried deep within himself.

I remember that when you were at camp I was confused by your quickness and sharpness in getting hold of people and things. I was afraid of it for you. It seemed to me many times that you were riding life with whip, boot and spur instead of letting life flow into you.

Oh damn. I wonder if I can make you see what I mean. Really to you and me this war, prison, none of the calamities that can come should have any effect at all except the effect of throwing us more solidly back upon our true level.

You see the real mind, the thing that is buried away in us, must be a wonderful thing. I sometimes think that our minds really record every little thing we see and hear in life and that we only confuse and perplex ourselves by not trusting absolutely the knowledge that flows in to us.

Am I talking like a fool. I am beginning again to live in a wonderful world. Things march in long processions past me. I wake and sleep and dream in a world full of significance. All the weary trivialities with which my hours in the office are occupied count as nothing.

It is because I am rested and can sustain the open door. I want you to be that way. I want you to ride life less. I want you not to whip and thresh your mind to action.

And in the meantime I want you to get well.

S.A.

MS. Penn.

1. Author and an editor of *Seven Arts*.

2. After spending the summer camping at Lake Chateaugay, N.Y., Anderson had returned to his job as copywriter for the Taylor-Critchfield-Clague Company (later called Critchfield and Company), an advertising agency in Chicago.

TO Caroline M. McIlvaine[1]

3 October 1917, Chicago

My dear Miss McIlvaine:

I have really published two novels, both more or less intensive studies of present-day Chicago life, and would be glad to present them to the Chicago Historical Society except that there is a matter of principle involved.

Really you know I suppose I have had already a hundred requests of presentation copies of both novels. That means about two hundred dollars to me. I am not a popular writer, at least the royalty checks from my publishers do not indicate that I am. My books are seriously discussed by our American deep sea thinkers but they are not bought by the man in the street.

Now you do know that no one is so poorly paid for his labor as the serious writer. I don't want to take myself too seriously but it is a joke to me that the Chicago Historical Society should want me to give them a copy of *Marching Men*. Make the publisher give you one if you can. Don't tackle the defenseless writer.

And please bear in mind this is not personal. I don't blame you but I'll be hanged before I'll give any institution a copy of a book I write.

Very sincerely yours,
Sherwood Anderson

TS. NL

1. Librarian of the Chicago Historical Society.

TO Henry Mencken

23 March 1918, Chicago

Dear Mencken:

Here is the story[1] trimmed down where it belongs. If you like it you must pay $30—that is, $25 for me and $5 for the young woman who types these things when she is supposed to be typing advertisements that I have written. The rights of small nationalities must be respected.

Ben Hecht[2] says you are coming out here sometime this summer. I have written a brutal sketch in which you are pictured as a man drunk and sodden with words wandering into a West-Side saloon late at night and begging one more drink of Theodore Dreiser.

Lane is publishing a book of my songs called *Mid-American Chants*. I bet you won't like it. I bet you're wrong.

Sincerely yours,
Sherwood Anderson

TS. NYPL

1. "The White Streak," published in *Smart Set* 55 (July 1918): 27–30.
2. Author and columnist with the Chicago *Daily News*.

TO Burton Rascoe[1]

3 June 1918, Chicago

Dear Rascoe:

I am sorry I did not have an opportunity to thump you harder about your inclination to wear yourself out at your job. Since I have known you it has seemed to me that you have been constantly more and more inclined to work intensely.

Chuck it. Play more. You cannot possibly open yourself up to receive impressions when you are so absorbed. Abah [À bas] the *Trib.* What does it matter?

About the biography matter. It is simple enough. Born at a place called Camden, Ohio, September 13, 1876—I nearly wrote 1776—spent most of my youth in the village of Clyde, Ohio, near Cleveland. Town poor family, village news-boy peddling papers, cheating people out of change etc.—all that stuff.

Came to Chicago at eighteen[2]—no work—common laborer until Spanish War broke out. Went into that.

Stumbled into advertising writing and have been there ever since except for five years when I got the great American idea of getting rich. Started a factory—got all my friends to put money in—bright young businessman, etc.

Scheme didn't work. Went nutty—had nervous breakdown—slight suspicion have been nutty ever since.

Started writing for the sake of the salvation of my soul and except for one or two slips—when I fancied I might by some chance hit on a popular note—have been writing for that end ever since. Don't know whether I'll make it or not.

Sincerely yours,
Sherwood

TS. Penn.

1. Then the literary editor of the Chicago *Tribune*.
2. He was nineteen or twenty at the time.

TO Trigant Burrow[1]

New Year's Eve [31 December 1918], Chicago

Dear Brother

Your letter with its enclosure reached me yesterday after having stopped at almost every point I have touched in the last two years. I am back in Chicago at the old grind after four months of glorious liberty during which I wrote a new novel and several tales.

I should have liked to see you in order to tell you how much of what you told me that summer up at the lake I have found to be true and how much you helped me by giving my mind many new slants. The difficulty with me is that I cannot learn things by being told but have to get them in my own way out of life.

I am publishing my Winesburg tales this spring, probably in March, and will no doubt have my novel ready for fall.[2] I call it *Poor White* and it is a study of the birth of a central western town. If the gods again give me some months of freedom I hope to follow it with another novel to be called "Immaturity," a study of a town born and passed into the second generation of industrial people.[3]

The poor little magazine called the *Little Review* will be publishing in a month or two a tale of mine called "The Triumph of the Egg" I am particularly anxious to have you see.[4]

With love and hopes for a good year to all of you from Tennessee and myself.

I am truly yours
Sherwood

MS. NL

1. Psychoanalyst whose talks with Anderson at Lake Chateaugay in 1917 provided the basis for Anderson's story "Seeds," *Little Review* 5 (July 1918): 24–31.
2. *Winesburg, Ohio* appeared in Apr. 1919; *Poor White* was not published until Sept. 1920.
3. This novel was never completed.
4. Concerned about the declining quality of the magazine, Anderson withdrew this story from publication. It was later published in *Dial* 68 (Mar. 1920): 295–304, and in *The Triumph of the Egg* (1921), where it is retitled "The Egg."

TO Burton Rascoe

[c. 9 June 1919, Chicago]

Dear Burton—

Whatever may be the truth about a lot of the fine things you have said concerning *Winesburg*, there is one thing very true and I can't help being glad you said it. Whatever is wrong with the people in the book is wrong with me.[1] I detest the damn paternalism of the writer who patronizes life.

Your review is, as you suggested, a challenge. It is this sort of thing that keeps a man pegging away and trying to work out his own vein no matter where it may lead. One doesn't feel like thanking a man for this sort of thing. The fact that you sense so keenly my impulse in writing shoots a lot higher than thanks. You will know how I feel about it.

Sherwood

I'll bet you what you will that the *Sun* reviewer is a woman.[2] I wrote Ben Huebsch[3] to look her up and please find someone to gratify her choked-up desires.

TS. Penn.

1. In a review of *Winesburg* in the Chicago *Tribune*, 7 June, p. 13, Rascoe had written: "Mr. Anderson says in effect, 'Here are human beings of whom I am one. Even our errors, our grossest weaknesses have about them something of tragic beauty. Are we not worthy of your sympathy no less than of your disgust?'"

2. The New York *Sun* published an anonymous review of *Winesburg*, "A Gutter Would Be Spoon River," on 1 June. Both it and the Rascoe review are reprinted in *Studies in Winesburg*, ed. Ray Lewis White (Columbus: Merrill, 1971), 26–30.

3. Head of B.W. Huebsch, Inc., which published *Winesburg, Ohio* and Anderson's subsequent books until 1925.

TO Ben Huebsch

14 June 1919, Chicago

Dear Ben:

Burton Rascoe told me yesterday that *Winesburg* was a best seller in Chicago this week. My God, suppose you and I should make some money. Ruin is staring me in the face. However, the book may go dead in a few weeks and we'll be saved. Here is an interesting development. There is a Weinsburg, Ohio.[1] I'll stay out of that town.

I'm obliged to your friend for knocking holes in my bad use of words. Every time one of these educated chaps attacks me they are always right. I'll keep track of these things and if there is opportunity for a second printing will send you a list.

Do you suppose you could buy the plates of *Windy McPherson's Son* and *Marching Men* at a low price? I might go in with you on such a deal. When you get a chance sound Jeff Jones[2] out. I've a hunch that one of these days *Windy* will sell more than it ever has yet.

Lord it's hot out here.

Very truly yours,
Sherwood Anderson

TS. NL

1. Anderson uses the original German spelling of the town's name, which had been changed to Winesburg.
2. Jefferson Jones, New York manager of John Lane Company.

TO Ben Huebsch

[c. 26 July 1919], Ephraim, Wisc.

Dear Ben—

What an interesting comment on people the reviews of *Winesburg* will make. Do keep them for me. They begin to constitute something like an essay on present-day American opinion. One has a feeling of standing aside and overhearing not his own work but the town life of his native village discussed.

Do you publish any juvenile books. Most of the children's books are such asinine sentimental nonsense that I have been thinking of writing out a series of tales of country life at the edge of a middle-western small town—little pictures of the actual life of the hay, the farm hand, the dog, the cow etc. I want to do these primarily for my own children[1] but would like to make a book of them for other children. If you do not go into that department of publishing I could find someone who makes a point of it.[2]

Mrs. Anderson has been ill and I have had her up north in the woods on Green Bay for 2 weeks. Now she is better and I will be back in Chicago by Aug. 1st. When do you go to Europe?

With love,
Sherwood Anderson

Address me at Chicago as usual.

MS. NL

1. Anderson's three children, all from his first marriage, were Robert, John, and Marion ("Mimi").
2. Although Heubsch replied positively to the suggestion, Anderson did not undertake this project.

TO Waldo Frank

Wednesday [27 August 1919, Chicago]

Dear Brother—

It is early morning and I have just got off a train, having just come home from the state fair at Springfield, Ill., where I spent a day with one of my clients[1] who was exhibiting his agricultural implement there. It was delightful to sit in the grandstand among the farmers, off for a day's vacation, and see the trotting and pacing races. The horses were beautiful as were also the fine steers, bulls, pigs and sheep on show in the exhibition sheds.

It has been very lonely here since you went away but I get good reports of Tennessee and that cheers me up. I am working pretty steadily.

All the time in the back of my mind I am working and working trying to devise some plan by which I may live and get out of business. It is going to be harder than ever for me to face the thing this year. Everything in me that is worth a damn draws away.

One plan I have is to try to raise enough money to buy a good sized tract of land up in Door County.[2] Then start a summer camp there. Take in both grown people and children. Employ a practical carpenter and a farmer and let the children work with them during the summer months. No doubt many grown people, if we got them up there, would be happy in working with the children also.

The work done could be in the nature of building little log houses for people, clearing the forests, improving the place, doing some farming, etc. It would take some money to get it underway but once underway I should be able to live there six months a year and have six months to spend in a room in New York or Chicago writing. Tennessee has genius with children and I could handle the grown-ups.

My problem has, you see, become something more than personal. Tennessee cannot stand the kind of work she is now doing for many years.

I am wondering if such a plan might not offer a handle by which I could take hold of a man like Emerson.[3] If I could get some man like him to back me in such a venture I am sure after a few years I could return his money and have left a means of making a living entirely outside the world of affairs.

In some way I have got to come to that.

Always there has been a kind of cunning in me. I have been able to sabotage very successfully but I grow very weary of it and I am losing my cunning. Often I feel that I should rather starve than stay another day at any occupation other than the occupation of the writer.

Well enough of that. I shall try to go to work at it and see if something cannot be done.

I do hope you and Margy[4] had a worthwhile time. All of these problems have been in the back of my mind all summer and in addition I saw Tennessee's illness not as a temporary thing but as evidence that her life did not suit her. In fancy I saw her breaking under the hard work she does every year. I keep feeling that I did not do my share to make you two happy and I wanted you to be happy.

I know however you will forgive me any shortcomings of mine.

You must not fail to come this way when you go west. Give my love to Margy. Tell her I will keep working on the children's things. I know your new novel[5] is going to be a big piece of work. May the gods be with you in making it. Write me whenever you are in the mood. Later I will write to Margy and send her some of the tales.

Sherwood

My regards to Mr. & Mrs. Cane.

TS. NL (ph)

1. W.A. Steele, owner of a ditcher and grader company in Owensboro, Ky.
2. In Wisconsin, on the peninsula between Green Bay and Lake Michigan.
3. John Emerson, childhood friend, later an actor, playwright, movie producer, and the husband of Anita Loos.
4. Margaret Naumburg Frank, author, educator, and wife of Waldo Frank.
5. *The Dark Mother*, published by Boni and Liveright in 1920.

TO Ben Huebsch

25 September [1919], Chicago

Dear Ben—

I am returning the plate correction proofs and the clippings. Hope you are still getting some sales for *Winesburg*.

My novel moves very slowly as I am seldom in the mood for writing these days. Business has rather got on my nerves. I keep wondering why the devil I should have to spend so large a part of my life in writing fool advertisement in order to live. You don't know of some intelligent man or woman who wants to be patron for an American artist, do you. Seems to me I've got a lot of good books in my system and I would like to get them out.

Chicago is a madhouse. The growing industrial unrest makes the middle class business men among whom I am compelled to live more impossible than ever.

Well little Sherwood, the sun is in the sky and the winds blow. If you don't like it why don't you go be a tramp.

Yours truly
Sherwood

TS. NL

TO Waldo Frank

Wednesday [19 November 1919], Evansville, Ind.

Brother

I write to you not to disturb your present solitude but because I feel you keenly these days. My voice is thrown out to you on a wind. It happens that recently I have had the 12 copies of *Seven Arts* bound into books. It is so characteristic of me that now I read *Seven Arts* for the first time.[1] I have been reading your articles. It is striking how often you have been a voice for me, how often you have voiced the gropings of my dumb years, do yet voice my dumb days.

I was up on the Ohio River last night, churning up the silent dark river on a little boat. The whole land out here is so little removed from its savage state that it wants but a flash to make it clear. The men, farmers and river town men sitting about, the thing man has invented, the puffing, stinking gasoline boat, the uncouth farms, blank faces—and out on the little ten-foot deck in the darkness, the stars and the country waiting for men to come.

As I am a little better physically, the jerking in and out does not violate me so terribly. I see the business game men play and in which I help as something far off. It is like lying on your belly and watching ant hills.

My mood of poetry goes on and I continue to make the testament—also I write the Mary Cochran stories.[2]

All yesterdays are dead.

It is time to make testament. It seems to me that in the last year I have come a little into your world and to understanding of you. To me that means a deeper love for your spirit.

Sherwood

MS. Penn.

1. *Seven Arts* had ceased publication in Oct. 1917.

2. One of these, "Unlighted Lamps," was published in *Smart Set* 65 (July 1921): 45–55, and reprinted in *The Triumph of the Egg*.

TO Hart Crane[1]

[3 December 1919, Chicago]

My dear Mr. Hart Crane.

What I wish as I read your letter is that you would take a weekend and come see me. I would go see you if I had money to do so.

Let me speak of your poem.[2] I can speak frankly because I have so little knowledge. It does not give me anything of yourself, the bone and flesh and reality of you as a man. Your letter does that so your letter is to me the better poem.

This poem coming and your letter too cut sharply down across a mood I am in in regard to poetry and that I am going to try to work out into expression in my *New Testament*.

Yesterday I was at lunch with a businessman who in a moment of frankness said,

> I was at my prayers
> And the lust for women came to me.[3]

That was to me a perfect poem. I went away and put it down as a Testament out of his life to all life.

About your father.[4] One is at a disadvantage there. Fathers, American fathers, can't be dismissed. I wish I knew him as well as you. I would like to walk with him for an afternoon as well as with you.

The arts he ridicules have not been very sturdy and strong among us. Our books are not much, our poetry not much yet. The battle has scarcely begun. These men are right too when they ridicule our pretensions.

I have that feeling about magazine efforts now. A magazine is in a way a heralding of victory. It is setting up a flag over the land.

Much more now what is wanted is the reality of individuals.

I wish you would read Waldo Frank's *Our America*[5] and ask your father to read it too. Do you know Van Wyck Brooks' *Letters and Leadership*.[6]

They get across something we all need to know here.

Akron is familiar ground to me. I have a friend there I have known many years, not young but very fine. Will you drop her a note and go see her. I will write her of you.

Miss Trillena White[7]
1032 W. Market St.
Akron, Ohio.

It would be fine if you could afford to take the time and spend the money to come here for a Saturday and Sunday.

Very truly yours,
Sherwood Anderson

The poem seems beautiful to me. It wants for me though the realities of you the man.

MS. NL (ph)

1. Anderson began corresponding with poet Hart Crane after Crane published an appreciative review of *Winesburg* in the September issue of *Pagan*.
2. "My Grandmother's Love Letters."

3. Anderson used these lines with some change in "The Minister of God," *A New Testament*, 50.
4. Crane's father, a businessman, was unsympathetic to his son's poetic interests.
5. Published by Boni and Liveright in 1919.
6. Published by Huebsch in 1918. Brooks, the critic and literary historian, had, like Frank, been an editor of *Seven Arts*.
7. A high school teacher in Springfield, Ohio, when Anderson attended Wittenberg Academy there in 1899–1900.

TO Ben Huebsch

[c. 25 February 1920], Mobile, Ala.

Dear Ben—

I am moving from Mobile to a single tax[1] colony down here called Fairhope. Address me there. Don't know anything about single tax but have a small house on the water at low cost and the town seems to be inhabited with nice people.

The novel moves along and I hope to have it ready to send in to you in a month. Why doesn't your new magazine[2] buy the serial rights. The *Nouvelle Revue Francaise* had made a big success of the idea of printing a novel in two or three issues of the magazine. They tack it right on at the back much in the way the *Nation* tacks on their foreign section.

The novel I am finishing will be called *Poor White*. It is really the story of the development of an American town into an industrial center and the effect of the coming of industrials on the people. It is not of course propaganda for anything but is the story just as I see it. The central figure is an inventor, one Hugh McVey, son of a Mississippi River raftsman and a descendant of Poor Whites of Kentucky. The story itself is I believe a rattling good one and the novel moves. It will contain six books and I am writing on the fifth. I would like to offer it as a serial to your magazine and to the *Dial*. If I could get some real money for serial rights, writing would begin to look not quite so hopeless a way to make a living. The *Dial* pays me $100 for short stories. Do you want to see stories of mine for your magazine and if you do what can it pay.

With love and good wishes.
Sherwood

TS. NL

1. A system of taxation based on land values devised by Henry George, a nineteenth-century American economist.
2. *Freeman*, a weekly magazine published by Huebsch from 1920 to 1924.

TO Burton Rascoe

15 May [1920], Fairhope, Ala.

Dear Burton—

I had a letter yesterday from Lewis[1] telling me of the attitude the *Tribune* had taken in regard to the free expression of your mind.[2] Although I have for a long time felt that something of the kind would inevitably happen, to have it happen is a shock. May the gods rot the balls of all newspaper publishers who aspire to a million circulation.

Anyway and as long as it had to happen, I am glad it happened over a thing like Christian Science. There is something terrible about the way the disease of that religion takes all humbleness and fineness out of people. A veil drops down over the eyes. A smug smile comes to stay on the lips. It is a kind of patent medicine religion. A scheme for bluffing the gods.

I wish I might go with you for a long two or three months' tramp over the roads of Missouri and Arkansas but I have had my playtime for the present and must go back to civilization (what a farce that it should be called by any such name) and make some money in order that I may run away again. Do by all means take advantage of the situation to get into the country for a long stay. Your fight is just begun. I can't tell you what it means to me that you have preserved your intellectual integrity and have not joined the tired ones who think nothing matters but feeding their damned bellies or making the cheap excuse that they can't be honest because they have children.

We have had a glorious three months here in this golden land. The town is impossible—a place where tired-out men and women from Iowa and Wisconsin have come to build themselves unspeakably ugly houses but we have not lived in the town but in a little cabin at the edge of the wood and right on the shore of Mobile Bay. I finished a novel—*Poor White*—and have sent it off to Huebsch. No one has seen it but Tennessee and Van Wyck Brooks but they both think it the best sustained thing I have done. Just between us I think myself it's a little dull but there is some damned good writing in it.

You should see how Tennessee has come out here. She is almost well and has taken up modeling. She does remarkable things in the beautiful red, blue and yellow clay we find here.

After I finished *Poor White* I began writing a rollicking Rabelaisian thing called *Many Marriages* that I hope will keep me happy and satisfied in a writing way for months. It will need good health and spirits to keep the thing up but I have hungered to do just some such a thing and will probably never be in better shape to at least begin it.

It was inevitable that something else happen here. The whole land is such a wash of warm glowing color—a golden land—that I had to begin painting. That has been more fun than anything. My painting is I am afraid like my poetry—a thing to puzzle the gods—but it is the most fun of anything I have ever gone into. The two or three conventional painters who are here look at it, shake their heads and then go home and take Epsom salts. That is no doubt the best way to take it.

We leave here the last of next week. Will go to New Orleans for a day or two and then Tennessee will go to Chicago. I have some work to do in Kentucky on the way home but will land in Chicago about June 1st. If you go away and I do not have a chance to see you, drop me a note at Critchfield & Company—10th Floor, Brooks Bldg.—Chicago. Give Hazel[3] our love. Hope I shall see you both soon.

Sherwood

Tennessee shouts from outdoors that I am to send you her love.

TS. Penn.

1. Lewis Galantière, critic and translator, previously of Chicago, then living in Paris.
2. Rascoe had lost his position as literary editor of the Chicago *Tribune* after publishing a book review that contained a slighting reference to Mary Baker Eddy's *Science and Health*.
3. Rascoe's wife.

TO Floyd Dell

Thursday [c. November 1920], Palos Park

Dear Floyd.

I still haven't finished reading your book.[1] I take it as one would step in to see a friend, talk for a time and then go away, liking his friend and thinking of him. Have no idea at all how it is going to hit but to me it is an intensely human book, filled with meaning and damn well done.

Your letter was like the book too.

I've never really felt any enmity between us but often I have felt in you a desire to attack something in me.

What you say in your letter today is exactly what Tennessee said after the one talk she had with you.

Seems to me we aren't aiming at different marks after all.

As a personality I'm made in a different way. To me writing is no road to fame, wealth, or even power. The truth is, Floyd, I began to write because writing was curative for me.

One thing I've known always, instinctively—that's how to handle people, make them do as I please, be what I wanted them to be. I was in business for a long time and the truth is I was a smooth son of a bitch.

I didn't want to be that and writing helped me face myself, helped me tell myself things.

The point of this is that actual writing and through writing to touch other lives was and is secondary for me. I did and do find writing helped me to live—it still helps me that way.

Perhaps you and I do need two different approaches to come to the same end. You may need to punish the poet in you. I may need to give my poet breath and life.

What I can't understand is this. What is so damned valuable in maintaining the fact that two and two make four. Suppose one were destroyed as a novelist but got hold of something—

The two notions don't fit in my mind but I put the case to you.

What have you done, what has anyone in the world done that they should command me, shout at me—"Don't take that road. You'll fall over the cliff." How am I to know you have ever been along the road?

You see what I'm driving at. It isn't personal.

Anyway I'm not saying what's in my mind. Some day we'll both be mature enough to talk it out, without cleverness, frankly, like two men who are sincere anyway.

What I've always been afraid of in your creative work is cleverness. I haven't found any of it in *Moon-Calf* yet. For me at least the gods grant I don't.

I'm painting and I'm afraid when you see my paintings you'll swear at me.

With love—
Sherwood

I've said nothing of what is in my mind. Some day I'll manage to do it. Your book drives clouds away from your personality and makes me love and understand you as never before.

P.S. I had a brother whose struggle was the one you have. My grip on reality frightened, terrified him. I kept thinking of him when Felix[2] lay on the bed and heard the girl moving about, waiting in the attic. It would have been to me simply inconceivable not to have gone up there. Felix didn't. Earl my brother wouldn't have.

How shall we ever know that the other fellow is wrong. The only thing that hurts me is when you want to change my impulse toward the strange and beautiful impulses in myself. My brother always fought me in the same way and on the same grounds.

MS. NL

1. Dell's recently published novel, *Moon-Calf*, which he had sent to Anderson in October.

2. Felix Fay, the idealistic young hero of *Moon-Calf*.

TO Sinclair Lewis
5 December 1920, Palos Park

My dear Mr. Sinclair Lewis—

I am writing to tell you how glad I am that you wrote *Main Street*. Hope it will be read in every town in America. As a matter of fact I suppose it will find most of its readers in the cities. You've sure done a job.

Very truly yours,
Sherwood Anderson

MS. Yale

TO Paul Rosenfeld[1]
Sunday 23 [January 1921, Palos Park]

Dear Paul—

You know how happy your wire made me. Of all the men I know in America it is you I should have picked to go with to Europe. This year it has been very hard for me to live in the Middle West. I can come back here to live but I have been deeply hungry to go into old cities, see old cultural things. You have opened the door for me.

Your wire of course does not say where you want to go in Europe. I suppose of course you'll want to go to Paris.

With my passage paid I'll be able to manage—the exchange rates are favorable. I will not need to live expensively there. Surely in Paris for example Copeau[2] can show me how to live at not too great cost. Perhaps you also know the trick of it.

I'll not come to New York now—first to save money for the trip with you—second to stay here and work.

I've finished a new 25000 word story.[3] Would you care to read it. I would like your mind on it.

Will you want to be bothered with the paintings.[4] I had planned to express them to you this week.

O Paul, I can't tell you what this chance and the opportunity it offers for companionship with you means to me.

Sherwood

MS. NL

1. Literary and music critic, who had offered to pay Anderson's way to Europe with him in May.

2. Jacques Copeau, French drama critic, editor, and play producer, who had previously visited Anderson in Chicago. See *Memoirs*, 361–64.

3. "Out of Nowhere into Nothing," published in *Dial* 71 (July, Sept. 1921): 1–18, 153–69, 325–46.

4. An exhibit of Anderson's watercolors was held at The Sunwise Turn, a New York bookshop, during the spring of 1921.

TO Felix and Helen Russman[1]

[early June 1921, Paris]

Dear Felix & Helen

The trip over on the *Rochambeau* was very quiet with no one sick but in the English Channel we ran into a heavy cold fog and I got a hell of a cold in the head. We came right up to Paris and have been on the go ever since.

I find myself loving Paris wholeheartedly and without reservation. The stories told about the Parisians being surly with Americans is all wrong as far as I can see.

As for cost of living, it is less than Chicago now. We have a big double room for about .75—American—a day and food at the smaller restaurants does not cost much.

There are a great many Americans here but one does not see much of them on the left bank—except students.

After we got up to town Tennessee was smitten with a cold and laid up for a few days but is O.K. now again. We are but about 5 minutes walk from the Louvre and I go there almost every day. No use telling you what there is. Really I expected to be disappointed in the masters but all of them I've seen have some[thing?] so fine and real that you realize there is a reason for their survival. It will be fun to talk with you of all these things when I see you this fall.

Yesterday I went to see an exhibition of Picasso. It is amazing stuff. I've an idea that the strength of the revolutionist movement is pretty well centered in him.

Now it is 9:30 in the morning and I am sitting under the trees in the Luxembourg Gardens. The sun is shining. A rather handsome French woman has come to sit on the other end of the bench and is flirting with me but with my meager French the case is hopeless.

As a matter of fact I get along pretty well as the French are so courteous and are always willing and ready to help you out. Taxi drivers sting you a few francs but it doesn't amount to much.

On Sunday we all went into the country with a French poet and his girl to a little 12th century town[2] where we ate out in a garden under trees and had a very happy time.

Almost every day I go off somewhere on an adventure. I put a few francs in my pocket and just plunge into the city to find what I can.

Next Sunday we go out to Fontainebleau and later we are going to Chartres to the cathedral and to other places here near Paris.

Plenty of good wine and at low cost but I have not yet had my French jag. Perhaps I won't want it when it's so easy to get.

Everyone here is being very fine and thoughtful and no one seems in a hurry. There is a really lovely feeling of leisure. I have met a good many of the distinctive figures in French writing but as a good many of them speak English about as I speak French there isn't much gained.

It will be fun to see you both in the fall and to walk and talk with you again on the hills of Palos.

Sherwood

MS. NL (ph)

1. Artist and his wife, friends of Anderson's in Palos Park.
2. Provins, which the Andersons and friends visited on 5 June.

TO Felix Russman

[7 July 1921], Cabourg, France

Dear Felix—

We are here in a little Norman town, about 2 hours from Havre, spending a few days swimming in the sea and sleeping before going to London. In Paris we didn't have much time to sleep. Things kept happening too rapidly.

All the gloomy predictions everyone made about France turned out to be wrong. Things cost more than before the war but with the exchange so much in our favor we did not suffer.

As for the French people—they have been fine and have done everything possible to give us a good time.

I've been impressed by the fact that Picasso is the most powerful living man among the painters of France. He is a Spaniard by the way. It interested me a lot to find that the moderns are more powerful than ever—their pictures sell.

To be sure the older painters have things their own way at the Salon and the Academy but everyone I saw agreed with me that the Salon show was dull, ungodly dull.

There are all sorts of rumors of life in Germany and of a strong new school of mystics growing up there. I wish I were going to Berlin.

The weather since we came to France has been the most perfect thing imaginable. Day after day of cool bright days with marvelously clear skies. Our place was on the left bank, just opposite the Louvre and we could run in there for an hour anytime.

As for French writing, I met a good many of the Frenchmen but none who struck me as much alive. Style has a tremendous grip on them and their language is naturally declamatory. There will have to something happen before there is anything fresh and naive comes in.

The Dada thing has run its course. The only good men in it have got out and it has become the plaything of silly empty fellows.

I saw [James] Joyce several times, a witty gloomy Irishman. [Ezra] Pound seems to be an empty man without fire. Of the French writers [André] Gide is the most powerful in himself and in his influence and he is a classicist.

I keep thinking of you all at Palos and of the night walks we took. I hope you are finding good companions in Wright and Bagg and that you'll be there when we blow back that way early in September. Give my regards to Mary, Wright, Bagg, the Bucks and my love to Helen and the children.

Sherwood

MS. NL (cc)

TO Lewis Galantière

19 October 1921, Palos Park

Dear Lewis—

I don't blame you for being a little sore at those fellows[1] for introducing the Greenwich Village flavor into your special and charming little cafés. Damn that Stearns, he should know better especially as he will probably be your guest for a long time. He's a real fellow but he sure has got the rep of making his friends bear the freight charges.

I'm in bad for not seeing Burton [Rascoe] on my way through New York but it couldn't be helped. I got a sudden call to Chicago when I had been there but a day or two and had to take the first train—a bread and butter matter. Had expected to stick about the town for 10 days and see Burton when I had leisure. About the holding up of his book. I understood it was because he had had a change of heart about some of his opinions and wanted to rewrite them. That was Ben Hecht's story. Madame Gay[2] has written me she has the translation finished and has also written giving a few American expressions she can't understand. Have tried to make them clear in a letter but if you do see her ask her to show them to you. You I know can clear them up.

Ben Hecht's novel[3] seems to be stirring up a good deal of talk. It's well written. Plenty of holes in it but it's good to see another man coming along who has some appreciation of the art of writing itself.

The *Triumph* will be out in a few days and I'll send you one at once. Also I'll sure tell Tennessee about the old woman.

Am up to my eyes in a novel[4] and hope to have it off my chest in a few weeks. If I can raise the dough I think I'll try taking a look at Mexico this winter. God I wish you and I could do that together. Wouldn't that be the blessed fun?

We both love you [with] all there is in us.

Give my love to Stearns and that red-headed monologist Lewis. Do you wonder that man writes long books?

Yours always.
Sherwood

TS. Columbia

1. Sinclair Lewis and Harold Stearns, who, Galantière complained, brought too many of their American friends to his favorite Paris restaurants. Stearns published *Civilization in the United States* in 1922.
2. Marguerite Gay, Anderson's French translator.
3. *Erik Dorn*, in which Anderson is portrayed as the character Warren Lockwood.
4. "Ohio Pagans," not completed.

TO John Peale Bishop[1]

21 November 1921, Chicago

My dear Bishop:

I have just been reading your article, "The Distrust of Ideas," in December *Vanity Fair.*

It is an amazing article. It makes me feel as one might feel sitting in his house in a lonely place in the country and having someone he thought a long ways away suddenly open the door and walk in.

In certain respects I feel as though you had not only done that but had taken the door off and made a bonfire of it so that every passer-by along the road could look in.

It is certain that you have done more than justice to me in this article but I doubt a little whether you have been quite so fair to Lawrence.

As a matter of fact, Bishop, I think the man that opened my eyes to what the possibilities might be in the development of my own vein was not Lawrence but Dostoyevsky who has always been the one great master to me.

However, I do not want to let you make me become absurdly serious about anything I may be able to do. There are such a lot of things I want to do I haven't done. Naturally, however, I do want to express my gratitude.

The closing lines of your article in which you express your suspicion that my own mind is like one of these grey towns out here is, I am afraid, profoundly true.[2] We are a long, long ways from bringing much of any beauty into these towns and the Lord knows I have a big enough job ahead of me.

With sincere gratitude to you, I am

Very truly yours,
Sherwood Anderson

P.S. I thought I had something for *Vanity Fair* the other day and had got it into an envelope to send you, when doubt crept in. Now I have laid it aside to be re-worked.

The thing was all right but was very slight and, I believe, can be a good deal enriched. As soon as I have done this I will send it on for you to look at.

S.A.

TS. Princeton

1. Author and critic, whose essay, "The Distrust of Ideas: D.H. Lawrence and Sherwood Anderson and Their Qualities in Common," appeared in *Vanity Fair* 22 (Dec. 1921): 11–12, 118.

2. The article concludes: "One suspects that Anderson's own mind is very like one of these grey towns, and that in it, as in these towns, there is a conflict, and that out of that conflict his books are made."

TO Ben Huebsch

30 November 1921, Chicago

Dear Ben:

Well my dear Ben, this coming out into the open has a distinct flavor of vulgarity, always present.[1] One cannot deny that. It has nothing to do at all with what I really want to do.

Achievement is all right, but how much is achieved. I have written a few stories that are like stones laid along the highway. They have solidity and will stay there.

And what is this in a life. What I mean to say is that there is old age and death in accepting the idea of achievement. Not what is done, but what is to be done.

I say this to you because I give warning I'm going to go the lowest limit in dining and speech making.

At that I thank you for the fine way it seems to me you are doing your end of the job.

Sincerely,
Sherwood

TS. NL

1. *Dial* had chosen Anderson as the recipient of its first annual award of $2,000 for outstanding contribution to American letters.

TO Paul Rosenfeld

Thursday [12 January 1922], Lexington, Kentucky

Dear Paul—

I stopped here for 2 days about some advertising affairs. It's quite dreadful. I'm becoming impossible. Nowadays when I sit listening to a man tell his schemes for selling something, my ears do not work and I can't keep the track of what he is saying. I keep wanting to break in and say, "For God's sake man, drop it. You have a little money, go play, learn to love someone or something." Am I to become a damned evangelist, Paul?

Last night I went riding over the hills with a man who was running illicit whiskey. We took chances of jail I suppose but it was fun to be with him after the businessman and to hear him talk of race horses. He is a man I've known for several years. He has been shot twice but never caught and he boasts that he can drink a quart of moonshine a day and that it keeps him from ever being ill.

One of the great joys of my stay in New York was you, Paul. You're O.K. I'm so damned glad to have you as friend.

Will send list of bookstores etc. from New Orleans.

Sherwood

MS. NL

TO Hart Crane

Sunday [15 January 1922], New Orleans

Dear Hart Crane—

I dare say you are right about the story in *Dial*.[1] It doesn't seem to come off, does it? I rather thought it did when it was in manuscript but when I saw it printed felt very much what you have said. There will be a story in the Feb. *Dial* that you will, I'm sure, find quite charming.[2]

I came down here after two or three weeks in New York to live and work in the old French Quarter here, one of the really charming spots in America. New York was exciting after the heaviness of Chicago and for two or three weeks it was good to see many people and indulge in much talk about the things going on in America but, having had my fill of it, I was glad to come away.

Here I have taken a room in an old house where I have a fireplace and a big table for my books and materials.

By the way I went to see the *Double Dealer*[3] crowd and found them delightful men. They gave me the July number with your article on my work, which I had never seen before, also one in which I found your poem "Black Tambourine."[4] It hit me as a very fine thing in print.

Of course you must know that I appreciate such a fine clear statement of what I am trying to get at in writing. It was beautifully written. God knows it is good to see a man willing to give some service to time in order to get hold of what he wants in song. We've had an ungodly lot of stuff thrown off and if your way is the slow way, it is, anyway, the clean honest way. As for myself, I've written a novel,[5] which hasn't seemed to me to quite come off so I've put it aside for the time, and now I'm at work on some long short stories or short novels, or what you will.

It may be indeed that I will come up to my feeling and conception of the novel in this way, something more nervous, exciting and intense than our accepted novel form. Anyway I shall be working toward that.

Write me when the mood comes. 708 Royal Street—New Orleans.

Sherwood Anderson

MS. NL (ph)

1. Anderson apparently erred; the story on which Crane comments is "The Contract," which appeared in *Broom* 1 (Dec. 1921): 148–53.
2. "I'm a Fool," 119–29.
3. A New Orleans literary magazine, founded in 1921 and edited by Julius Friend, Basil Thompson, and, later, John McClure.
4. Crane's article was "Sherwood Anderson," 42–45. "Black Tambourine" appeared in the June 1921 issue, 232.
5. "Ohio Pagans."

TO Karl Anderson

1 February 1922, New Orleans

Dear Karl—

I am living in an old house in the old Creole section of New Orleans, surely the most civilized spot in America. The houses and the people, Italians, French Creoles and Negroes, are charmingly unambitious, basically cultured and gentle. Where else in all America could one spend a day, as I did yesterday,[1] working steadily all morning, going to see the oyster opening championship of the world settled after lunch, walking on the wharfs among singing Negro laborers in the late afternoon and seeing Panama Joe Gans whip his man in an out of doors arena in the evening. And at that I missed the horse races. Do you not suffer of envy.

There is a story of mine in February *Dial* you must see. I'm sure you'll like it.

From what I hear things are doing fairly well for me. In the Modern Library *Winesburg* has sold in a month as much as in its first year and the *Triumph* is going into its third printing.

As to the new book,[2] if it comes off—as pray God it may—it may have to be printed in a special limited subscription edition—as already much bolder and I believe more penetrating stuff has gone into it than into anything else I have printed.

At any rate I am very much the workman these days, trying as I never have to make every day count.

And surely few men have been so blessed of the gods. Now, for a time, I have money enough on which to live and a strong body that does not tire too easily. I have already had more recognition than I expected to get in a lifetime. Naturally I'm trying hard to make the time count.

When I'll go north I can't say. Not while the work goes as it does now.

But too much of S.A. I began writing to say that if you get free I should think you might enjoy running down here, even for a few weeks.

Give my love to Helen[3] and the children and to others there and thank Helen for the good Christmas time.

By the way, I loaned Jamie[4] one of my prized little colored handkerchiefs to blow his nose while we were out for a walk. If it happens to show up will you ask Helen to mail it to me.

With love.
Sherwood

MS. NL

1. The events Anderson mentions actually occurred four days prior to the date of the letter. The oyster-opening contest and the boxing match, in which Panama Joe Gans defeated Oscar Battiste, took place on 28 Jan.
2. *Many Marriages*, published in Feb. 1923.
3. Mrs. Karl Anderson.
4. James Anderson, Karl's son.

TO Jerome Blum[1]

[2 February 1922], New Orleans

Dear Jerry—

Of course I'm damned sorry you turned back at Mobile and didn't come on over here. Don't know what kind of a pal I'd have made but not bad I guess. Have been going like a house afire ever since I hit town and it would have been fun to have you here too.

My room is on the third floor of an old house down in the center of the French Creole section and is run by a strong young French Creole whose husband is a mechanic. Pretty bare and all the better for it. There is [a] picture of the Virgin over the mantle and beside it two glass candlesticks, in the form of crosses with Christs on the Cross in bronze on them. I've become a good Catholic therefore and lead a virtuous life. In the morning the woman or her husband brings me up toast and coffee and I stay put until noon.

Not a bad lot of fellows down here too. There is one, a Memphis newspaper man who is a good loafer and likes the niggers as I do. We spend a lot of time together loafing on the wharfs.

There is a little magazine down here called the *Double Dealer*, run by the sons of several rich men, and I have played with them some but now have rather cut them out. Their playing is largely with society women. Never got into touch with that crew before so thought I would play with them a little and see how I liked them. Now I've seen and I know and I don't have to [do] that again.

It's all right but one goes evening after evening among these women—at least these fellows do—and there is a constant and pervading sense of the feminine and one never goes to bed with one of them and gets clear. As far as that is concerned they will go further without going anywhere than any people I ever saw. Perhaps you know them better than I do.

My new book—if I write it through as I feel it—the gods be good and permit me this—will be something anyway. But I guess I'd better not be bragging about that.

As for the niggers. One can't get anything from the whites here. They all lie blindly and don't know when they're lying. Best thing I think is just to loaf where they are and watch and listen. Sometimes at night I go walk in the part of the city where they live. Little houses. No pavements in the streets. Broken sidewalks. Laughter in the darkness back of the walls. The one thing they constantly do for me is to rest something inside me. I've really been going like hell and sometimes at night I can't chuck it and sleep. Well I go where the niggers are at work and watch their bodies and my own body gets rested. There aren't any other people in America [who] know anything about physical work. They have the key to it, the secret to it.

Don't know whether or not I'm romancing but I've a notion they know I have a somewhat different attitude toward them than most of the whites. There is a kind of something in their eyes, both men and women, something like surprise and pleasure.

Well, it's big shooting whether I get anything or not and in the meantime I like being right where I am and doing just what I am. Can't beat that much. Give my love to Lucile.[2] She's solid with me for good.

And love to you.

Sherwood

TS. AAA

1. Artist, formerly of Chicago, whom the Andersons had visited in New York the previous December.
2. Blum's wife.

TO Ben Huebsch

[c. 15 February 1922, New Orleans]

Dear Ben—

I think you are dead right and a very charming and sensible kind of publisher for one Sherwood Anderson to have.

What you say about the greasy fingered book-leggers gives me the fantods.[1]

But Ben I've got a terrible Rabelaisian book in me (not this one but another), one about race horse men and whores, and bartenders and country doctors and other fine profane gentry I know well.

As for this book—here is the sense of it.

It will be called *Many Marriages* and will be in the form of 3 to 5 episodes.

The first episode—now nearing completion—will be nearly a volume in itself. I've written 50000 words since I came here. The book itself may go to 2 or even 3 volumes.

The thought back of the book is something like this.

There is within every human being a deep well of thinking over which a heavy iron lid is kept clamped.

Something tears the lid away. A kind of inner release takes place. In other words the man cuts sharply across all the machinery of the life about him. There is, in the old Christian phrase, a rebirth.

Is this man in his new phase sane or insane. He does new things, says new and strange things and his words and actions fall with strange illuminating power on those about him. To some they are sentences of death, to others invitations into life.

What I aim to do you see is to show step by step the process of this rebirth in a man and its effect on those about him.

The whole thing is so absorbing to me that "Ohio Pagans"—almost complete—had to be put away. It won't come out until this book is written and published. That may be 3 months. It may be two years.

The machinery of the tale is bold. It will cause a howl of pain from many quarters I'm afraid.

But I like the self-respect of your attitude and I'd rather be hung on that tree than sneak up an alleyway.

The point I think, Ben, is this.

Some years ago I wrote the little book *Mid-American Chants* and that led directly into the impulse that produced *Winesburg, Poor White* and *The Triumph*.

For two years now I've been at work on another thing I call *A New Testament*.

And that has led directly into *Many Marriages*. If it comes off—the gods grant it may—it will be the biggest, most sustained and moving thing I've done.

As to the method of publishing—I'll forget it and trust to your judgment when I can lay the book before you.

I think the new prose is going to be unlike any I've written. I am struggling to get a quick nervous rush to the thing, something intensely suggestive of modern life.

Will I achieve all this?

The gods know.

There is one thing. The *New Testament* might perhaps be brought out at the same time we bring out *Many Marriages*.

The complicated rhythms and the rush of imagery I have worked for in these things would be better understood after reading the same impulse in prose and the prose would be better understood in the light of the *Testament*.

It's all woven together you see.

The story or rather stories or episodes of *Many Marriages* will be striking and stirring I believe.

Anyway I write all this to let you know I'm working like hell and what direction my work is taking.

On some days I have had to fairly force myself away from my desk and have worked until I was almost too weak to walk.

I'm after big game anyway, Ben, and will forget the whole matter of publishing problems until I come through.

With love.
Sherwood

Thanks for statement for income tax.

About children's books—what about the ones I have written.[2] My own notion is that the American mind isn't far beyond childhood.

MS. NL

1. Huebsch had warned Anderson against limited-edition publishers, "book-leggers" who cater to erotic interests, and urged him to write for the general public.

2. Huebsch had admired Anderson's capturing of a youthful perspective in "I'm a Fool" and suggested that he write a children's book.

TO Lewis Galantière

[late March 1922, Palos Park]

Dear Lewis—

Have just finished revising my new book. For the present am somewhat confused about it—too near it I suppose.

Burton [Rascoe] was out here last week and Jerome Frank[1] gave a party for him up in Hubbard Woods. I got very drunk and you should have seen me jazz. I sure learned to throw a wicked hip down in New Orleans.

The apartment house in which Tennessee has been living so long is to be revamped, dolled up, apartments $200 per each. She's got to dig out. I've invited her to Palos Park for the summer. Am I not a generous cuss?

Ben Hecht had a story in the *Daily News*.[2] He and I are sitting in the back room of a saloon. A waiter approaches. "What will you have to drink?" he whispers.

"Nothing," says I, knowing he (Ben) was broke.

Everyone says it's a perfect picture of me.

I hear you are in thick as thieves with Gertrude Stein, Mary Reynolds,[3] Bones[4] and all my girls. That's a hell of a way to act.

Burton was piped all the time he was out here but looked well and seemed to be enjoying life. He is to leave *McCall's* and become book editor of the New York *Tribune*.

God knows I'm glad you've got Mary, Gertrude Stein, Bones, Ernest etc. instead of Harold Stearns. Life must be going a bit pleasanter.

It's a god-forsaken time in Chicago. I don't like the damn town much—have been hopelessly vamped by New Orleans, the sweetest town on this continent. Am going to live there sometime and be an old son of a bitch. Maybe I'll go whole hog and be a nigger.

Except a few of you they're the nicest people I've seen yet.

Sherwood

Don't be so damned stingy about letters.

MS. Columbia

1. Chicago lawyer, later a member of the Roosevelt administration and a judge.
2. The story is in Hecht's column, "Around the Town: A Thousand and One Afternoons in Chicago," in the Chicago *Daily News*, 17 Mar. 1922, p. 48.
3. Chicago friend, living in Europe.
4. Hadley, first wife of Ernest Hemingway.

TO Newlin Price[1]

15 April 1922, [Chicago]

Dear Mr. Price:

I am very glad indeed to have the opportunity to write you a few things about my brother, Karl Anderson. You must, however, bear in mind that I am dictating this hurriedly, and in this connection I will be very glad to give you permission to make any changes you think would add to the literary or news interest of what I have to say.

In our family, there were 5 boys, of which Karl is the oldest. We were born and raised in a little town in Ohio.

Karl Anderson
COURTESY OF ELEANOR ANDERSON

As a matter of fact, our parents must have desired to give us all separate birthplaces, as they seemed to have moved about from town to town through the state, perhaps with the intention of making as many towns as possible famous or infamous, by having one of us be born there.

Our father was a southern man[2] and, as we all remember him, a delightful person, with, however, a streak of the gypsy in him that made it impossible for him to make a living.

We boys were all bound out to learn some trade and, as it happens, Karl served his apprenticeship in the harness making trade.

There was, of course, no artistic life in the town, but as he sat on his harness maker's horse, Karl Anderson must always have been seeing things, as he soon began drawing pictures on the wall of the shop and later went away to Cleveland, where he began his life as an artist.

I can well remember how proud we all were at the thought of this older brother of ours living an artist's life. In fact so much did the life he had taken up influence ours that all, at one time or another, tried to be artists.

As a young fellow I remember Karl coming home to our town with the city's way about him and always seeming a little strange and far away to the rest of us.

I have no doubt he endured many hardships during that period, but almost from the first he had success in his new life, as not only ourselves but all our old town soon began to be proud of him.

Later we began to see drawings he had made appearing in the pages of magazines, and we younger brothers carried these around in our pockets in order that we might brag and strut before the other boys, because he was our brother.

During all this period Karl not only made his way as an artist, but managed in some way to chip in generously toward the support of his younger brothers and even managed, in the midst of all this, to get together money enough so that he could go to Europe and finish his art education there.

Of his adventures as a young art student and later as a practicing artist, I know little. It is, you know, characteristic of the American race that no one knows as little about one as one's own family. The choice little adventures of life that so feed and enrich the memory are always told to friends and never to younger brothers.

However, Karl was never the high and mighty one with us and I have no doubt was eager enough to bring into our little world the adventurous stories of that greater outside world in which we always fancied him living.

Karl Anderson's life has been somewhat unusual, for an American, in that he has always been an artist, from boyhood, has never cared about anything else, nor has he even done anything else.

The two or three years working as a harness maker's apprentice, during his boyhood, really do not count.

I think it a very characteristic thing in my brother's personality that, although he has always been what we call a representative painter, I have never known a man more open to the impressions and influences from whatever source seemed to him to lead to beauty.

And now you see I have been unable after all to tell you much about the adventures of his life. I think I have explained why. It is because I am his brother and brothers so seldom tell the real adventures of their lives to one another.

The hard struggle of this man, unknown in the cities, the trying periods when he had no money, the long struggle to get money enough to go to Europe and the slow coming of recognition, well, all these things, you see, are necessarily seen and felt from the outside.

As a matter of fact, I would be perfectly delighted to lie about the matter and tell you gigantic stories of the wild adventures of my brother's youth, if it were not for the fact that one's fancy never succeeds in playing about the figure of a brother. Cannot you get some friend to give you this part of the story?

As I see his story, it is primarily a story of a patient, determined struggle under adverse conditions and of a determination that has never weakened.

Yours sincerely,

TS. NL (cc)

1. Director of the Ferargil Galleries in New York.

2. Although Sherwood, like his father, often made this assertion (see letter to Hansen, 29 Nov. 1922), Irwin Anderson was actually a native of Ohio.

TO Lewis Galantière

[late June 1922, Chicago]

Dear Lewis—

I am sorry if I have unloaded my depression on you. What happened to me? Perhaps I worked too intensely on my last book, *Many Marriages*. And then a kind of fame suddenly came to me and that made me a little ill perhaps. I have been drawing away from people more and more. For some weeks now I have been living alone on the South Side and have seen few people. Tennessee has gone off to Wisconsin and, as I am to go east next week, I shall be alone all summer. It is what I seem to want.

I own a Ford and am setting out in it. Perhaps I shall see Burton [Rascoe] in New York, perhaps not. I think of him now as being surrounded by the literary groups and I do not want them. Him, as a man, I love and perhaps I shall be able to see him that way.

There is a kind of dreadful thing happens with recognition as a writer over here. Some men, Lewis, Sandburg and others, seem to prosper on it but it makes me sick. I even think sometime of passing out altogether, becoming someone else—Joe Bumblebee, for example.

So far this summer I have written little but there is a book stirring in me. Perhaps I'll get at it during my trip, which may last three or four months. I have no very definite plans as to where I am going.

Raymond O'Neil,[1] whom you met in Paris, is here and is starting a theater among the Negroes on the South Side. He comes often in the evening to walk about with me, a very charming, sensitive man.

I shall try to make Europe next year, perhaps Italy. It depends upon money. If I can rake enough together I shall go. The trip last year had an odd effect on me. It made me want to go back to it as a babe wants the breast while I do not think it killed America for me. What it did perhaps was to make me see things from a somewhat different slant.

What shall I tell you of Chicago. I have seen practically no one for months. Last winter in New Orleans I played and worked violently. When I begin to do the same thing again I shall be a more cheerful correspondent.

Give my love to any of the people you see over there that I know and one of these days, thank God, I'll be seeing you and Europe again. My love to Griff Barry[2] when you see him and above all to Ernest and Bones.

Sherwood

Better address me % B.W. Huebsch, 116 W. 13th, N.Y.

MS. Columbia

1. Playwright and producer.
2. Griffin Barry, American journalist working in Europe.

TO Paul Rosenfeld

8 July [1922], Cleveland

Dear Paul—

As I am here without my machine I shall have to put you to the bother of reading my scrawl. I got hold of a Ford and left Chicago last week. Intend to wander along looking at the country for a time and will then settle down, somewhere in the east, and I hope will go to work.

Seldes[1] has written me that he has just returned from a delightful five days with you.

As to the matter of my going to pieces. I hardly know whether your analysis of what is wrong is the correct one for Sherwoodio or whether as usual it is all my own fault. What I think is that I have allowed people to make me a bit too conscious of myself. A certain humbleness toward life in general, that has always been my best asset, was perhaps getting away from me. One begins to be taken up by people of little or no intelligence and soon cannot discriminate. I have thought the remedy to be a long period of being unknown—even if necessary losing my name.

Well enough I know, Paul, that we have done little enough and I have seen what seemed to be the effect of the sort of thing of which I am speaking on Sandburg and Masters. In both these cases I am of course speaking from reports only.

At any rate I suddenly find myself in a somewhat new position in life—the prize, the *Literary Digest* writing me up,[2] *Vanity Fair*[3] etc. The thing penetrated down into channels of life it had not reached before. I want, you see, a period of living a pretty obscure life although God knows I need my real friends.

And there is Chicago. It has been pretty ugly this year. Perhaps Europe did make its ugliness more pronounced. It has lowered over me like a great beast ever since I came from New Orleans.

By the way I shall perhaps go there again next winter and I wish you would consider undertaking the adventure. It might turn out to be great fun.

[Raymond] O'Neil came to Chicago and got into the social, literary life there—trying to start his theater. As a relief I suggested he try starting it among the Negroes in the Negro section of town—which, by the way, is huge.

He took up the notion eagerly and has the things well under way. I would like to write some plays for it.

And incidentally he has made a remarkably fine play out of the story "The Egg." The man has a real brain. I became very fond of him.

And so, Paul, I shall perhaps be seeing you after a few weeks. There seem to be many things I want to talk with you about. Will let you know when I am anywhere near you. Seldes is to send proofs of *Many Marriages* here and for the next 10 days, while I am in northern Ohio, I will get my mail % Richard Laukhuff[4]—40 Taylor Arcade—Cleveland.

With love.
Sherwood

MS. NL

1. Gilbert Seldes, managing editor of *Dial*.
2. "An Exponent of the New Psychology," *Literary Digest* 73 (1 April 1922): 33.
3. See letter to John Peale Bishop, 21 Nov. 1921.
4. Cleveland book dealer and friend of Anderson.

TO Harry Hansen[1]

29 November 1922, New York

Dear Harry,

I have your letter, sent to me in care of Ben, and I am answering it from Ben's office. If you or Ben Hecht come to New York, my address is 12 St. Luke's Place.

As you know, I came down here in a Ford in August, and when I got here, sold what was left of the Ford. Have been living on that ever since.

I never have read Ben Hecht's new book,[2] because I am waiting for him to send me a signed copy, but on all sides I hear nice things about it. Please tell him to hurry up.

After I got here I was in rather a nervous state, due to the excitement of life at Palos Park, I suppose, and got a chance to make an ocean trip to New Orleans and back, so I did it. Now I am back here and at work, and will be out to Chicago one of these days—just when I don't know. I heard Carl Sandburg was in town while I was away, but I didn't see him.

Now as to the questions:[3] I was born at Camden, Ohio, which, I understand, is not on the banks of anything. I have never seen the place, and some time ago the editor of a local paper at Camden tried to dig up my parentage, without success. I am afraid my father was a drifting kind of a man, who moved whenever the rent came due, and I just happened to have been born at that place. There were seven children, and no two of them born in the same place, which rather gives him away. My father came from a southern family, or at least he said he did, and there was Italian blood in my mother's family. Mother died when I was about 14.[4]

My older brother is, as you know, a painter. Shortly after mother's death he went away to Cleveland, Ohio, the family at that time living at a little place called Clyde, Ohio, and I became, in a way, the father of several younger children. Afterward I worked as a laborer in factories, and out-of-doors in various cities, and later, through the influence of my older brother, who had become a magazine illustrator, got into the advertising business, in which warm nest you found me when you first knew me.

I really suppose, Harry, that I always wanted to be a story teller, and in fact, among my fellow advertising writers, was always known as a notorious liar. I kept scribbling away, did several novels which were never submitted to any publisher, and finally found publication through the enthusiasm and voluntary help of Floyd Dell.

As to my life after that, Ben Hecht knows a lot about it, but please don't ask him.

As to *Windy McPherson's Son* and *Marching Men*, the first two novels published, I myself believe that these novels were written largely under the influence of my reading—not under the influence of my observations of life.

Later I wrote an unsuccessful book of poetry, called *Mid-American Chants*, but I myself believe that the writing of this broke me into a second period that might be covered by *Winesburg, Poor White* and *The Triumph*. Then I wrote another long book of poetry which I have had the hardihood not to publish, and I believe this broke me into a third mood in writing, the first expression of which is the new novel, *Many Marriages*.

Oddly enough, if I were to name the books I have read most consistently, it would not be the Russians. I have always been a great admirer of George Borrow,[5] and I suppose I have read all of his books 25 times, and, without any pose in the matter, I think I can honestly say that I have had a tremendous lot of joy out of the Old Testament. When I travelled around as an advertising writer, I used to take my knife and cut books out of Gideon's Bibles in hotels, and carry them in my pocket.

I suppose that the reason the Russian influence has been spoken of so often in connection with my work is that my own approach to writing is very similar to the Russian writers, but for just this reason I perhaps admire most something not quite so much like my own work.

As a single piece of work, I think the story "The Egg" in *The Triumph of the Egg* the best thing I have ever done.

In this connection, I would like to call your attention to an Irish horsedealer I once knew who said, "The best horse I ever owned I own now." Really, I think *Many Marriages* far ahead of anything I have ever done before.

As you know, there was a great deal of row raised when *Winesburg, Ohio* was published, and in one New England town I was told that it was publicly burned in the square, before the public library, to satisfy the people in the town that the two copies accidentally bought by the librarian were safely removed out of the community and could contaminate no one any more.

However, any abuse I have had has been more than offset by appreciation. I have been mighty well used, as you know, and have no kick coming.

As to the question regarding the change of *Windy McPherson's Son*, I thought the end of it as it stood in the first edition sentimental and untrue, and changed it for that reason.

I think the meanest possible thing anyone ever did to me was in a little church community somewhere in the Middle West, where they once took me up in prayer meeting and sent me a copy of their prayers, typewritten. It upset me a good deal to have them act as my agents before God, and I really think that was the meanest trick ever done me.

Now I urge you to come to New York soon; drop me a line a few days before, and, as you know, I will be glad to give you any additional dope I can.

Please give my respects to Smith[6] and to Carl, when you see him, and you might tell Smith I would be charmed to have a copy of his new book.

Sincere regards.

Sherwood Anderson

TS. NL

1. Literary editor of the Chicago *Daily News*, who was gathering material for his book *Midwest Portraits* (1923).
2. *A Thousand and One Afternoons in Chicago* (1922).
3. Hansen had asked Anderson to comment on his birthplace and parents, his early reading, the influence of European authors (especially Russian) upon his writings, the revised ending of the 1922 edition of *Windy McPherson's Son*, and "the meanest possible" reaction to his work.
4. Anderson's oft-repeated claim that his mother was of Italian ancestry is, like his father's alleged southern origins, apparently without basis. She died on 10 May 1895, when Sherwood was eighteen.
5. English novelist, author of *Lavengro* (1851) and *The Romany Rye* (1857).
6. Henry Justin Smith, writer for the Chicago *Daily News*, who had just published *Deadlines* (1922).

TO Jean Toomer[1]

22 December [1922], New York

Dear Jean Toomer—

Your work is of special significance to me because it is the first Negro work I have seen that strikes me as really Negro. That is surely splendid. I wanted so much to find and express myself something clear and beautiful I felt coming up out of your race but in the end gave up. I did not want to write of the Negro but out of him. Well, I wasn't one. The thing I felt couldn't be truly done.

And then McClure handed me the few things of yours I saw and there was the thing I had dreamed of—beginning.[2]

You are right about McClure. He is the real thing—one of the most fundamentally sweet men I've seen as is also Julius Friend of the *Double Dealer*. It gives me joy that the *D D*—a southern magazine—is bringing you forward.

You speak of a book—are you ready to publish a book and will you have any trouble finding a publisher. I would be so glad to go to bat for you—that is to say go see and talk with any publisher you wish me to.

Also if my writing an introductory scrawl for you would be of any help—call on me.

In London I met a woman of your race[3] with whom I had some good talk and with whom I have had some correspondence but in the end I felt she was a bit too Negro.

I felt something like this—that she was inclined to overestimate everything done by a Negro because a Negro had done it.

In you, that is to say in your work, I have not felt anything of the sort. It is really one indication of a rather too great inner humbleness expressed in an outer too great race boldness—isn't it.

Anyway—thank God I haven't seen or felt it in any things of yours I've seen and I will be only too glad if you will let me see any of your other things.

Will get Dec. *Double Dealer.*

Do come to see me if you get to New York.

Sherwood Anderson

MS. Fisk

1. Toomer, living in Washington, D.C., was then working on *Cane* (1923).
2. *Double Dealer* published "Nora" and "Storm Ending" in its September issue and "Harvest Song" in December.
3. Ruth Anna Fisher.

TO Harry Hansen

[c. 26 December 1922, New York]

Dear Harry.

There were several novels written that were not published and none of which were offered for publication.[1]

When I came back to Chicago from my manufacturing adventure in Ohio about 8 years ago I had four novels—*Windy McPherson*—*Marching Men*—a novel called "Talbot Whittingham" and one called "Mary Cochran."

Later when after and through the efforts of Floyd Dell *Windy* was published I did revamp *Marching Men*.

Then I had a severe nervous breakdown and went off down into the Ozark mountains. This was before *Windy* was published however.

While there I wrote a novel which I threw out of the car window on the way home.

And as for this matter of unpublished novels—I wrote most of one last year which will never be finished.

It's an odd business this novel or story writing with me. For example I went home the other evening here and on the way home just the form of a longish short story I've been waiting to write for years came to me clearly.

I sat down when I got home and wrote until three in the morning—went to bed—slept until seven and got up and went to the house of a friend.[2]

I was tired and he had some good whiskey.

At his house I sat and wrote in a heat until about 3 that afternoon—that is to say almost 7 hours more.

It was a curious experience. When I got through most of a quart of whiskey was gone but the story was fixed as I wanted it.

Perhaps I had written 12 or 15000 words. I don't know yet.

I was perfectly sober until I had written the last word and then suddenly I was drunk and went and fell into bed and slept for several hours like a dead man.

As to that story I've tried to write it a dozen times and it wouldn't come—that is to say just the swing and rhythm of the prose to fit the theme wouldn't come.

That happens about novel writing sometimes. For example I wrote a novel last year called "Ohio Pagans," threw it away and then went to work on *Many Marriages*.

All this might sound discouraging if it were not for the fact that I love passionately the mechanics of writing, the blank sheets before me, the smell of ink.

You see as to those earlier novels—they really belong to a period of my writing that is past. I couldn't go back to work over material conceived in one mood when my whole writing mood has passed on to something else.

What I myself believe is that—if I am of any account as a writer—and I do think I can sometimes tell a story in first-rate style—is that my career as an individual writer began really with *Winesburg*.

What I mean is, Harry, that the previous books were too deeply influenced by the work of others—my own mood as a writer did not appear clearly enough.

This is a long-winded scrawl but you have brought it on yourself by asking for it. I really like to gossip about my craft, you see.

And here is the point about those unfinished things—they weren't just clear straight-forward story telling.

You see, Harry—where most writers fail—and this is not clearly enough understood—is because they aren't at bottom story tellers. They have theories about writing, notions about style, often real writing ability, but they do not tell the story—straight out—bang.

You see after all, Harry, style—well the devil—it's like the dress worn by the actor—the way he walks across the stage etc. etc.—important to be sure—

But—if the man is thinking too much of these things—and isn't feeling within himself the part he is to play—

Well what I am trying to say is that style should naturally grow out of the content of the thing itself.

And that brings me back to these destroyed books. The story in them was not clearly put across and I suppose I wasn't ready to put it across. Then I went off into experimental things—the books frankly were no good.

And it's always better to throw such work away and not try to fool with it. In fact I have got so nowadays that if a story does not come fairly singing out of me—if it stops dead—I let it go and go walk and look at the ships in the river.

It takes patience to do this but it works. Why, do you know man, I've got stories tucked away inside myself that have been there ten years and I can't tell them yet. There are things I don't understand about them. I'm not ready. Someday perhaps I will be ready.

I don't know why I'm taking this roundabout way to answer a few simple questions—only I think the throwing away of these things had a kind of significance. I suppose I'm really explaining it to myself as I write to you.

No I never used any part of any of the books but the characters—some of them—did remain living things in the world of my imagination and every now and then one of them pops up and insists on being put into a story but always into a quite different story than the one told originally—and that happened to have been Mary Cochran's experience.

Sherwood Anderson

MS. NL

1. Hansen had asked Anderson about "Mary Cochran" and other early unpublished works.

2,. The friend was Stark Young. Anderson describes this experience in *Memoirs*, 434–35, and identifies the story as "The Man's Story," published in *Dial* 75 (Sept. 1923): 247–64, and in *Horses and Men* (1923).

TO Paul Rosenfeld

Thursday 15 [March 1923, Reno[1]]

Dear Paul—

Elizabeth[2] tells me you have decided not to make the trip—but anyway I did have the joy of anticipation. Very soon now she will come west and I shall be able to see her from time to time.

In the meantime I work—rather intensely. As for the actual work that creeps out from under my pen—I can't be sure of it yet.

But a process is going on—a sort of process of internal adjustment perhaps. On these days, sometimes I feel as though it were a kind of inner distillation with the hope perhaps of finding some new primary colors on my pallet when it is all over.

The effect of the year, [with] its devastating intensity of feeling, is—O I hope—just a little more knowledge, more wit—I devoutly hope—in seeing things and people.

A kind of poetic fervor for life I have always had but I want knowledge too, all I can get, nor do I care to be protected from any possible devastating effect of it.

It is a thing I know you have and that I love you for having—even when it cuts the ground out from under me.

I've thought a lot out here—thought and felt a lot. In a sense and for the time being my body has been a quite secondary thing. I walk so many miles—breathe so much air, put my feet down on the ground and see houses and hills as one might look at them in photographs.

There are all sorts of attempts at adjustment—looking at things of my past—bringing them into relation to myself as I stand today—on my two legs—as closely as I can.

Elizabeth also wrote me she had seen you for an afternoon and that made me happy. I cared about your knowing her a little better a lot.

I've been thinking of you too, Paul, and a quality you have that distinguishes you from all other men I have known.

There is something. Many men can feel—as you do—the beauty of a passage, a vase, a painting, a rug, but who but you quite gets into the realization of beauty, so subtile an understanding of the difficulties of creating beauty.

That rare and delicate quality in you has made you invaluable to me, dear friend, although I know I have expressed my feeling of it sometimes so lamely and crudely.

As for Elizabeth, I think you will know why I wanted just particularly you to feel her beauty and what it has brought and is bringing to me.

I did a bold thing—asked Stieglitz[3] to let me have—to hang in my room while here—one or two of his things.

Alas Paul. I've become, I'm afraid, civilized. I can't quite live without touches of beauty from other men's hands about me.

And I wonder, sometime, when you are there, if you would mind getting for me another copy of the dry point I got from Miller[4]—the young girl's head. If he has one I may have—I'll send you [a] check. The one I got I gave to Elizabeth's brother.[5]

I rather have to have small things on account of the difficulty later—of getting them about. I may be gone for a year—you see. But I do hope to come back then and to be near you.

I am to have David Prall—Elizabeth's brother—for three days next week and that will be a help.

As a matter of fact I've written a good deal—have plowed straight in thinking to go back and balance and weigh what I have done a little later.

And are you working. I had two reactions when I got your first wire—first, joy in the thought you might come—second, fear that things were not on the swing for you and that you might have cause for personal unhappiness.

With love
Sherwood

By an odd chance I haven't seen the book yet but Huebsch says he has sent another copy.[6]

MS. NL

1. Anderson was living in Reno to obtain a divorce from Tennessee Mitchell.
2. Elizabeth Prall, then working in New York, who in Apr. 1924 became Anderson's third wife.
3. Alfred Stieglitz, photographer and art exhibitor.
4. Kenneth Hayes Miller, New York artist.
5. David Prall, a philosophy professor at the University of California at Berkeley.
6. *Many Marriages*, published 20 Feb.

TO F. Scott Fitzgerald

[mid-March? 1923, Reno]

Dear Fitz—

One of my brothers sent me your review of my novel[1] and I read it with delight. It's a kind of satisfaction to get broken away from the "realist" notion.

It is pretty evident I did not handle with entire success the notion of the little stone given the daughter by Webster or the fellow in *Poor White* sitting in the train and playing with the handful of bright stones.

You see it may well be that the idea I have isn't well digested in me. Maybe I'm a serious ass. Vulgarity and ugliness often hurt me physically like sitting on a board full of nails.

And at such times some little thing—a well made chair, a bit of jewelry, a touch of color remembered from some painting—seems to cheer me up and make me grin again.

Wish I had had some chance to talk with you—with neither of us tanked.[2]

Did Boyd[3]—Minneapolis—tell you the charming ironic story—how I went about saying you could write but your style bothered me and your people seemed to me insignificant and not worthwhile, while you were, at the same moment, taking the same shots at me, in the same words.

I grinned with joy when I heard it.

Am in the west—having chucked our well known centers of civilization for the time. Some day I hope really to become acquainted with you and Mrs. Fitz.

Sincerely
Sherwood Anderson

MS. Princeton

1. "Sherwood Anderson on the Marriage Question," a review of *Many Marriages* in New York *Herald*, 4 Mar. 1923.

2. They had met at a party given by Theodore Dreiser while Anderson was in New York, an occasion described in *Memoirs*, 454–55.

3. Thomas Boyd, author and literary editor of the St. Paul *Daily News*.

TO Paul Rosenfeld

[late March 1923, Reno]

Dear Paul—

You are a beast for never writing and I would swear at you but that I have had a feeling perhaps you are ill or unhappy. Do let me know how you are.

I'm getting into pretty good shape myself. When I first came here the high altitude and my own state of mind—that had for so long kept me tense and upset—would not let me sleep at night. I took the sun and wind cure for it—staying at my desk from eight 'til twelve and then spending all the rest of the day outdoors.

The sun shines every day here and the days are warm and the nights cool. In the valley the grass is becoming green and leaves are beginning to show on the trees.

The book is rather fun.[1] I've never let myself say some of the things I wanted to and now I'm rather letting go all holds and pouring it out.

As I see it now the book will separate into three sections—

1. Youth—the call of the material world—the call of the life of the imagination—
2. The period of the attempt to go out to the world—to take it at its own valuation—the muddle of sex—etc. etc.
3. The beginning of the realization of surfaces—the significance of the artist's life etc.

I think of calling the book "Immaturity"—a protest. The writing runs along in comments—narrative—observations etc. as one would talk to a dear friend.

It may come off. I've already written the first section—some 40000 words—through the first time—so you see I haven't been idle.

Reno begins to amuse me. Such a place you have never dreamed of. Some 700 to 1000 divorcees, many lawyers, small hotels, Indians in gaudy blankets, flappers with dogs—pretty girls on horseback, cowboys, gambling houses, bootleggers, sage brush deserts, trout fishing and the snow clad hills looking down and grinning at it all.

I've picked up a young chap—rather a gentleman—relative of the Gould family—and we knock about together. He stays here, becomes engaged to be married to pretty divorcees and then they marry and go away and he gets another but in the afternoons he likes to tramp and that's the side of him I get.

I haven't much idea at all as to how *Many Marriages* is being received but I believe some 7000 or 8000 have been sold in the first month. It may go to 12000. For the time being I keep away from thoughts of it. When you are ready you must write me your impressions. Does it now strike you as a real piece of work or doesn't it.

Don't be afraid to hit me. I like it. I want to do my work well, if I can.

As regards the situation, I'm glad I have done what I have this year. It is going to prove the healthy thing. Something dark, afraid is gone out of my life. I look forward to the days to work—to love—in life.

And I do want to know you are all right. You mean something to me, I fancy you know.

Sherwood

MS. NL

1. The book later entitled *A Story Teller's Story* (1924).

TO Harry Hansen

[27 May 1923, Reno]

Dear Harry.

Your question is perplexing—largely because I am afraid I grow always more and more a bit sheepish about discussing seriously my own efforts.

I should say, wouldn't you, that prose always opens new vistas to one working in it. Hardly anyone cares enough to work long and patiently—I suppose because they are after results—praise, fame or something of the sort.

One who writes however out of pure sensual delight in white paper, the smell of ink, sentence forms, etc. etc. might try all sorts of purely experimental things.

Why not think of the Testament therefore, Harry, as pretty much the prose writer's experiments in rhythm—of words, emotions, thoughts.

I believe it to be just that. You see, I have never given it book publication—although there is a great deal of it.[1]

I go back to it now and then, trying to break it into new rhythms, new freedom of imagery.

Will it achieve form of its own?

Will it sometimes break into real poetry?

That I should say is on the knees of the gods and for the present I am content to let it lie there.

Sincerely,
Sherwood

MS. NL

1. Anderson published his "New Testaments" in magazines from 1919 to 1927, when they were collected in *A New Testament*.

TO Georgia O'Keeffe[1]

[29 October 1923, Reno]

Dear Georgia O'Keeffe—

You know something of this country out here. Yesterday I was up on the mountains—go almost every day. It is a land of strange phenomena. Some of the mountains are altogether bare, others with sudden little upland valleys wooded with big pines. Almost anywhere you come on flocks of sheep attended by a silent Basque. These Basque came here in the early days with the Spaniards and are very successful with sheep—having cared for sheep on their own hills in Spain for generations. Many of them grow rich and ride around in expensive automobiles but they remain silent sheep men anyway. They have little restaurants of their own where, if they are not suspicious, you may have good white wine.

The book on which I have been working here is done and I have half a notion it has something to say, now I am at work on some tales that have been in my head for years but never would come straight, couldn't just get the tune, now perhaps I shall.

Will get through here in the next month or two one way or another.[2]

Don't too much care anyway. If the woman fights I'll let her hang on to the form of marriage. It's all a queer business. Such a fuss about nothing. What asses we all are—children, Stieglitz would say.

I have sent Stieglitz my new book of tales *Horses and Men* to his New York address. There is one tale, at least, in the book I think he'll like and perhaps you will too—the one called "The Man Who Became a Woman." It's all about horses and niggers and other things of the sort.

As for the natives here, cowboys, ranchers, gamblers, etc., they are rather crude, noisy, brutal children who seem to get a real satisfaction out of hurting animals. I like the silent sheep men better.

It would be fun to come out there in the fall. I'll probably stay out here during the winter and come east with the early spring. Want to get myself some kind of a little house where I can have some painting and other things about.

Love to you both.

Sherwood Anderson

MS. Yale

1. The artist, who married Alfred Stieglitz in 1924.
2. Anderson's divorce from Tennessee Mitchell was granted in Apr. 1924.

TO Ben Huebsch

[c. 9 December 1923, Reno]

Dear Ben

Thanks for sending the Newton Arvin article.[1] Great God, he is intelligent, isn't he. He gets what I am driving at. Who is he. I am so far out of the world I do not keep much in touch just now.

Since the long book has been finished have attempted several short stories that did not come off.

Then one day last week got into a real story and finished it—first writing—10000 words in two days. It will be a peach of a story when I have inked it in.

And then bang—right on top of that I got the new novel theme for which I have been feeling about in the darkness for months. Oh, it's lovely—a real story.

Do sell a lot of *Horses and Men*—10000 anyway. I'll need the money. Am not broke but pretty bent. Did hope the Feb. check would go to $2000 but hell, I've no kick coming.

Isn't it fine old [Van Wyck] Brooks is to have the *Dial* prize. He has deserved it a long time.

Harper's have my long thing. They should decide in a week or two.[2] Sold a pretty good tale to Mencken for his new *Mercury*.[3]

As regards the story book—Miss Newman—she is, as I suspected she might be, all wrong in choosing "The Other Woman" from among my tales.[4] O'Brien made the same mistake. He chose that story for his Best Story book[5] in the same year I wrote the tale "The Egg," an incomparably finer thing.

These people go wrong because they have their eyes too much on conventional technique. "The Other Woman" is so decidedly French in technique and spirit. It's a clever story—no less. I wrote it partly with my tongue in my cheek—bad little boy stuff. In a sense just wanted to show the mutts I know their damn technique.

Here are a list of stories—real stories—"The Untold Lie"—*Winesburg*, "Hands"—*Winesburg*, "The Egg"—*Triumph*, "Out of Nowhere Into Nothing"—*Triumph*, "I Want to Know Why"—*Triumph*.

In *Horses and Men*—"The Man's Story" and "I'm a Fool."

Solidest of all my tales "The Egg."

Second "Untold Lie." Here is a tale overlooked—solid as a rock.

To be sure Miss Newman is doing the book and I'm only telling you and her. And, Ben, I'm much more conscious of technique etc. than the critics think I am. It's pretty childish to think an artist gets results without knowing what he is doing.

On my list Dr. B.H. Caples—Masonic Bldg., Reno—never got his copy *Horses and Men*. Will you try another.

I wrote to Stein.

How is the baby. Regards to Mrs. Huebsch.

With love
Sherwood

Working like hell. Sell 'em *Horses and Men*. I'll need lots of oats.

MS. LC

1. "Mr. Anderson's New Stories," *Freeman* 8 (5 Dec. 1923): 307–308.
2. Harper's was considering a plan to publish *A Story Teller's Story* serially in *Harper's Magazine* and later as a book. The magazine rejected the manuscript, however, and Huebsch published the book in 1924.
3. "Caught," *American Mercury* 1 (Feb. 1924): 165–76.
4. Frances Newman was editing an anthology, *The Short Story's Mutations from Petronius to Paul Morand*. She changed her selection to "I'm a Fool" before the book was published by Huebsch in 1924.
5. Edward J. O'Brien, ed., *The Best Short Stories of 1920* (Boston: Small, 1921), 3–11.

TO Jean Toomer

[3 January 1924, Berkeley, Cal.]

Dear Jean Toomer.

Cane came along to me at Christmas and last night, when I had got into bed, I plunged into it and finished it before I slept. It dances.

It made me feel—what did it not make me feel? Once I lived in New Orleans and I'm going back there to live, for keeps, one of these days. There I used to spend hours on the docks, watching the ships come in and most of all watching the blacks at work.

They sang, their bodies sang. I used to go blessing them—saying to myself it was glorious there was not a neurotic among them but now I can no longer say that.

You I am sure belong to us, nervous distraught ones, us moderns, and it is quite wonderful to think you belong also to the men I saw working on the docks, the black men.

I never tried to talk to them, never approached them.

Perhaps I did not know how much I wanted a voice from them.

When I saw your stuff first I was thrilled to the toes. Then I thought—"He has let the intense white men get him. They are going to color his style, spoil him."

I guess that isn't true. You'll stay by your own, won't you.

It is just a little crack opened of the thing you have got, that no one else can get—yet.

It is very very fine to me.

I've often wondered—do you paint. God what a painting story your people have got—for someone.

Sincerely
Sherwood Anderson

℅ Max Radin,[1] 2597 Buena Vista Way, Berkeley, Calif.

MS. Fisk

1. Law professor at the University of California whose wife, Dorothea, was Elizabeth Prall's sister.

TO Jean Toomer

[18 January 1924, Reno]

Dear Jean Toomer—

The ill health you speak of finding in New York has I fancy been in every capital of every civilization always—don't you think? Sometimes I think it is inherent in what we call intellectuality.

A man like yourself can escape. You have a direct and glowing genius that is, I am sure, a part of your body, a part of the way you walk, look at things, make love, sleep and eat. Such a man goes rather directly from feeling to expression. He has hellish times but keeps fairly well cleaned out. I dare say you won't stay in New York. The warm south, no matter what its attitude toward you, will call you back.

I have myself—having Italian blood in me—have a constant call southward. Something pagan and warm comes to me on a train going southward. I spent two long periods, one at Mobile, another at New Orleans. I dare say I had advantages there you couldn't have had. On the other hand I missed much.

The Negro life was outside me, had to remain outside me. That may have been why I wanted to paint. There was less mind, more feeling. I could approach the brown men and women through a quite impersonal love of color in skins, through the same kind of love of line as expressed in lazy sprawling bodies.

That perhaps led me to the attempt to paint. I haven't done much with it since. Think I shall be back there next summer. Would like, I fancy, the breathless summer heat of it.

It may be someday you will approach painting as you have writing—in those moments when you are so fully yourself. If one could forget what has been taught about painting, much might be done.

I myself had, I thought, an advantage as I could not draw. I went for line and spaces only and the color I could lay into them. Subconscious things I fancy welled up. I owed nothing to painting, to the traditions of painting, being no painter, being just a fellow with a brush in my hand and pots of color before me. I used water color. It's cheap. $12 or $15 would outfit me.

What I got offered nothing, I dare say, to anyone but myself. There were, however, happy, excited hours, just the tenderness of a bit of color coming up—like the things in your book, when the smoke from the sawdust piles drifts over one of those terrible little Georgia mill towns at evening.

And the roads—your people laughing and walking in the roads, the significance of roads in the south, to your people, brought out like color in a painting.

I speak of it at length only as a possible additional joy to you in life, something added.

Your problem is bound to be hellish. That hellishness won't fail to come to any artist in our time but you are pioneering I think more than any of us. The ungodly ghastly emptiness. White men only about 11 or 12 years old, the best of them perhaps.

Write me now and then and tell me of your thoughts, where you are and what you are doing.

Sherwood Anderson

MS. Fisk

TO John Gould Fletcher[1]

[early July 1924, Berkeley, Cal.]

Dear John Gould Fletcher.

Your note got to me at Berkeley, Calif. and I write at once to tell you my European trip for the year is off. I was rich and suddenly I am poor. Had sold the ms. for the serialization of my new book at a good price but the magazine—a new one—is reported about to bust.[2]

For myself I think that "I'm a Fool" is a first class but not important story. There are better stories in the book.[3] "The Man's Story" is far beyond it.

You see this is not addressed to you to refute what you say because you haven't read the others.

But isn't it rather stretching a point to call me—because I live in an adolescent civilization and write sympathetically of adolescence—an eternal adolescent. It doesn't seem to me that if I were that I could even be on top of my subject enough to write of it.[4]

That at least is my slant.

I've an idea I shall be in New Orleans at 504 St. Peter's Street when you get over here. It may be I shall also be in New York for a few weeks in the fall.

At any rate when you get over here drop me a line as to your own plans.

And I do hope your own work will come clear and fine for you.

It would be fun to see you.

Sherwood Anderson

MS. Ark.

1. Arkansas poet living in England.

2. *Phantasmus*, a short-lived magazine published in Pittsburgh, printed two excerpts from *A Story Teller's Story* in its May and June numbers before folding.

3. *Horses and Men*.

4. Fletcher replied that he had meant to compliment Anderson on his youthful point of view.

TO Henry S. Canby[1]

[mid-July 1924], New Orleans

Dear Henry Canby—

I have just moved into my new quarters in New Orleans, my things are not unpacked and I have nothing at hand but this light yellow paper.

However I want to answer your fine letter as best I can. I believe you had a note from me about the matter of the publication of *A Story*

Teller's Story.[2] That matter was quite settled by circumstances and I am not sorry.

The other matter covered by your letter also touches me closely. We started to speak of it when we last met at Berkeley but circumstances prevented our going deeply into the matter. I am sorry. I should have liked to make my position clear to you.

In that conversation as in your letter of today you spoke of a kind of obligation to the public. I wonder if our minds do not take a quite natural turn in two directions here.

It is a matter on which I have thought a good deal. Perhaps I may have seemed to you at times perverse, purposely flaunting something offensive to a great many people, making myself disliked when being disliked was unnecessary. You may often have thought I might have gone with lighter and more cautious tread through the halls of the house of my fancy.

If you, dear Canby, think I have wanted to defy public opinion, that I have wanted even to make myself disliked, you have been greatly mistaken in me.

I have tried to be, as far as I could, an experimental artist working in the medium of human emotions expressed in words. Many times when I have got up from a piece of work, having had the clean feeling of having done the job as well as I could, and then later when the work shocked many decent, nice people, I have been amazed. Can anything be unclean when the workman does not feel unclean in doing it. I think you will bear me out in the assertion that I have never been smug, self-satisfied, a smart-alec.

But dare I at all begin to bring the public into my workroom. Dear Canby—what is this public? Where is it to be found?

I confess to you I know nothing of it. I know only individual men and women.

For example after I had published *Many Marriages* and you had praised it[3] there was as you know a chorus of condemnation from other New York critics.

But do you know, man, that private letters I got from men I think the finest artists in America, painters, musicians etc. etc., more than agreed with you while the very men who had formerly condemned as bitterly books like *Winesburg* and had now only praise for them went to the other extreme.

Where is this public? What of it? What does it really think?

I grant you there are men who have a quick ear for public attention. They may be valuable men to publishing houses. Would you ask me to trust them? I think you would not.

Dear Canby, I have no desire to make a lot of money—do not want it. I live on the scale of a plumber, have my corner in which to work. I have had some financial reverses this year and for a time was scared but have got over my scare.

Even since I have written you things have happened. My books are coming out in Russian. The Germans are printing four of them for which they pay me advance royalties. Sweden has bought the rights to *Poor White*. The Tauchnitz[4] (spelling doubtful) are going to bring out my books. Perhaps I shall have a European public if I cannot get a large one here.

At Berkeley I delivered a lecture on modern writing before I left. Although my books had not sold much there, over 1200 people came to hear what I had to say. Perhaps, if I cannot sell largely enough to support myself, I can talk for a living and keep in the experimental mood, as regards writing itself, that means so much to me.

Anyway I do appreciate your own kindness and generosity. My speech at Berkeley covered the very subject you say you would like me to write on in the *Post*. I could very well make one article of it. Would you like me to try?[5] It is a somewhat important matter to me. The article would run to 6000 or 7000 words but perhaps could be split. What could you engage to pay.

I shall probably be in New York in the late fall—and in the meantime I am, just now, struggling with proofs of *A Story Teller's Story*.

My best regards to Mrs. Canby.

Sincerely
Sherwood Anderson

MS. Yale

1. Editor of *Literary Review*, a supplement to the New York *Evening Post*.
2. Canby had been involved the previous year in the unsuccessful negotiations with Harper's to publish *A Story Teller's Story*.
3. In a review in *Literary Review*, 24 Feb. 1923, p. 483.
4. A publishing house in Leipzig, Germany, which in 1926 reprinted *Dark Laughter*.
5. "A Note on Realism" appeared in *Literary Review* on 25 Oct. 1924, pp. 1–2.

TO Roger Sergel[1]

[c. 22 July 1924], New Orleans

Dear Sergel—

It is good to think of you off in a quiet place and away from papers and lectures.[2] I am myself, just now, deeply buried in proofs of *A Story Teller's Story*.

We have come to New Orleans to live and have an apartment in the old part of town—just now very hot—very charming—and cost not too great.

Have had so much financial bad luck this year that I have come to the place where it is a choice between going back to advertising writing and going—for two or three months a year—on the lecture platform (if there is a demand for me there).

Have therefore got a manager who is going to try to make engagements for me[3] and if there are any organizations in Pittsburgh or other town that should be addressed and you know who they are let me know. At any rate I could see you.

I've a sort of notion—and it may be wrong—that I'm a sort of public character and they'll come to see & hear me. It will be of course exhibitionism but it seems to me the best way out.

My 16 year old boy[4] has been quite ill and I have been upset about him but now he is O.K. again and as soon as I have got proofs off my hands I hope to be able to work again.

Hope the summer is panning out for you and that Mrs. Sergel and the children are well.

With love
Sherwood Anderson

MS. NL

1. Then English professor at the University of Pittsburgh, later head of the Dramatic Publishing Company in Chicago and Westport, Conn.
2. Sergel was vacationing at Boswell, Pa.
3. W. Colston Leigh, of Leigh Lecture Bureau in New York.
4. Robert Anderson.

TO V.F. Calverton[1]

[late July 1924, New Orleans]

Dear Mr. V.F. Calverton—

I received your note and the copy of *Modern Quarterly*—with your article and the Ernest Boyd introduction.[2] Your approach sounds sound. I myself, as a matter of fact, had my chance at a bourgeois life, as a comfortable, well-to-do manufacturer and turned aside from it. My instincts have always been altogether in another direction. However I instinctively hated the sentimentalizing of working people. It seemed to me a sort of insult to them.

What I do feel, my dear Calverton, is that you, like most men who make the scientific approach, may, in treating the individual artist, consider him too much from one point of view. In the desire to analyze, most scientists miss—it often seems to the artist—the whole point. You are too detached and not detached enough.

May I illustrate?

Roger Sergel
COURTESY OF ELEANOR ANDERSON

You write me under date July 21 saying, "I consider your work, and then Mr. Dreiser's, the most important that has appeared in America in twenty years" etc.

In the issue of your magazine Summer 1924 you publish—page 78—a review of my last published book signed "O.L." that is a kind of brief funeral sermon of my remains as a writer.[3]

There is a seeming detachment here—from the magazine of which you are editor—that is amazing.

Or are you also writing a funeral sermon?

I do want you to know that the man working with certain materials cannot be any kind of workman at all if he cannot detach himself, view things objectively sometimes. The man who just floated with the current having no objective at all in sight would naturally just drown.

You will see that what I do dread is an entirely scientific mind. I dread it because I'm afraid it would make me dislike you.

Sincerely
Sherwood Anderson

TS. NYPL

1. Critic, author, and editor of *Modern Quarterly*.
2. "Sociological Criticism of Literature," 2 (Summer 1924): 1–21.
3. The review of *Horses and Men* asserts that Anderson "has said his say; his sun is setting—too rapidly."

TO V.F. Calverton

Monday [25 August 1924, New Orleans]

My dear Calverton—

Your letter came this morning and I put it aside until I had finished my morning's work so that I might think about it a little. I have been through this novel once, rather at white heat, often writing four or five thousand words in a morning. Now I am back into it for a second writing. It has so absorbed me that I do not see how I can possibly promise you anything for the fall number. I shall not want to think of anything else until this book is out of the way and it may well keep me tied up for two months yet. I shall be fortunate if I can get it all down in that time as it may be rather a long novel.

You see, *Phantasmus*, after offering me a very good price for the serial rights to *A Story Teller's Story*, got the book and then did not pay me. That is the reason I shall probably have to do some lecturing this winter—if anyone wants me—a dollar and cents matter. You must know that the popular magazines do not often buy my things and I have three children to support besides myself. My books do not sell very much. I say all this to explain why I am so anxious to do this book and nothing else during these early fall months. If I go lecturing, it will be impossible to maintain the rather intense application necessary to keep the book as alive as I want it to be.

The book *A Story Teller's Story* will be published as a book by Huebsch in October. We recently got the ms. back from *Phantasmus* and Mencken wants to use some of it in *Mercury*—October issue—if it is not too late. He wrote me yesterday that the magazine was all set up but that he was going to try to get an installment in. Whether or not he will succeed I can't say. He lives, I believe, in Baltimore and has the ms. there. Why not see him? If he is not going to be able to use any of the book, perhaps you could find in it something of what you want for your fall issue.[1] When will your fall issue be published? Even if he is going to use some of it there might still be something you would want. Fragments of it have been published in *Phantasmus* and in *Century*[2]—August issue. Any details of price to be paid or anything of that sort would I fancy have to be carried on with my business agent—Otto Liveright, 2 West 43rd Street—New York.

I am suggesting this because it does not seem possible to me now to get at anything else for your fall issue and I hate to seem ungracious. You will, however, understand my position.

It is very curious that in this novel—which I think I shall call "The Lovers"—I am doing a death scene—a murder in fact. I myself always rather liked the murder scene in the harness shop in *Poor White*—didn't you?

As for my philosophy—Lord man—that's a large order. I've a sort of notion that men—in our day—having—because of the coming of the machine—got rather far away from their own hands, bodies, eyes, ears—having rather depended too much upon intellectual development, have got into a jam. There is partial development or none. Men remain immature. Immaturity is no doubt the note of our own American civilization.

I got that feeling myself when I was in business and sought for a way out, if I could find it. Perhaps I only turned to prose, to story telling, because that was a sort of natural trend in me. Also I have done some painting and perhaps, had I the thing to do over, might have gone in for that.

As I have gone along naturally there has come to me a growing feeling for words—word texture, a sense of the book as a thing in itself—as a whole thing if one can make it whole.

Do you not think that in an older day, when men were artisans rather than factory hands, there was a closer connection between the man and the things about him in nature—trees, the land, other men, women, buildings—the facts of life?

Like all the so-called moderns, I would take the fact into myself, color it with my own thinking and feeling, and get it out of me again through the fingers, in words, color, line. You get my drift. I think the arts—practised—are a sort of cure for the disease called living. Living becomes a disease when you remain immature mentally and emotionally after the years when your body comes to physical maturity.

It is rather a question, isn't it, of attempting to live fully, all over, with the mind, the emotions, the body.

The development of artists in America now may be a matter of physical stamina, of physical strength. Take into account men like Sandburg, Dreiser and the others, or a man, outside the arts, whose life has nevertheless been a sort of artistic development—a man like old Clarence Darrow. They are all rather horses physically.

If you are an American you have got to fight it out, inside yourself, with things American, with life as it is, here and now, or you have got to slip off into a book world—live in books—and that means living in a European civilization really. It means something false, artificial. We have surely had enough of that over here.

You see, Calverton, what I have had to contend with is an inclination on people's part to look upon me as something rather unhealthy. There is a dreadful fear of the actuality of life here. People are afraid of it. If you approach it at all closely it seems to others something dreadful. They shrink from it. That I fancy is why our people so love books about life on some other planet, or in a lumber camp or a cow camp.

And if you feel a thing intensely enough to make the people of your book world live in the book, people then confuse what you have done with what they call Realism.

This however is aside from the point. My own desire is to develop my own sensitiveness to life to the highest possible point. To get into myself as much as I can of nature and the people about me and then to be able to so function with my mind and body that, as a workman, I can transmit something of what I have felt to others.

That is about all there is to it. I won't succeed, of course. The trying keeps me more or less happy and healthy I believe and that's why I am at it. It's the best fun I know in life.

The little thing of your own has charming quality—particularly the first part of it, where you talk of the feeling of the teacher.

Sincerely
Sherwood Anderson

TS. NYPL

1. Neither periodical used any portion of the book in its fall issue.
2. "When I Left Business for Literature," 108 (Aug. 1924): 489–96.

TO Alfred Stieglitz

[4 September 1924, New Orleans]

Dear Stieglitz:

I am having another one of my little bad times. They last 3 or 4 days.

What happens is that I work so intensely that all of a sudden I have to stop. It takes the form of a cold in the head—something of that sort. I am simply tired or I need to do some quiet thinking about the work I am on.

Here it isn't difficult to rest. You walk a block to the Mississippi. Big ocean steamers are coming and going. The niggers are working, laughing, sweating and singing. They have the real flair for physical things. One of them rolls a heavy barrel of oil down a sharp incline. He plays with it as a cat with a ball—never letting it quite get out of hand. In all handling of heavy loads in difficult places they are as clever as a good boxer. The load never quite gets the upper hand. When it is on their shoulders or heads there is a remarkable play of the body muscles, giving to the load—controlling it. Often a Negro with a heavy load, walking on a narrow plank, does a little dance step to show he has the upper hand. I hope Harry Wills defeats Firpo—the Argentine Bull.[1] I have come to have a real feeling of nearness—not to any particular Negro but to them all. They rest me, playing with life as they do.

I am sorry you were put to the bother of making the picture—for publicity—but am glad Huebsch is to have it.

The agent—for my lectures—wanted to print a circular. Your photographs were still in the West—not having been shipped yet. A painter here came forward and offered to make a little sketch and like a fool I let him. It was terrible—ugly. What was I to do. Could I tell him how ugly it was? I hadn't character enough. I hope you do not see it.

After a time perhaps I shall grow strong enough not to let little painters paint me.

There is a son of a rich southern family here[2]—lives alone in an old plantation house in the country and paints. Quite lovely still life things. Fine delicate feeling for line & color. He came to call on me and began suddenly to talk—of [Marsden] Hartley, Rosenfeld, O'Keeffe, [John] Marin,[3] Stieglitz. They were the people of importance. Why could not the South have a few such people—etc., etc.

It was very amazing coming from a man buried away in a little southern town. You see Stieglitz how far your influence has gone—for these are all children of yours. The man knew that too.

We are moving into another apartment—540 B, St. Peter Street, about Sept. 15. Rather it is not a move. We have only camped here.

There we will have some things about, pictures, books, a few sticks of our own furniture.

Love to you both.
Sherwood Anderson

Huebsch will send you a copy of the new book in late September.

MS. Yale

1. The fight between Harry Wills, a black heavyweight from Louisiana, and Luis Firpo on 11 Sept. 1924 was declared "no decision."
2. Weeks Hall, of New Iberia, La.
3. Stieglitz exhibited the paintings of both Hartley and Marin.

TO Ruth Kelso[1]

[12 March 1925, New Orleans]

My dear Ruth Kelso

To say that the teaching of writing is impossible would, it seems to me, be sound enough—to say however that the proper approach to writing cannot be taught is absurd.

Really I would have no quarrel at all with all you are doing. However I think there is something that might be stressed. We all do seem to need to be so plagued utilitarian. Yesterday a young boy came into my study. He has been walking on the docks among the shipping men for days. With all his heart he wants to write. He goes to walk on the docks, sees the shipping, reads a story by Conrad and tries to write of the sea. Then he reads the *Saturday Evening Post*—or *Adventure* magazine and tries to write of business or a detective story. There is a fever to get published, to begin making money by writing.

Doesn't it really come down to a question of whether the student wants to write as an easy amusing way of making a living or whether he wants to approach writing as an art.

The arts are as you know intangible challenges to the whole of life. There is this queer thing called "the imagination." What may not be done with it.

I know a man who, after several years' futile attempt to do what might be called "good writing," decided to go in for money making. He read the *Saturday Evening Post*—nothing else—tried to train his imagination to work along certain definite lines and succeeded.

A rather dreadful thing happened however. If you have not done so, read the Epilogue to *A Story Teller's Story*.

You see it gets down, doesn't it, to what you want to teach. Our universities, it seems to me, go so far in the way of what they call "equipping people for life" and seem to mean so much one thing—that is to say equipping people to make a living easily—in some slick way.

If you could only teach love of craft for its own sake—brushing out of the minds of the students—as far as that is possible—the idea of success, of putting it over.

So many people in life who have no devotion to anything—so many smart slick men being produced.

Lordy I do not blame the men and women who are working in the schools. Sometimes I think many of them are the only sincere workmen we have left. What is startling is the almost overwhelming preponderance of the other sort of thing.

So much bad sloppy work everywhere. My secretary is ill. That is why I am subjecting you to this horrible script of mine. Work is piled up and an agency has sent me three different women—all presumably able to go out and do their work. Not one of them able to write one clean page.

Dozens of plays being successful in New York. Not two of them felt through, thought through.

In story telling so many little fake ways to arouse temporary emotions, grounded in nothing.

I just wonder if students may be made to know that there is no good art without giving, giving the best of yourself—all of yourself. The relationship with an art should be like the relationship with someone you love.

You see I only talk vaguely. It is so hard to be definite.

Have you read Brooks—*Letters and Leadership* and his *America's Coming of Age*. It seems to me they might say so much more than I am saying about the things I know you care for.

Sincerely
Sherwood Anderson

MS. NL

1. English professor at the University of Illinois who had written to Anderson describing her approach to a proposed course in narrative writing.

TO Julia C. Harris[1]

[c. 1 April 1925, New Orleans]

My dear Julia C. Harris

It was good of you to send me the article—in print[2]—and the letter.[3]

Indeed I did hear from Mr. Wade[4] and forwarded his letter to my lecture agent—one of whose circulars I enclose.

The manifesto too was exciting.[5] It seems to me sometimes that all over the South there is evidence of awakening spiritual and intellectual life.

Often one grows deeply discouraged. I myself have periods of slump when it seems to me I reach the absolute bottom.

I dare say though that my own difficulties are largely a matter of bread and butter. It is a precarious life, this living by the pen, when one does not go in for the sort of thing people think they want.

One sinks into periods of deepest gloom and then one finds people like yourself and your husband.

And then the letter you were good enough to send. Do tell him for me to go ahead with his study of medicine and practice. It will be a real chance to touch people's lives. Also when he comes to writing he will not have to depend on it. Chekhov did that and I have always wished I might have been a doctor myself. It is from such men—who get themselves into a position where they do not need to live by the pen—from whom the most can be expected.

Thank you for writing and sending both articles and the letter.

If I do go to Athens I shall count on seeing you.

Sincerely
Sherwood Anderson

MS. Smith

1. Mrs. Harris and her husband, Julian, son of Joel Chandler Harris, edited the *Enquirer-Sun*, a newspaper in Columbus, Ga.

2. "The Spirit of Revolt in Current Fiction," which she had published in the *Journal of Social Forces* 3 (Mar. 1925): 427–31.

3. That of a young relative of hers in medical school, who wanted to be a writer.

4. John D. Wade, English professor at the University of Georgia, who arranged for Anderson to lecture there in October.

5. A statement of student protest over the selection of a new chancellor at the University of Georgia.

TO Horace Liveright[1]

15 April 1925, New Orleans

Dear Horace:

I am in receipt of your letter of April 11, together with the contract, copy of which I have signed and initialed, and am returning to you, enclosed.

In this same mail I have written to Ben Huebsch, telling him about the contract and making it plain to him that you took this matter up with me at my request. By the time you get this letter he will have the letter telling him that the contract is signed.

Between ourselves it may seem a little unfair to you that I should

Sherwood Anderson with Mr. and Mrs. Julian Harris
COURTESY OF THE NEWBERRY LIBRARY

switch publishers without giving Mr. Huebsch more chance to meet an offer made me by another publisher, but, as you know, I did not feel like shopping around. I have been with Mr. Huebsch for six or seven years and I simply felt that if he had any better proposal to make me, he should have made it long since. As a matter of fact, Horace, you know and I know that his failure to do better with my books is a matter of organization and ability to place them. That has been discussed and we understand each other in that, so I think you will agree with me that I have not been unfair to him.

As for yourself, Horace, I feel you are taking a gamble on me[2] and I am going to give you the best I have in shop. Before this matter came up I had arranged for a lecture trip next winter but after this one trip I will devote all my time to writing and to giving you the best in me.

Now that I have come with you I want to build up in you a feeling of confidence in me, and want you to know I will be just as loyal to you and your house as I possibly can be.

On the other hand you know, Horace, there may be times when for a month or two I will slack off and be unable to produce as I should. That sort of thing seems to be a part of creative work but I, myself, believe that with the worry off my shoulders I shall be able to make this contract more than worthwhile to you and your house.

I sincerely hope that you will be able to get the other books from Mr. Huebsch and, as a matter of fact, Mr. Huebsch owes it to me to give you a good proposition on these books. You are taking chances with me that he could not or would not take.

Now Horace, any time that you can use my judgment in literary matters or anything else, use it. If at any time there is anything I can do for your house, let me know. For one thing, I was for years an advertising writer and a pretty good one. If, at any time, you are booming a book and want to get my notions on this, and when you have time, send the advertising down to me and let me see if I can help make it stronger or better.

As the *Childhood* book[3] will not be ready for publication until next year I think I had better switch off of it and devote the next month or two to the novel,[4] getting that out of the way and in your hands early in June. This will give us a little more time to think about the title and if I have any more ideas about the title I will submit them to you and if not I will go on your judgment and use the title "Deep Laughter." I am a little afraid that the word "Deep" is a little pretentious and it seems probable to me that just the title "Laughter" might be better.

What I most of all want to impress on you, Horace, is that in going with you I go all the way and want you to feel that if there is anything in sincere intent and loyalty I will make your gamble a good one for you in the next few years.

I will leave the matter of handling of any books for the Modern Library[5] to your judgment after you have talked with Mr. Huebsch.

Sincerely yours,

TS. NL (cc)

1. Head of Boni and Liveright publishers and brother of Otto Liveright.
2. Anderson was to be paid a drawing account of $100 a week for five years and was to publish a book each year.
3. *Tar: A Midwest Childhood.*
4. *Dark Laughter*, which Liveright actually received on 26 May.
5. *Poor White* was reprinted in the Modern Library edition in 1926.

TO Horace Liveright

1 June 1925, New Orleans

Dear Horace.

Smith may be right.[1] Anyway I never intended writing a solemn history of the river. How many books have been written about Christ, or Lincoln. I'm not going to be ready for it for some time now as the *Childhood* book will keep me busy for a time. It may be a straight book of adventure when it comes.

Huebsch may be sore but I can't think he would make the kind of remarks the book salesmen attribute to him.[2] It doesn't sound like him. Immediately after you left here I wrote him but did not get an answer for about ten days.

Then he said that he thought I might have let him know before the news leaked out in New York so that he had to get it second hand. How it could have leaked I don't know as I of course wrote him at once. Did some one from your office talk of it? It doesn't matter greatly now.

Of course Ben is sore. Lawrence, Joyce, a dozen others have left him just as I did. You can't expect him to think he isn't all right as a publisher. A man has to justify his job you know Horace but I am sure any soreness will wear off. A man can't stay sore about such a matter.

You know I liked old Ben, always did. You know how I hung on. I wanted to go to you before but my loyalty to him kept me sticking. I guess I'd be sticking yet if I hadn't thought you were being as fine with me and giving me a better chance.

Had your wire and am delighted you are liking the book. Had a nice note from Hemingway. Stark Young wrote and wanted me to say something on the cover of a book I understand you are to publish for him.[3]

That young Bill Faulkner I told you about down here as the one writer here of promise has finished a novel. He calls it "May Day."[4] Do you want to see it. I think he is going to be a real writer.

As ever.

MS. PC (cc)

1. Thomas R. Smith, Boni and Liveright editor, reacting to Anderson's idea of writing a book about the Mississippi, had pointed out the great number of books already written on the subject and recommended that Anderson's book should be fictional rather than factual.

2. Liveright reported as gossip among book salesmen that Huebsch had referred to Anderson as a Judas.

3. Anderson's blurb appeared on the dust jacket of Young's *The Saint*, published by Boni and Liveright in 1925.

4. The novel, later entitled *Soldiers' Pay*, was published by Liveright in 1926.

TO Julia C. Harris

[c. 12 June 1925, New Orleans]

My dear Julia C. Harris

We will hardly manage to go to the trial at Dayton, Tenn.[1] although I should like to hear it and in particular to hear Darrow whom I much admire. The town will, I'm sure, be crowded, the trial may be slow and involved. Bryan is such an old fool.

I know your husband is a born southerner. I wonder if you are. The point is that, after the book on which I am now at work, I want to write a novel about a certain phase of southern life. It would touch just all of the people of what you might call the middle south. The far south, at least New Orleans, is I am sure something special. Ships come and go, there is a large French, Spanish and Italian infusion. I am thinking in particular of Mississippi, Alabama, Tennessee. Of Georgia I know nothing but the article regarding educational conditions makes me think it is the same thing. I wish I might talk to you two about it sometime. I have made some notes of people, conditions etc. Among people who are what one would think of as the upper classes, the gentlemen if you will, there seems to me a strange lack of any grasp of reality, no real touch with the soil. The Negro matter is involved in all this. I have touched on it a little in the novel to be published this fall—not much.

Did I tell you I had to give up Ben Huebsch as a publisher. I have never sold enough to support me. Liveright thought he could do it, in fact guaranteed to do it. I hated to quit Ben who felt, I'm sure, that I had betrayed him by leaving. Do you know him. A very fine chap.

I liked the article. You must make many fine enemies among the stiff-necked.

We are a little puzzled about the summer. Do you happen to know of any good place in the mountains of Tennessee or Georgia where there might be some fishing, where one could live economically. We would like to go somewhere—that doesn't cost a lot—for a month or two a little later. It may be that Virginia would offer the best chance.[2] My regards to you both.

Sherwood Anderson

TS. Smith

1. The "monkey" trial, in which Clarence Darrow defended John T. Scopes, and William Jennings Bryan represented the state of Tennessee.

2. At Mrs. Harris's suggestion, the Andersons spent part of the summer with the John Greear family of Troutdale, Va.

TO Adam Hull Shirk[1]

28 August 1925, New Orleans

Dear Mr. Shirk:

Please convey my thanks to Mr. Bill Hart for the charming photograph he sent me. There has been something of a crime wave in New Orleans and I feel safer with it in my room.

It was delightful of him and you.

Sincerely yours,

TS. NL (cc)

1. Publicity agent for William S. Hart, cowboy film star. The photograph, apparently sent in response to Anderson's admiring mention of Hart in *A Story Teller's Story* (119–20, 428), is inscribed: "For Sherwood Anderson, whose tales give folks a heap of enjoyment and make them a whole lot kinder to everybody. From William S. (Bill) Hart."

TO Ferdinand Schevill[1]

[mid-September 1925, New Orleans]

Dear Ferdinand—

I have sealed your letter. So many things I want to write you about. I take to the pen—my natural medium. About your own book. The few words you say stir me up.

In the novel I am trying to get and give just the slow after effect of war hatred on the emotions of people. You can see how elusive such a theme. I have had to create a style for it.

Dear old Carl.[2] Just my own feeling is that—win or lose—I can't go on writing always in an old mood—the naive people of a small town.

My own feeling is that there has been—in America since the war—a new influx of Europe. It is not so much people coming now as European moods. Cynicism with a sharper tang—the beginning of sophistication here—in the young—in everyone.

Do you agree.

Wish I could talk to you of it.

I don't think it's anything special yet. The question is what it will be. The book is rather biting away at that thought. It is about your own theme isn't it?

Sherwood

MS. NL

1. University of Chicago professor of history. He and his wife, Clara, were close friends of Anderson.

2. Carl Sandburg had commented to Schevill that the entire setting of *Dark Laughter* should have been a small town.

TO Henry Mencken

29 December 1925, New Orleans

Dear Mencken:

I am almost through gabbing. Have to go out to California yet and then that's all—for keeps I hope.

Had I known I would ever have a book that would sell would never have done it.

Have been at work on a spring book—little essays, notes, etc.[1]

When I get back here—about the middle of February—I hope I may be doing something you people may like.

You certainly have got the back country. Everywhere I went they asked me first—what do you think of Mencken?

After that they go to marriage, flappers, why did you write *Many Marriages*, etc.

No matter what I said they put their own opinions in the paper under my name. In one town they made you eager to join the Rotarians and the K.K.K. I think you were blackballed. Anyway they attributed the tale to me.

Need I say that the Anderson herd fell hard for both you and your whiskey?

Sincerely,
Sherwood Anderson

TS. NYPL

1. *Sherwood Anderson's Notebook.*

TO Mary Blair[1]

15 February 1926, New Orleans

My dear Mary Blair:

I am in receipt of your letter of January 23rd and sincerely hope that Wilson has recovered from the measles.

About the play—I only wish you were here so I could talk the matter over with you.[2]

A year ago last winter I was tremendously excited about writing just such a play as you describe in your letter and I remember talking to Wilson about it. I have since that time thought the whole thing out dozens of times but have never tried to put down the words of it.

Three things in New York excited me that winter, that is to say in connection with the theatre. Your own playing in O'Neill's play, Paul Robeson and Lawson's play at the Guild.[3] I presume that the trouble with me is that I have never gone to the theatre much and my imagination has never played very freely within the confines of the theatre and when I am in New York and if I am lucky enough to see a good play or two, I get all stirred up again and when I come away the excitement oozes out of me. I get caught up by some novel or story and the theatre is quite forgotten.

What I really need, I daresay, is someone about who would drive me at it and keep up my interest in the theatre long enough to at least make an attempt. Whether I could do it or not would be another matter.

Have been lecturing this year and kept it up for three months and out of it and also out of *Dark Laughter* got money enough to buy a little farm in Virginia. We are going over there the first of May and will be there all summer. When we get away from people it is just possible that I may get back to this effort to write a play and actually put something down. As I said before I wish you or someone equally interested and with a real flair for the theatre were around and would force me to at least make the attempt.

It is very kind of you to have kept this interest in the idea and if I ever do get at it I want you to see it. With sincere regards,

Sherwood Anderson

TS. NL (ph)

1. Actress and wife of Edmund Wilson.

2. She had asked about a rumor that Anderson had written a play about a black woman and white man and, if he had, whether she might act in it.

3. In 1924 Mary Blair played in O'Neill's "Diff'rent," which was presented along with "The Triumph of the Egg," Raymond O'Neil's adaptation of Anderson's "The Egg." Paul Robeson appeared in *The Emperor Jones*, and the Theater Guild presented *Processional* by John Howard Lawson.

TO David Karsner[1]

Easter Sunday [4 April 1926, New Orleans]

A bright warm morning.
Dear Karsner . .

I am very glad to give you the information you want. I was born at the place called Camden, Ohio. It must be a very small town. I have never been there since my mother carried me away as a boy. After I was born the family lived in several other small towns. My father was then a small harness maker having a shop of his own. Later he went broke and became finally a house painter. I was the third of a family of five boys and two girls. The boys are all living. The girls both died, one as a babe, the other as a grown woman.

All of my boyhood was spent at Clyde, Ohio, where the wandering family finally settled down. Perhaps there was never enough money to get out of town. The place is very charming, a small farming community that has never been successfully industrialized. All my memories of it have a pleasant flavor.

As my mother died when I was very young—perhaps fifteen[2]—and as father was irresponsible I like all my brothers had to go to work.

I sold newspapers, worked in the fields of nearby farmers, went about to fairs with race horses, went with a threshing crew to thresh grain in the wheat harvest, worked in the cabbage and corn fields.

Later I went away to cities and worked in factories, tramped some, beat my way about on freight trains.

When the Spanish War came on I went into it—not I believe from any great desire to grasp Cuba out of the hands of Spain but as an adventure. It was a rather good one. A lot of the work I had been doing had been too heavy for me. In the army I had leisure. The war as a war was rather a joke as everyone knows.

After the war and for a few years I continued to knock about as an unskilled laborer—but in the army I had found that I did have skill, of a sort. I could get along well with other men, make them rather do as I wished.

After a short time in a little Lutheran college at Springfield, Ohio—called Wittenberg—I got into the advertising business and began to prosper.

There is a certain plausibility and slickness in me of which I have always been ashamed. However I used it and got in.

After some years in advertising I became a business adventurer, organized companies, thought up slick schemes for getting money out of people. Some of my schemes succeeded—others failed. When one succeeded it wanted but patient following to make me rich but I had no patience.

A time of intense inner dissatisfaction followed. I became moody, drank a great deal—at one time promised to become a drunkard. Instead I hit upon writing novels, poems and stories.

My absorption in this new diversion was so great that my schemes did not interest me. It is quite true I walked away from an Ohio factory and never went back.[3]

I was a writer but could not live by my craft. Very well. I went back to advertising writing and kept it up until a few years ago. All my notions for stories have of course drifted up out of this kind of varied life among all kinds of people.

As to the novels I wrote five of them before one of them was published. Of the five *Windy* and *Marching Men* were later published, the others thrown aside. They were probably pretty bad. I can no longer remember the order in which they were written. Floyd Dell and Dreiser finally got me published.

I am sure *Marching Men* did come out of something got by being a soldier. I was a private and later a corporal.

I do hope all this will give you about what you want. You may be sure it is a pleasure to me to have you interested in writing of my adventures.

Very sincerely,
Sherwood Anderson

TS. Camden

1. A writer with the New York *Herald-Tribune*, Karsner was doing a series of profiles of authors and had asked Anderson about his life and works. Karsner published his article, "Sherwood Anderson, Mid-West Mystic," in the *Herald-Tribune Magazine* on 16 May 1926, pp. 8–9, 16.
2. He was actually eighteen at the time.
3. Anderson left his factory on 28 Nov. 1912; he remained in Elyria, however, until Feb. 1913.

TO Karl Anderson

[c. 4 April 1926, New Orleans]

Dear Karl—

I just got your letter about Irve and Earl[1] and will answer it right away, while I am at my typewriter. Irve has improved immensely while he has been here and tells me he is going back to Baltimore at the end of the week. We haven't been able to make it very lively for him. In the first place I have been working pretty steadily and Elizabeth hasn't been well. She had four teeth taken yesterday and I am sure that is at the seat of her trouble. They also were infected.

As for Irve's going to Europe it isn't in the cards. It would seem too impossible to him and anyway he wouldn't get out of it what you or I would. He would be too lonely.

I have watched him down here. He doesn't seem too comfortable with me or I fancy with you either. It's because our lives have been different, more reflective. I'm pretty sure that, deep down, Irve also wanted to be some kind of an artist. He has an intense and sweet nature and not having been able to find what he wants in life has concentrated on his own work, not because it really interested him, but because he didn't have anything else.

One can't try to interfere in such a man's life much, not at his age. He will have to stick at his work because he will never get anything to take its place and for pure economical reasons. If he were to quit now—because of ill health—he would get a pension—from the company he served so long—but he would feel a defeated man.

What has happened to him happens to many men in modern industrial life. Such a man can't take it out in mysticism—which is what all religious escape means.[2] A man's life is his work, his relations to his work, what he lets of himself go into it, how it helps him grow and learn to handle his human relations.

If either of us had known this earlier in life we might have been of greater help to both of these men brothers. We didn't.

I feel something of a dog, realizing that Earl is better off with you than he could be with us now because it means an additional burden to you I would like to share more.

At that it may serve to draw us closer to each other in the long run. We ought to do our own brother business better than we do. I fancy it has been largely my own fault.

Mechanically we will of course be upset this summer. We will have to half camp out while our house is being built. It would all be fun for Earl, being a part of it—if he were well enough to be up and about and take part. In the fall I would like to go to Europe with Elizabeth for two reasons. My own European vogue is just beginning. My appearance over there would help just now. There are many men I want to meet and talk to. One can't do that sort of thing always by correspondence. For another thing E. has never been over. I want her to go.

Irve says Earl can stay with him for the winter. We could perhaps have him the later part of the summer. Our house should be ready I should say by late July or August. Then of course we would be back there in the spring. I am sending you and Earl some snaps of the country in the winter. It is very lush, warm and quiet in the summer.

Even if Earl can't come as soon as we hoped, it is possible you could run down there for a few weeks of rest and quiet. You might be able to do a good deal of work there. It is very isolated, very quiet. The country has character.

I think E. has been good for Irve. They find a common basis and talk more freely than he can talk with me. The man himself has real brains and sweetness but feels himself defeated. It is because of a queer inferiority complex he has always had but now he realizes it. That realization is in itself a help however. O Lordy aren't these human beings a strange lot. Do you wonder I have become so absorbed in thinking about them and trying to write them.

And I haven't half expressed my gratitude to you and Helen. Don't let me impose on you and do let me know promptly what my own financial obligations are in the matter.

With much love.
Sherwood

TS. NL

1. Irwin and Earl Anderson, brothers of Sherwood and Karl. Irwin, a factory manager in Baltimore, was visiting the Sherwood Andersons while recovering from a nervous condition. Earl, after a disappearance of thirteen years, had suffered a paralyzing stroke in February and was staying with the Karl Andersons in Westport, Conn., prior to hospitalization.

2. Karl had suggested that religion might be of help to Irwin in relieving his preoccupation with himself and his work.

TO Alfred Stieglitz

[14 May 1926, Ripshin Farm]

Dear Stieglitz

We came out so much better than we deserve. Right around the cabin we have both pink and white dogwood, flowering ivy and lots of mountain laurel. Log wagons go down the road past the door. The neighbors—farming men and woodsmen—come to visit. The women work in the fields with the men. Uneducated sweet people with plenty of character. It is mostly English stock—much of it uncrossed.

The man who is doing our building[1] would go wonderfully as one of the grave diggers in *Hamlet*—a rakish old fellow with the real workman instinct.

This summer we'll live in the barn while he builds the house *Dark Laughter* paid for. At least I hope it will pay for it.

The novel on which I am at work gradually takes form.[2]

I get rather nice letters about *Notebook*—some of which go in strong for the essay about you.[3]

You know I'm glad you like it.

Both you and Georgia in the cabin here. You go well with the green hills seen through the window.

Am glad you will both and soon be in the country.
Love to you both.

Sherwood

MS. Yale

1. The builder of the house at Ripshin Farm, Marion Ball, whom Anderson discusses in *Memoirs*, 493–98.
2. "Another Man's House," never completed.
3. "Alfred Stieglitz," *Sherwood Anderson's Notebook*, 151–59.

TO Ernest Hemingway
[19 May 1926], Ripshin Farm

Dear Ernest Hemingway.

I am sending a man, Ralph Church, to see you, a friend of mine who wants to know you and admires your work.[1] He is a California man I knew out there last year and is going to spend a year or two in Europe. Please see that he meets Pound, Joyce and some of the others. I am giving him also a note to Galantière and to Gertrude Stein.

I guess you know how much I admire the solid fineness of your stories. They tell me you are coming back to America to live. I have bought a farm in the Virginia mountains and am building a house. If I have any money left in the fall will come over to Europe for a few months. If you come across before that and go west, stop over here, both of you.

Sincerely
Sherwood Anderson

Troutdale, Virginia. It is away down in the southwest corner, near the North Carolina and Tennessee lines.

TS. Kennedy

1. Anderson sent this note to Church, a philosophy student at Oxford, who carried it to Paris.

TO Ernest Hemingway
[14 June 1926], Ripshin Farm

Dear Ernest Hemingway,

I bought a farm at Troutdale, Va.—had just written you a note suggesting that you and Hadley stop here on your way to Arkansas.[1] Thought you might be going this summer.

However I hadn't your address. All my letters files still packed. If

Ripshin Farm
COURTESY OF ELEANOR ANDERSON

you weren't coming over soon, I wanted to send a young fellow—friend of mine from California—to see you. I'm giving him a note to you. His name is Church.

About the book[2]—your letter—all your letters to me these last two or three years—it's like this. Damn it, man, you are so final—so patronizing. You always do speak to me like a master to a pupil. It must be Paris—the literary life. You didn't seem like that when I knew you.

You speak so regretfully, tenderly, of giving me a punch.[3] You sound like Uncle Ezra [Pound]. Come out of it, man. I pack a little wallop myself. I've been middleweight champion. You seem to forget that.

Honestly, man, you sound like a chap I met once in Cleveland. He also had been drinking and talking with literary guys. He went home and wrote an article. The whole gang worked on the Cleveland *Plain Dealer*. Then he came down to my hotel, still drunk, and cried on my shoulder.

"I tore the article up," he said. "Great Christ, it was good. After I wrote it I sat down and read it. I knew, if I published it, you would never write another word and no one would read you any more."

About the little plug I put in for you with Liveright.[4] I'm sorry I even mentioned it. I've done the same for men I hated and I like you. The only reason I even spoke of it was to let you know I liked your work.

Tell the truth, I think the Scribner book will help me and hurt you. Spite of all you say, it's got the smarty tinge. You know it. Fitz & Dos[5] must have baited you.

But in your turn now, man, don't get sore at me. If you are going to wallop, you've got to take yours. You started it. I didn't.

We are trying to build a house on our farm—in the Blue Ridge. If we have any money left in the fall, plan to come to Paris. Anyway when you start—for Arkansas—find out if we're here and if we are stop and see us. It's on the way to Arkansas all right—will prepare you some.

Sherwood Anderson

D'you ever hear of Kid McAllister—the nonpareil—that was me.

MS. Kennedy

1. Hemingway had planned to visit Piggott, Ark., home of Pauline Pfeiffer, who in 1927 became his second wife.

2. Scribner's published Hemingway's parody of Anderson, *The Torrents of Spring*, on 28 May.

3. Hemingway had written: "You see I feel that if among ourselves we have to pull our punches, if when a man like yourself who can write very great things writes something that seems to me, (who have never written anything great but am anyway a fellow craftsman) rotten, I ought to tell you so" (*Ernest Hemingway: Selected Letters*, ed. Carlos Baker [New York: Scribner, 1981], 205.)

4. Anderson had encouraged Liveright to publish Hemingway's *In Our Time* in 1925.

5. F. Scott Fitzgerald and John Dos Passos.

TO Ernest Hemingway

[17 July 1926, Ripshin Farm]

Dear Hemy . . .

Speaking of that—I see by the papers that "pop 'em" Paul Berlenbach got popped last night by Jack Delaney.[1] You miss a lot in Troutdale, Piggott, Ark. or Paris, I guess. Would like to have seen that one. An ox cart with two of the finest looking black and white oxen you ever saw just rushed past my door.

If you got $500 . . . At that, man, the whole Winesburg book brought me just about half the $300. They're a swell lot, the publishers and the reading public. If a man did it for them he'd die of discouragement before he got a start. What I always felt in you is a sense of vitality—the ability to take it. Most so-called artists haven't enough juice to get through the first few years.

I'm glad you are coming back over here to live. Whatever it is, it's our own mess. I rather like the whole show myself and I think you do. You've got a reputation already. It doesn't go down to the buyers and perhaps never will but some of these days the publishers will begin to think it does and there you are. They begin to sell you I guess when they begin to be afraid not to.

Get here when you can, both of you. It's as quiet as God and nothing but the simple life going on as far as the eye can see. One reason I like it is that they think I'm rich here. They call me a millionaire because I bought a farm for eleven hundred and didn't mind being cheated about three hundred. I liked the place and you both will.

If we have money enough to go to Paris we won't stay long and won't go anyway until late November. Back in March.

As ever
Sherwood A.

TS. Kennedy

1. Delaney won the light-heavyweight boxing championship from Paul Berlenbach on 16 July in New York.

TO Earl Anderson[1]

[mid-August 1926, Ripshin Farm]

So many things to say after my rotten short visit. I came away wanting only to go on talking with you for hours. The silly necessity of schedules. I had engaged to be back home for the weekend—some laborers building my house—to be paid.

To think I even hesitated about coming—going first to consult Karl. There was some notion in my head—you might not want to see me.

Thank God now I can write you often and more freely. In spite of all my early stupidity—and I must have been terribly stupid—you have always been the brother to whom I most clung.

So odd that I came away from you with no feeling of illness in spite of your horrid illness. There was only something grey and vast like the sea—the terrible vast complication of life.

That it should have swept us so apart. Love me if you can while we both live, dear Earl. I need the feeling of you loving me in spite of everything as I need nothing else in this world.

It won't be so long for either of us, I dare say. A few summers, winters, days, months, years—what does it matter.

If I were a praying man I would pray daily that you may be able to come here in the spring—a few months under apple trees—talking many things out.

You did not go up there, dear man, because you in any way offended Helen. She is a good woman but a fool I've always thought. In fact—in a curious way you have brought Irve, Karl, and me together.

O, it is all muddled, muddled. God help us all.

It isn't to be well. You may never be that. It is to be well enough for a long quiet summer here—near me. This not for you but for me. My roots are in you, have always been in you in spite of everything.

Regrets, regrets. What good are they.

My mind cannot accept God as a part of physical life—your poor paralyzed leg and arm—my own stodgy body.

God in our world of fancy—in our poet's world—I do accept—worship always.

I cannot write a line without going back, back. It's what made you cry. You don't want to.

It's no use. As you say, "Let it go."

Dear man, love me now. I love you.

I'll write again soon.

Cornelia's address?

MS. PC

1. Anderson composed this letter, apparently without recopying or sending it, in the back of a book in his library.

TO Earl Anderson

24 August 1926, Ripshin Farm

Dear Earl:

A steady drizzle of rain. Karl and Irve are both here. Karl is doing a portrait of Irve and me. He talks of coming to Newport[1] to paint you into the canvas.

I think of you every day, every hour of every day.

Writing, writing, work. It is the only thing I can do that will keep something inside me quiet. Novels, stories, articles. I have tried to write an article about the Modern Great Factory. It does not satisfy me. Nothing does.

Nothing will pay me back for things missed.

It is true of you.

Your illness is mine.

I feel it in my legs, my body.

To love is everything. To love is terrible.

Irve has something beautiful in him covered up. It may be he never dared love. Karl is in a strange way a shadow. How shall I explain. Perhaps you know.

Rain. You in that place, facing the gray sea. The men about.

For the sense of beauty you gave me I can never pay you—dear man I love.

TS. NL (cc)

1. Earl Anderson was then a patient at the United States Marine Hospital at Newport, R.I.

TO Karl Anderson

[early September? 1926, Ripshin Farm]

Dear Karl . . .

I am still swimming about in a sea of uncertainty about the novel. It forms, dissolves and then forms again.

Yesterday my nerves went rather to pieces. Always when I am trying to get a novel into writing shape I have to go through times like this. The actual writing is nothing.

The house seems empty without you. While you were here I tried to say something to you that I did not get said. Yesterday I tried to write it.

It is something about our past relationship. I feel I have often been so unfair to you. You left home when I was so young. I have never had you where I could see you day after day.

It might have been that you were an older brother and an artist for years before I began. You have a faculty of self abnegation I have tried very hard to get and without much success. As an actual fact, now, your relationship with your work seems to me much purer and finer than my own. I wanted to say it partly, I'm afraid, as a sort of apology. There is a spoken relationship [that] goes on between people and an unspoken one. It is that unspoken one I want thus to clear a little if I can.

I am blundering in doing it. I have to say something. You do not feel that I owe you anything of the sort but I feel it.

You here and at work, where I could see you at work day after day, made me ashamed. I was ashamed of spoken and unspoken thoughts.

What a difficult family we are. You will forgive me what I am accusing myself of before I accuse myself but that doesn't help me.

If I can make you feel I admire you intensely that will be some consolation to me anyway.

Do come again whenever you can. I hope this may become a painting place for you and that you may come back here to work often. Elizabeth hopes the same thing.

Our best to Helen.

Sherwood

TS. NL

TO Burton Emmett[1]

[4 October 1926, Ripshin Farm]

Dear Man . . .

After all the point of view,[2] if I held it, would be horrible. If I could live as I wanted to I would do away forever with the whole notion that what one man does is more important than the work of another. We are all caught in the same trap—most of necessity leave about us a great litter. You may be quite sure that I would not write you if you did not interest me as a man. That you are a collector has nothing to do with the matter. In the morning I come to my cabin to work. On some days a fog lies over my mind. The amount of stuff I write and throw away would amaze you. Suppose I write to you, sit thinking of you. Is that not as important as anything else I can do.

At least I try to maintain this point of view. Because I may have written a few things having a certain merit is no reason that I should surrender. Suppose I sat pompously on this hill thinking—I must not waste my time. What I do is of such importance that I must guard every moment. What a complete ass. And this in the presence of things in nature. Other men all about me—the farmer going off to town with a load of corn, the little country girl going along the road to school.

At least my life should be a little [like] a thing held carelessly in my hand, not overvalued. I am quite sure that the baseball pitcher who has something on the ball does not grip it tightly for fear of dropping it.

For one thing I think that you do not realize just how unusual is your own attitude. You are, for example, a business man. I have been a business man myself. Well, you are a bad one. You are not trying to get something for nothing. Man you should see much of my correspondence—the bad writers who send me long volumes, asking criticism,

Burton Emmett
COURTESY OF ELEANOR ANDERSON

suggestions. Men wanting this and that. I would like at least to be half as generous as you are.

As for the Dreiser incident.[3] Frankly I do not understand it. There was some absurd slip. As he was out of the country I tried to keep it as straight as I could. My own private notion is that the man—perhaps as an exercise—tried to put some of my prose into verse form. He might have left it lying about, forgetting in the end the source. Some such thing happened. It does not matter except that it must make him feel very foolish and uncomfortable when it comes to his notice. I do not know him well personally. I admire him greatly. I hope at any rate that the incident is closed now.

I will be in New York the latter part of November and hope we may meet.

Sincerely.
Sherwood Anderson

TS. NC

1. New York advertising executive and collector of art, books, and literary manuscripts, who had written Anderson about acquiring his manuscripts and who later became a close friend.

2. Emmett had stated that an author's manuscripts were a part of his business interests.

3. Dreiser had recently published a poem, "The Beautiful," which was apparently plagiarized from Anderson's story "Tandy." See W.A. Swanberg, *Dreiser* (New York: Scribner's, 1965), 313–14.

TO Ernest Hemingway

Sunday [10 October 1926, Ripshin Farm]

Dear Hemingway . .

I am sorry you did not get to see Church. He is a fine one all right. Have a suspicion he is in Paris about a girl. That may have kept him occupied.

My God man, I have always thought of you as a horse for strength. It shocks me to hear that you don't sleep. Aren't there any real huskies in the world? Will be looking for the novel.[1] Am wrestling with one myself.[2] You may not like it. Anyway it will not be printed until next year.

Last year I went lecturing, trying to get money to build me a house. Well, I've almost got it—although not half paid for. I won't lecture this year though—or at least damn little. Would rather write ads.

Think some of publishing my *Testament* in the spring. Can't quite make up my mind. It may be poetry and may not. God knows.

Anyway old dear don't take me from the chatterers. Most of the time I don't know a thing. I get older in my body but can't seem to get it up into my head. No one gets very wise I guess. At least I know I don't.

It looks now as though we could not leave here until about the 20th November. That should mean sailing about December 1st. We should be drifting into Paris along about Christmas.

Can't make out from your letter. You say Piggott shot to hell. Does that mean the plan for coming back over here to live is shot too.

Love to you both.
Sherwood Anderson

TS. Kennedy

1. *The Sun Also Rises*.
2. "Another Man's House."

TO Burton Emmett

[15 November 1926, Ripshin Farm]

My dear Burton Emmett

Mrs. Anderson and I will be leaving here about Thanksgiving day and will sail on the *President Roosevelt* Dec. 1st. During my few days in New York I will have to go up to Newport to see an invalid brother up there. My son John—17—is to join us in New York and go to Europe with us. I will be back the first of March and will, I hope, spend some time in New York then. Perhaps we can have at least an hour together when you and Mrs. Emmett return from Cleveland.

It is just possible I can see the exhibition of prints in New York. What is likely is that I shall have to go to my brother in Newport as soon as I arrive.

As you may suppose there will be many things to do in a few days.

About the early articles, tales etc. As a matter of fact I have kept no record. Just now everything is half packed and in a sad jumble.

It has been so all this year. We have lived only in temporary quarters while building was going on.

For a long time now I have been trying to get straightened out in my head—perhaps as the theme of a novel—the thing that happens to men. It is unavoidable—I dare say—as you suggest in the clearly written introduction to *Fifty Prints*[1]—that the bases of sales mark also the bases of appreciation.

Artists do need a response. That you are moved or stirred by things I write is the only justification I know for writing.

The significance of money in life is a dramatic and moving story. I wish I could get to the bottom of it. I want really to make it the theme of a novel.

I am sending you a copy of my new book.[2] It shows, I think, in a certain lack of flow in the prose, the effort of trying to do two things at once—build a house and a book.

I enclose a copy of proof—an introduction to the special edition of Stephen Crane Knopf is doing—that is to say to one of the volumes.[3] I will send you the manuscript of this later.

Sincerely
Sherwood Anderson

MS. NC

1. The catalogue for an exhibition of prints by the American Institute of Graphic Arts. Emmett's introduction, later reprinted as the foreword to *Fifty Prints* (New York: John Day, 1927), states, "A healthy volume of sales is the only tangible encouragement which any country can give to continued production of distinguished work."

2. *Tar: A Midwest Childhood.*

3. Anderson wrote the Introduction to *Midnight Sketches and Other Impressions*, vol. 11 of *The Works of Stephen Crane* (1926).

TO Burton Emmett

19 January 1927, [Paris]

My Dear Burton Emmett.

I am writing with a lead pencil because I have a feeling that I am about to write you a long letter and my pen is in bad order. We got to London after a quiet passage but did not stay there long.

Perhaps I was more tired than I knew. In London I was struck down by a cold which, after I got to Paris, developed into flu.

And so there I was, flat on my back in a small Paris hotel. I have been up for some time and about but my strength has not come back.

I am in a curious state of mind. Perhaps it is that I want to talk to you about.

And why to you. You have shown an interest in my work. You are an advertising man. For years I was one myself. You have an interest in other things that interest me profoundly.

We are all as you know, my dear Burton Emmett, caught in a slam bang world.

Most of my work as a writer has, as you no doubt know, been done while making my living at something else. I retained a sort of loose connection with advertising writing until three or four years ago. After that, not feeling myself strong enough to keep doing the two things, I cut loose from advertising. My *A Story Teller's Story* did not sell. I was in New Orleans, in debt, and Mr. Horace Liveright came along.

He proposed a connection with his firm. I had just finished a long novel—*Dark Laughter*—which he took and published.

The book was for me a commercial success. I took the money it brought in and built me a house in the country. However, as you well know, there is always a sting in these arrangements with these big commercial houses.

The firm in question for example advances me money enough to live very comfortably, but it is implicit in the contract I'm afraid that I am to grind out books fast enough to keep them even.

It might not be too much to do if the feeling of being under obligation did not come in. Frankly what I am afraid of is that it will lead me into cheap hurried writing.

For example I am sure that my *Tar* should have had another year in my hands.

Surely you, so deeply interested in writing, know what happens. In England I met Bennett, Swinnerton[1] and others. Seeing what has happened to them made me a little ill.

My own writing, when it is as I love it to be, experimental—done for its own sake—does not sell largely. I happen to be the sort of writer talked about and not bought largely. Often my best things are at first condemned.

When I was younger and stronger, all this I did not mind. Now I do need to live in comfort and have leisure. I must work more leisurely if I am not to become a hack.

Is it sentimentality. My keeping in the track does seem to me to have meant something.

As for Boni & Liveright—or any other commercial publishing firm—I cannot blame them for their attitude. They want to make money—for themselves and me. I think their attitude is very kindly. If I may say so, however, I am sure there is a point of view I cannot expect them to quite get.

I am writing all this to you as a practical man. There is a good deal of wealth in America. Do you think it would be possible to get some wealthy man or woman interested in American writing to put up enough money to insure me—say $2000 or $2500 a year.

Now that I have my own home almost paid for and with what income my books and incidental writing naturally bring, I could I believe live very comfortably with such an income assured.

I could write experimentally and at my leisure.

This being constantly in debt to publishers does an odd thing to me. I have a queer sort of puritanic money conscience. The least bit in debt I am always harried and nervous. You see how un-American I am.

I am putting this to you as a practical man. Will you not tell me whether or not the idea is impractical. How would a man go about it to put such a thing through. I am, I'm afraid, but a poor man to court favor with the rich and yet I know many people with money are really seeking investments that may pay something in other things than money.

Am I presuming in asking you to think of this matter. I shall return to America in early March and perhaps then we can talk of it.

I have an idea myself that if something of this sort cannot be done I will return to some kind of advertising writing. It would be so much more honorable in me than to join in the hurried careless grinding out of books.

Sincerely
Sherwood Anderson

You will be pleased to know that four of my books—the *Notebook, Winesburg, A Story Teller's Story* and another book of tales[2] are to be done in France this year. Two stories—"The Man Who Became a Woman" and "A Man's Story"—have been done here and have had a distinct literary success.

MS. NC

1. Arnold Bennett and Frank Swinnerton, English novelists. Anderson had met Swinnerton on the boat to England. In *Memoirs* (438) Anderson refers to Bennett as "gone too obviously into cheap romancing."
2. A collection of stories from *The Triumph of the Egg* and *Horses and Men*, with the title *Un Païen de l'Ohio*.

TO Georgia Church[1]

8 April 1927, Ripshin Farm

Dear Mrs. Church—

I hardly know whether or not it is fair to ask you to try to read my script. It is raining and Elizabeth—with our Mary Ball—is at work in the kitchen. Elizabeth came on down to the farm shortly after we landed in New York, and I went lecturing. Now that is over and I am here.

The spring is well advanced—almost too well. The alarmists among our neighbors all say we will have a late freeze and kill all the fruit.

They may be right. The apple trees are putting out leaves. The plum trees are in blossom, violets bloom along the creek and yesterday Elizabeth brought a great handful of arbutus from the woods.

I have been having brush fires and breaking up about four acres of new ground for corn.

We bought another saddle mare and now have a pair. We shall have to raise enough grain to feed them. Claude[2]—our farmer—has a cow and two pigs. Elizabeth has three turkey hens and one cock—three geese and one gander. Already she has two turkey hens sitting on forty eggs. God knows how that will come out. One of the unbelievable miracles of nature to me—that an egg can become a huge turkey—or a hissing gander.

I landed in New York only to find that my invalid brother had died the day before. It was a release for him. He had been through several strokes—the result of some injury—perhaps in the war—and lived only to suffer too much.

What I really want to do—my purpose in writing—is to grow eloquent again about this country—I want to tell you how the streams sound at night—how quiet it is—the sound the wind makes in the pines.

It is such an odd satisfying feeling to look at a proud old turkey cock and say—"He's mine," to look at an old goose and say the same, to walk on land and say it.

I am suddenly very well. I work. Who knows whether or not to good ends?

I write then I go talk to a queer gentle little man[3] who is making us a flower garden. He was in the war—in France. When we tell him we want stone walls it does not seem silly to him. He has seen old French towns.

We are to have a baby on the farm within a month—the farmer's wife. I predict it will be named Sherwood. I will dedicate a book to it.

I presume Ralph knows David's[4] bad news. He did not get the Guggenheim.

Well, I had some good luck. Tell Ralph I sold the 10th reprint of "I'm a Fool." It will amuse him—my greatest story etc. Anyway tell him it is more reproductive than a rabbit.

I also sold 15000 reprints of *Dark Laughter*.

I half hope also I have managed college scholarships for my two lads—John & Bob. I want to give them at least a chance at college if it can be managed. It may turn out like David's Guggenheim.

I fancy Ralph will be back from London soon. O, for an evening with him at Lipp's.[5]

Tell Ralph I got the first copy of *transition*.[6] The format is rather ugly—too bad. It looks meaty. I've dipped into but one thing—having been—as I said—scribbling—a poem by Robert Desnos—translation by Gene. It's lovely.

Between just you and Ralph and me, Joyce makes my bones ache. He's up the wrong tree or I'm an egg.

Lecturing was rottener than ever. I was offered a good contract to gabble next year but almost kicked the man down stairs.

O well, we'll get you and Ralph here yet.

Sherwood Anderson

MS. Cal.

1. Mother of Ralph Church.
2. Claude Reedy, then the caretaker at Ripshin Farm.
3. Probably Felix Sullivan.
4. David Prall.
5. Brasserie Lipp, a Paris bar.
6. Paris magazine of literature and the arts, edited by Eugene Jolas and Elliot Paul. It began publication with the Apr. 1927 issue, which included two poems by Desnos, with English translation by Jolas.

TO Alfred Stieglitz

[18? April 1927], Ripshin Farm

Dear Stieglitz

I found out the O'Keeffe was all right. The paper had become wrinkled and the glass not too clean. Elizabeth has had it restretched. It's fine now.

God, but the country is lovely. This year I do not have to wrestle with workmen. I sit, smoke cigarettes and look at things grow.

Apple trees, peaches, cherries, plums, already in full bloom. Robins setting. I'm planting a field to corn, one to oats.

Bluets, white and blue violets along the creek.

The second year in the same little valley is like living with a lovely woman after the first fervor of passion and when the little nice things about her begin to come out.

Love to you both from us both.

Sherwood

MS. Yale

TO Stark Young[1]

[late May 1927], Ripshin Farm

Dear Stark—

How nice of you.

We are buried away here in the country and loving it more all the time. To the present moment we only have 30 acres but we are thinking of buying another 30.

Presently we shall be like peasants—land hungry.

There is always, near you, a wood you don't want cut, a field you can't bear having spoiled.

I think, in the end, we'll go in for raising sheep—being shepherds.

Now we have 2 horses, 4 turkey, 5 geese, 2 pups.

I went to see Mr. Croly[2]—*The New Republic*—about my boys. They should go to college. I can't quite see them through without some help. I don't want them to quite have to earn it all. Mr. Croly thought he knew a woman, lousy with money, who might help them, say $300 a year each.

It however fell through.

You don't know any lousy and careless rich do you.

It's a little absurd because I could, I fancy, make quite a lot of money by writing some stuff I am not going to write.

It's been 6 months of sheer struggle with me—trying to get straight with this novel.

I kept superimposing myself on it too much.

As far as I can see, Stark, a bit of fame, recognition etc., while very sweet and all that, is also a damn handicap.

There is something, a kind of direct, simple approach to your materials, that gets quite lost at times.

No fun writing if you can't make it sing and jump along like a little river—as you know.

I had my theme all the time—"Another Man's House."

You can smell the provoking possibilities of that.

Anyway here it's simple enough. Most of the people can't read. I told a man yesterday about the Nebraska boy flying to Paris.[3]

He was digging. "Did he?" he said. "I wouldn't want to."

Little piles of shaving in most any room you go into. Two carpenters and a painter still here. Men digging in the yard.

You have to be careful or the pups will chew up your sox.

Lucile Swan—that was Mrs. Jerry Blum—is visiting. She has taken a small house near to paint. It is being whitewashed for her.

Elizabeth is well and happy—I think. We all send you love and hope some day you will be getting off a train here.

Tell your brother in God there that I am going over to Springfield—to Wittenberg—to get a doctor's degree in early June.[4]

Sherwood

MS. Texas

1. Playwright, novelist, and critic, originally from Mississippi, living in New York.
2. Herbert E. Croly, editor of the *New Republic*.

3. Charles Lindbergh completed his nonstop flight from New York to Paris on 21 May.
4. Anderson received an honorary Doctor of Letters degree on 5 June.

TO Karl Anderson

[5 June 1927, Cincinnati, Ohio]

Dear Karl—

I got your note yesterday, at Springfield. Am staying over here a few hours and then going back home.

You have been on my mind a good deal this spring and summer. I remember that two or three years ago you passed through a bad time but, when you were with us last year, I thought it had passed.

You seemed to me then working along with a pretty steady hand and definite purpose.

I myself went to pieces during the winter in Paris. Am not right yet.

Of course, with both of us, it is the same story. Perhaps as we grow older we realize more fully the terrible limitations of ourselves compared to what we want to do.

I have myself got a certain amount of fame. It is detrimental to me. New elements come into a man's work. The past challenges as well as the future.

I don't know the solution. Vulgarity on all sides and in ourselves too. Earl is a good deal on my mind. His life seems to me now a kind of living picture of all the more sensitive lives of our times.

There is some delicate balance we both want and, having got, cannot hold very long.

For myself I write desperately.

If—in what we want to do—there is not salvation where is it?

I am rather glad you did not come to Springfield. The weather was hot. The marching through the very lovely college grounds, the doctors of divinity and myself being crowned, the speeches and prayers under the trees.

And all of it as far away from myself as Mars.

What had I to do with it. What had it to do with me.

The word "God" constantly reiterated.

Afterward, coming down here to Cincinnati, a young professor sitting with me.

A sense of his stupidity and vulgarity as contrasted with my own.

When I think of Earl of course I think of a painter's life. I don't believe a writer's life is any different. It is all so crammed full of disappointments and futility. Perhaps that's our own fault. I don't know.

As for your coming down to us—you know we want you. Young

Maurice[1]—at whose house I met you in New York—has been in the hospital with ulcers of the stomach.

He is coming out about the 15th and has asked us if he can come down and we have told him to come.

Paul Rosenfeld is coming too.

I think it would be better, if you can make it fit in, for you to come in early July. We would have so much more time to ourselves.

However, Karl, come when you need to come. That is the sensible thing.

If you are tangled up and tired I wish to God I had something clear in me from which you could get something.

I'm so damned doubtful these days about that.

MS. NL

1. Probably Maurice A. Hanline, poet and editor.

TO Burton Emmett

[19 August 1927, Ripshin Farm]

My Dear Burton

I wish you would find it possible—you and Mrs. Emmett—to run down here. I've an idea we would find a real basis of friendship. Friends—real ones—are pretty hard to get. I wouldn't like to miss the chance.

This morning I am a very inelegant young man. I am sitting at this moment in my bath robe with a hot water bottle on my belly, having got out of the bed with a roaring headache.

I have even been so inelegant as to vomit a bit.

Still as you see I am scribbling. It is an incurable disease with me.

About the Morris thing in *New Republic*.[1] Do you know I think the man is right and you are wrong. The Sherwood Anderson of *Winesburg, Ohio* has surely been dying for a long time now.

I have also an idea that the kind of criticism embraced in this article is what we need most in this country. We are all too damn tender. I am always being tender with myself. I don't want you to think, dear man, that I am any hero. The article, when I read it, made me sick to my soul.

I spent a couple of days in hell, trying to deny to myself what the man said. In fact I have hardly recovered yet. The fellow doesn't quibble at hitting below the belt. My present belly ache may be due to one or two punches he landed.

But let us admit the Sherwood Anderson of *Winesburg* not only dying but quite dead. For one I have spent too much time already over the man's funeral. Well, let him die.

The question that interests me is as to whether there is another Sherwood Anderson coming slowly to life.

I guess I'll have to work that out myself. If I can't work it out I may be in New York one of these days looking for a job as an advertising writer. You might give me a job. We might have some fun together.

In the meantime however I am at the job, hot water, belly ache from body punches and all, trying to find that new Sherwood Anderson.

I half wish I were writing this to the man Morris and to the *New Republic* rather than to a friend but I do not exactly like to predict a new emerging Sherwood Anderson who after all may never be born.

God bless you anyway.

However, put it down in your note book that I am at bottom all right.

And do come.

Sherwood Anderson

MS. NC

1. An article by Lawrence S. Morris, "Sherwood Anderson: Sick of Words," *New Republic* 51 (3 Aug. 1927): 277–79, concluding, "The author of 'Winesburg, Ohio,' is dying before our eyes."

TO Ralph Church

[August 1927, Ripshin Farm]

Dear Ralph—

We still amuse and comfort ourselves by thinking of the neighboring farm as belonging to you and your mother. We ourselves have extended our holdings by another 25 acres. Elizabeth bought it. She is going to try to raise some sheep and turkeys. It is a high upland piece and we have some men there at work clearing off the brush and plowing preparatory to getting a meadow. This land, with a little help to get it started, raises bluegrass, a very rich feed for all kinds of stock, that seeds low on the ground, so that even when pastured it seeds itself and makes a continuous sod.

I am working away but hardly dare talk much of what I am doing. It brings bad luck.

I think we will probably stay on here until very late in the fall, possibly all winter. We haven't had a winter here and the idea is attractive. We should see one year quite through. Now at last our house is about done and the men gone.

As there were lots of stones we built a high stone wall about the flower garden in front of the house and will have a pool fed from a spring on a hill above. Margaret[1] came for a visit of about four weeks and then Max and Dorothea [Radin] stopped for about ten days.

So you see we have had company most of the summer. My son Bob comes next week. He is going to the University of Virginia this fall.

Some day, I'm sure you will come to country life, with perhaps the outlet of a part of the year in some city.

I gathered from several letters from Gene [Jolas] that he had been going through a change of heart. Poor muddled man. He is so nice and such a fool. I can't think yet of some of those evenings last winter without getting sore.

My *New Testament* was well received and in some quarters thoroughly roasted. *New Republic* had a leading article announcing that I had died as a writer, or had quite passed out. It didn't affect me much. They mourned because I had not kept on writing in the tone of *Winesburg*. It's the old story I think. If you do one thing that pleases they want you to go right on doing just that whereas, succeed or fail, the only fun is in trying to push on into something else.

Well, I hope neither you or your mother get completely wedded to France. In the long run you have to be an American and live in America. I must say we live pretty well. We do not have Lipp's here—alas—but we do have wine of several kinds in kegs in the cellar and after a time you even become hardened to an occasional shot of moon.

Some of the old timers make it pretty well here.

Is there any definite plan for your coming this way. Little chance for us going that. We would so like to have you here for a look at this gorgeous country. With affection to your mother from us both.

Sherwood

MS. Cal.

1. Margaret Prall, a sister of Elizabeth.

TO Henry S. Canby

[late September? 1927, Ripshin Farm]

My dear Henry Canby.

Now that I have read the article,[1] which I take to be an extract from his book on me, I do not believe I can well answer it. The article seems to me to contain the sort of feeling I most dislike—I mean a certain sort of manufactured smartness. Well, here is a man making himself an article or a book. He does it with a certain distinct cleverness and plausibility. This is a private letter to you.

O, my dear Henry. What makes these fellows so sure. He accuses me of so much uncertainty as to the nature of art, of beauty, truth etc. One feels in his writing of my work a certain distinct pleasure that it is not more successful, that I am not a bigger and better man. As I read I gather that this man knows all of the things about life I do not know and have been unable to find out.

Why is the fellow not at the job of writing a book, making it all clear to me and others who are so often puzzled? It would seem a much more important task than bothering with poor me.

Between ourselves, Henry, I have a feeling just now that I have been too much praised and too much blamed. I am rather tired of the public attention I have got. There is too much centering upon me. I have no wish to add to it.

However I want to do what I can for you and your plans. Later you will think of some other subject on which I can perhaps write with more gusto. It would be better I am sure.

Sincerely. .
Sherwood Anderson

TS. Yale

1. Cleveland B. Chase, "Sherwood Anderson," *Saturday Review of Literature* 4 (24 Sept. 1927): 129–30. His book, *Sherwood Anderson*, also appeared in 1927.

TO John Anderson

[10 October 1927, Ripshin Farm]

Dear John.

These are rather busy days for me. As I suppose you know I am going into a new venture. How it will turn out I don't know. Anyway for a long time now I have felt that there was something very much wrong with my position. I can't go on depending on my writing for a living. I am a bit afraid of the temptation toward just becoming a hack.

What am I saying? As a matter of fact I am very much afraid. And so I have bought, or am buying, some little weekly newspapers over at Marion[1] and, beginning with November, will run them. It will be all new to me.

Well, I have to do something. Had quite made up my mind that I must make my living in some way rather than grind out writing. There is too much temptation to be sloppy. Whether or not I will have energy and strength enough to do this new work and have left enough freshness to produce worthwhile work in my own field I don't know. But anything is better than to get sloppy in the one thing I care most about.

And so here goes for the new thing. Sometimes I feel very guilty that I have not, in all of these years, made enough money so that you, Bob and Mimi will not be in your turn faced with the same problem. It

John Anderson
COURTESY OF ELEANOR ANDERSON

would be so very nice if I could now make you both a sufficient income to live on and let you just have leisure to go ahead and develop in your own way.

Often enough you are going to find yourself annoyed that it has not turned out so but as you see it hasn't.

Anyway, dear John, even at the expense of some time, do learn to do something by which you can live outside painting. What it will be I don't know.

As a matter of fact I have nothing but advertising writing and I can't well go into that because anyone for whom I could work would be rather bound to exploit me and my name for commercial purposes.

Well, it is the inevitable problem of life—to those who are not rich. I dare say they have another problem. It is good that you are happy and working at what you want to do, for the time being anyway. Perhaps if you go carefully about marriage and such things and learn to live with little money, you can escape most of it. I don't know. Am glad you have been seeing Bab and Mary.[2] Give them both my love.

Write often. I am afraid I will not have much time to write. Show this letter to Mimi. Give her my love too. I intend to renew her income—that is to say her spending money—soon. How are you financially. Damn finances. How inevitable they are though. Give my love to Cornelia too.

S.A.

TS. NL (ph)

1. The Smyth County *News* and the Marion *Democrat*.
2. Marietta ("Bab") Finley and possibly Mary Rose Himler, editors at Bobbs-Merrill publishers in Indianapolis.

TO Burton Emmett

[c. early May 1928, Marion]

Dear Burton Emmett

It must be good to be back but being back does mean the work again, doesn't it? Things seem to be moving along here. We got through the first six months with enough money laid aside so that we can make the payments as per program.[1] After the first year it should be better.

There was a subscription drive just before we took hold, with two automobiles given away and everyone paid up a year in advance. These papers we have had to deliver all of this year without pay for them. It should mean an additional three thousand the second year.

Subscription growth is steady. We might go ahead and give the papers a more or less national circulation but have decided not to do this. It seems better to let them remain local.

The man from whom we bought had about six weeks before we closed, after negotiation began. He let all the stock run down to nothing. We have put some six or seven hundred into that. Also we have made mechanical improvements and paid for them.

If I were a younger man I could see where a tight little fortune might be made. Our local papers here are so obviously an improvement on those in nearby towns that we have been urged to start papers in these towns. The chain idea, so successful in other things, is succeeding in the local weekly field. You simply manufacture in one spot, having a spot man in each town.

This idea however would kill all of the purpose for which I bought the papers. They seem to be serving that purpose, to give me something to do outside the practice of my own art.

In the American scene now the artist has no place. These papers do give me a definite place in the life of the community. When I have got them a bit nearer paid for I shall get a young man to do many of the things I now have to do—that is to say following up advertisers etc.

Besides my work on the papers each week, and I do most of the writing, I do a monthly article for *Vanity Fair* and I have a novel underway. I hope within a year or so to have a novel and that may so clear my skirts that I can ease off some.

I am pretty confident the definite purpose for which I got the papers will be served.

All of this about the situation here. Well, I know you are interested and that Mrs. Emmett will be interested.

I took the liberty of publishing the long letter you wrote me from the boat.[2] People in a small town love to have such letters from far places in the papers. I know you must have had a real rest and I hope you may find it possible to bring Mrs. Emmett and motor down here this summer.

I did accept an offer to lecture for two weeks in the fall and another two weeks in the spring. This to make quite sure I shall have money to meet things as they come along here.

I have sent some mss. along during the winter but there are still some piles of it at the farm. Soon we will be going there for weekends and I can get at it and go over it.

At any rate dear friend I work. When the writing does not come as I want it to I do not sit, twirl my thumbs and eat myself up with remorse that I cannot do more and better work.

All of my respect and regards to you both.

Sherwood Anderson

TS. NL

1. Emmett had lent Anderson $5,000 in Oct. 1927 to buy the two Marion newspapers.

2. The letter, written on a ship near Java, was published in the Smyth County *News* on 19 Apr. 1928, p. 6.

TO Charles Bockler[1]

[early 1929, Marion]

Dear Charles—

The painting "Bottles and Apples" is very living. I needed it. It is in my room, over the desk where I work. The other, "Trees," is in the print shop, over the folding machine. I have the Cézanne in the room upstairs with "Bottles and Apples." It stands up—I mean your own painting—in this distinguished company.

You know the one with the grapes. Please varnish this for shipment. I have a chance to sell it for $250.00 to a rich merchant here. If I succeed put it in a gold frame before shipping. The thing may not come off but, on the other hand, it may. I think it would be better to dispose of a few this way than to fuss with a show, for the next few years. Let the show come two or three years from now.

I remember so sharply my own experience[2]—all such asses as that one you saw and heard at the packing place, mulling over your work, pawing over it, patronizing you.

"Pretty good for a young man" etc.

"He has good color but cannot draw."

"If he could only paint." In time you get hardened to it of course but it is a bad time.

I have been thinking of Kath[3] almost constantly these last few days, loving her a lot.

Of course I was just playing with the story you and Kath told. It happens that way. You jump off from Kath and have Helen. Well Helen is not Kath. You understand.

Often you write a sentence. Let us suppose I start with Mary.[4]

I write—"She was a slender woman with red hair."

Now where has Mary gone. This red haired woman is not her.

It is like a new color, introduced into a painting.

I shall be in New York between the 15th & 20th of March.

If the picture sale should happen to come off I'll wire. It is worth the gamble of varnishing.

Lots of love.

MS. NL

1. Young painter encouraged by Anderson, then working in New York as a bank clerk.

2. Anderson's paintings had been exhibited in 1920 and 1921 at bookshops in Chicago and New York.

3. Katharine Bockler, wife of Charles Bockler, whose usual nickname was "Kack."

4. Probably Mary Vernon Greer, Katharine Bockler's sister and friend of Anderson.

TO Ferdinand and Clara Schevill

[16 January 1929], Marion

My dear Ferdinand & Clara—

I have an altogether charming feeling about my visit to you—as though I had been swimming a long time in winter, in an icy river and had got ashore—only to find your warm friendly house.

I have a feeling I misrepresented my own attitude. I emphasized too much—in my present troubles—the money side.

All of this wild purchasing was purchasing of baubles, of course—to compensate perhaps for love I could not give.

Alas I am not true. I am not dependable. I walk about often at night and think—"This sheer loneliness I feel is a part of my materials too. It is like paint. I shall brush it onto a canvas tomorrow."

I only mean that poor E. is very very nice—much nicer than I will ever be—and I do not want her anymore.[1] C. & T. were nice too. Why should I not face myself—a wanderer.

People give I think what they can give and take what they can hold. I never see you two without a feeling of being filled with something warm and good for me.

That you love me a little as I love you helps my poor self-respect. It may not be good judgment on your part but it is good for me.

Sherwood

MS. NL

1. The Andersons had separated.

TO Dwight MacDonald[1]

8 March 1929, Marion

My dear Dwight MacDonald . . .

I recently saw, for the first time, an article by you in the *Yale Literary Magazine*, printed last July. As a matter of fact I seldom see the reviews and am not a great reader. I long since gave up the notion that the thing aimed at would be likely to be understood by the average reviewer.

May I thank you for the fine intelligence of your article. Naturally I was sorry you felt compelled to deliver the funeral oration but I have rather a notion that you were but rounding out your article.[2] And you may be right.

However I am not an old man. I am still experimentally minded. You say that, in *Winesburg* and some of the other tales, I got at something. There may still be something more complex and difficult to be got at. The best I can do is to try constantly new approaches.

And I am not sure but that in some of the later things—as for example some chapters in the little book *Tar*, notably the chapter about the old woman dying in the wood[3]—I have hit as closely as I ever did or will. There may even be something in the *New Testament* that has not come into your own consciousness yet.

But I am not writing to rebuke or criticize you. A man, at this time, works constantly in the midst of difficulties. Prose in general is so bad. There is little understanding of the very thing you have pointed out so clearly and that I believe I have not seen pointed out before.

Sometimes really I have the temerity to think of myself as a sort of Cézanne in prose, that is to say—"the primitive of the way." I like to think that I have still much courage for new experiments, whether they succeed or not.

With me it seems necessary to live first what may possibly later be distilled into what I want and need. But living is very very difficult. It is however a very distinct contribution to my own living to find this article of yours. You are speaking of prose in a language I can understand and that is more helpful than you perhaps realize.

Sincerely
Sherwood Anderson

P.S. My great objection to the funeral oration note is that it has been done to me from the first—even before *Winesburg*.

TS. NL

1. Then the managing editor of the *Yale Literary Magazine*, which published his article "Sherwood Anderson," 93 (July 1928): 209–43.
2. In discussing Anderson's writings, MacDonald traced in *Dark Laughter* and subsequent books a decline in quality.
3. Ch. 12, the story which Anderson later called "Death in the Woods."

TO Burton Emmett

10 March 1929, Marion

My dear Burton Emmett:

I am writing this letter to you on Sunday morning. I got your letter out of the post office last night and it upset me of course. In spite of your great kindness I could not help reading into it your own sense of disappointment in me.[1] I do not blame you. You are quite right.

If you will remember back to our first correspondence a year or two ago you will realize again how difficult it is for me to get into my consciousness a sense of what you want. I wrote you at length about the matter at that time, about my inability to take seriously the collector's passion when applied to myself and I think told you how silly it made me feel. I guess you must know that my whole struggle for twenty-five years now has been toward a goal very seldom attained and even under the best circumstances very seldom attainable.

How often I have wished that I were a painter or a musician. Then I could work toward an abstract thing in which human beings were not involved.

Always my own life has been complicated by the want and need of money but wherever in my relationships with my fellows money has become involved it has led to the kind of disappointment you now feel and the kind of guilt I feel.

I believe that of all the writers living now, at least in America, I am the only man who has written prose having in it a kind of singing quality that is necessary to its continued life in the consciousness of others. To do this has involved every phase of my being. It has involved and constantly endangered my relationships with women, with my own family, and even with my children.

This is difficult to explain. The only time I attain to the mood in which good work comes requires a kind of isolation and cruelty along with a queer sort of tenderness.

I think you ought to bear in mind that works of mine which have cut the deepest have brought me practically nothing. This is not true of you. You have managed, out of the helter skelter, to obtain money enough to be safe.

When I came to you something more than a year ago about these collector's items I had no doubt of my being able to obtain them. I myself had not saved many of my manuscripts. There were some, I thought, in the hands of my first wife. I had sent them to her. Others I presumed to be in the files of my publishers. Immediately after my return home I wrote to the publishers and to my first wife. A manuscript of *Winesburg* had been in the hands of Mr. Huebsch. Mr. Huebsch later sold out to the Viking Press. I got in touch with Mr. Huebsch, who said that the manuscript with other material out of his old files had been thrown away.

There were other disappointments at this time.

As I told you at the time I had been in correspondence for the last ten years with a good many of the more notable figures in American life. You thought some of these letters would be valuable to you and I tried hard to see your point of view.

As a matter of fact I have been disappointed in those of my old files I have gone through. Often letters of no importance at all, from your point of view, were kept because there [was] some revealing human touch in them valuable to me. On the other hand, evidently many letters I thought I had and that might have been valuable to you were thrown away because I had so little sense of this other world of values.

There are still numberless pages of old handwritten manuscript, attempts made that turned out disappointing, etc., that I have not gone over.

It has been a bad year for me in many ways. The papers here are going off successfully and we have more than met our schedule as far as they are concerned but my personal life has been rather a wreck. I have been married three times and evidently cannot make a success of marriage. My last marriage has fallen to pieces during the last eight months. This has hurt me a good deal more than anybody has known. To try in the midst of it to run the newspapers here successfully and to keep some hold on my real work at the same time has kept me in a distraught, upset state.

Time and again I have set myself to work over this old matter and see what out of it I could obtain for you. To tell you the truth, it has seemed to me always like turning over old rags when I wanted the living garments of life itself. I have to be frank with you. To have been able to help one young painter of talent paint uninterrupted by necessity for a few months means more to me than all the collector's items in the world.

You will say, and rightly, that as I feel this way I should not have taken your money for these items, or rather, the loan. It is quite true. I was in a desperate situation, not necessarily financially but for something definite to do that would carry me through this distraught time. If it is any satisfaction to you I think I can say to you that owning these papers has perhaps saved me from insanity.

In addition to this I have done something through them and with them. I think you could not come here without feeling that the life of the whole community has been touched and changed by these papers during my editorship.

I have been remiss in my obligations to you. I know it and feel it. Now I am trying to sell the country place I have here and I have some hope of success this summer. If I succeed I will pay off this obligation at once and I will not again I hope get into such a position. I mean by this that I will try as earnestly as I can not to bring finances into my relationships with people. No doubt I will not succeed but I will succeed as far as I can.

I do not mean by this that I am not going to try to give you all I can of the things you want. Just how soon I will be able to do it is hard for me to say now. As I said before time and again when I have caught myself ready to get seriously at it, either some impulse toward writing swept me away from it or some complication of my personal life had the same effect.

I do hope that things may turn out so that I can return the money advanced me this year. If I can get the papers paid for here I can make of them a sort of mainstay for my children and can then go my own way toward work. I need terribly now long months of quiet life in which to work out the other side of my life. I probably won't get them but to get them is, I think, about the only chance I have to go on producing as an artist.

I have written you this long letter to try to lay down before you my own situation and to try to explain a little what must have seemed my brutality towards you and your wishes. I sincerely hope that out of the muddle I may retain your respect and friendship and I think I can quite safely say that you are not in danger of losing the money.

Sincerely,
Sherwood Anderson

P.S. I have got also out of the papers here a book which should be out of the press within the next month. I have taken the liberty of dedicating this book to you and Mrs. Emmett[2] as it was through your generosity that I was able to get hold of the papers here and also out of a feeling of sincere affection to you both.

TS. NL

1. Emmett had expressed some dissatisfaction with the extent and quality of the manuscripts that Anderson had thus far sent him. Their value was to be applied to the repayment of Emmett's loan to Anderson

2. *Hello Towns!* is dedicated "To my friends, Mr. and Mrs. Burton Emmett."

TO Baroness Marie Koskull[1]

[late July 1929, Dykemans, N.Y.]

Dear Dear Baroness—

Your letter, sent as you were leaving Germany for the visit, via Baltic, to your old home, made me full of love for you. In it I felt all of your splendor and the richness that made you able to give love to many people, and to receive it richly too.

"It is that Hilda, that Baroness," I cried to myself. "O, she should be glad and happy that she is of big frame, that her skin is fair and takes the light—that she is a painter's woman."

Then I was glad anew that you were my new friend and ashamed that I must have written you a craven letter.

But I am not craven nor dead dear woman. I had got so low. Marriage—American marriage—a curse on it.

It had sunk me so low—a crying woman. "But you do not love me."

O hell.

I came away from Marion the first of this month. Damn such luck. There was a young painter friend.[2] He and his wife were to take a house in the country. He was to paint and I write. As he was poor as hell—a man of talent—my little financial help was to make his summer possible.

And so I came—into a tiny New England town—really upper New York State. By God—the wife had got pregnant.

Some women vomit when they are so—they whine, they have morning sickness. The house we had taken was tiny. By God.

Echoes of my own married life.

The poor thing trying to cook for us.

Her whining voice in the house too. Curses.

The painter's summer gone too.

Then—

You see, my dear Baroness (Hilda)—I had been wanting a certain kind of prose. Once I got near it—in *Many Marriages*—a glorious book—(That is the one that most should be in German.)

I wanted a loose rhythmic prose, laughter under it, buried down under the words.

On the surface the prose so simple no one but a master would quite know what I had buried in it.

And so I began to write—under the conditions I have described. Of course I pitched everything too low.

The prose growled—it had dirt in it. There was nothing aristocratic in it.

God damn.

One day I went off into the hills alone—as low a man as you ever saw.

Something happened. Perhaps I saw God's face on the surface of the rocks.

Anyway I came home and began to write. I am a man you would not be ashamed to know. If I sell the house in the country all right. If not I shall give it to the Baptist church.

It is not money that makes a man write. He does it by God's grace. Or by knowing people like you.

Don't lose me. We have a popular song in America.

"Stick to me Lulu.
Stick to me Lulu."

Write me from away down south there.

We'll meet again.

Sherwood A.

MS. NL

1. German friend whom Anderson had met earlier in the year in Washington. She had gone to Germany and then to Argentina.
2. Charles Bockler.

TO Ferdinand and Clara Schevill
[c. 31 December 1929, St. Petersburg, Fla.]

Dear Ferdinand & Clara.

I have decided not to come to the funeral,[1] not just knowing whether, to Tennessee's sister, I would be a welcome sight . . . in her time of trouble . . . not just knowing what an ex-husband's status is, feeling also that any kindness from me would have been better disposed of by putting it into effect with the living woman.

The whole thing has been rather terrible and as usual I have been in a rotten state of punishing myself. I think I was doing it in Chicago.[2] In spite of a certain crudeness of approach she really wanted from me there a little love and comradeship and I didn't give it to her.

Well.

I could wreck myself forever on this shore. The whole coast is alive with the jagged rocks of my own unkindnesses. I guess Clara understands this better than you, Ferdinand. I'm damned if I think, in your whole life, you ever have been unkind, as either Clara or I might be at any moment. Excuse me, Clara dear.

I have chucked the novel.[3] It's a long story. I wish to God you and Clara could run down here for two or three weeks, right now. We'd sit on the beach or fish off the pier. The cold is all gone, the sun shines, the sea is marvelous.

Since I chucked the novel I've been writing short stories . . . some rather nice ones, I think. My plan is to stay here until about Jan. 15th and then perhaps I'll go to Miami. I've got a wild Irishman laundry friend[4] over there.

I wish I could see and talk to you both.

Just now I'll but write to thank you for your kindness in wiring me about poor Tennessee. Everyone was very very kind.

Will you inquire if there is any mail for me and have it sent on. And do come down. Why not? I would be so much better company than you found me in Chicago.

Love.
Sherwood

Hotel Detroit.

MS. NL

1. Tennessee Mitchell Anderson had died from an apparent overdose of sleeping pills.
2. Anderson had visited in Chicago earlier in the month.
3. This novel, "Beyond Desire," was never completed. Anderson reused the title for his novel published in 1932.
4. Maurice Long, who owned a laundry in Washington, D.C.

TO Paul Rosenfeld

11 January 1930, Savannah, Ga.

Dear Paul—

I have in mind inflicting a letter on you and think, with some sympathy, of your suffering in trying to read my scrawl. It came about through my having picked up a *New Republic* containing an article by you . . . "Mozart in His *Don Juan*."[1] As always your writing excited me.

It has been an odd winter. I stood Marion as long as I could and then lit out, going first to Chicago. Of course you have heard of poor Tennessee's death. I was in Chicago for two weeks . . . my daughter is in the University there . . . and talked to T. several times on the phone. She was to have dined with Mimi, Ferdinand Schevill and myself on Saturday night but at the last some guest arrived and she couldn't come.

So I did not see her. I am afraid that, as usual, I was rather unkind. She was very anxious to have me come to her, at her apartment, but I did not go. I made excuses. Between ourselves I think she had some sort of notion that I might come back to her. I remember that you suggested that, as a possibility, when we met in New York but it never was a possibility.

My thinking that she thought it was made me shy about going to her. There was nothing except, well, you know, certain things in her voice, when I spoke to her on the phone . . . She had also begun suddenly, after five years of silence, to write me letters.

I left New York for Florida after the dinner to which she did not come.

She died in her bed evidently a few days later. She was living alone there and her friends were under the impression she had gone out of town for the holidays. A friend wrote me that she was probably dead for six days in her bed before the body was discovered. I did not go to the funeral. That would have been rather too much.

This fall I went to Washington and Richmond and wrote a long novel. It had a few glorious spots in it but on the whole, after I had let it lie awhile and reread it, I decided it would not do. It was to have been called "Beyond Desire." I doubt if I shall ever write it now.

The theme itself has lost point and interest for me. Again it was an attempt to find some sort of answer to the man and woman problem. I've really thrown up my hands on it I think.

In the meantime, under the southern sun, I have begun to crawl about a little. The explosion of my theme in my hands, followed by T.'s death, had rather floored me. I began writing some little things I called, in my own mind, "A Don Juan's Book of Hours." I have been playing along with these, not taking them too seriously, trying to get little flashing pictures . . . they would be etching really if done rightly . . . out of a wandering, rather adventurous life.

They should give, if I go on with them and they are done as they should be, a picture of a rather naive, good intentioned man, moving restlessly among men and women, blundering of course, getting nothing but life itself, a sort of George Willard of Winesburg become a man of fifty. I do not want to say anything about them to anyone, except a few close friends.

Once word of any sort of literary adventure gets abroad there are publishers who write and wire—"How about it. When may we have it?" etc. It puts me out, upsets me. That, I presume, is why I am not more in New York. There is, it seems, money to be made out of me.

In the meantime I have another interest. As you know, Paul, I came from working people. The socially acceptable and the great American middle class interest me but little. I have been too much with them and a part of them these last five years. The great difficulty of life with Elizabeth was that she did love baubles. We were always being in debt for antique furniture, dresses, fur coats, houses etc. and more being purchased constantly. It kept me producing stuff when I was not ready, wasting by skimming the milk before the cream had time to rise.

Almost without exception it has been my experience that women I have loved, having been attracted by the poet and artist in me, have afterwards tried valiantly to kill the thing that attracted them. It is perhaps inevitable.

Lately I have been thinking that, as my central interest seems to be working people, small farmers, factory and mill people, and as the position of all such peoples becomes more and more insecure and uncertain in the American industrial system, that with mass production, speed-up systems etc., the real living drama of American life now lies with them.

I have come up from Florida . . . the yellow and white sands, the sea, the palms and the sun are wonderful there but such people . . . they are nearly all old with a dreadful kind of slack middleclass oldness . . . not like Stieglitz . . . not like old working men and women . . .

dreadfully old . . . they play shuffleboard and talk of money all the time.

I have come up from Florida and have stopped here in this old town for a few days. I am to be with a friend here.

I am thinking of drifting from here into the North Carolina mill towns. There a whole race of people, working people, small mountain farmers, are being brought into modern industrial life, beaten by it.

It keeps sticking in my mind that I should begin now and devote what there is left of life in me to people like this, finding my stories among them, devoting myself to digging out the drama of these lives.

Liveright is planning an omnibus volume of all my short stories, published and unpublished, in one volume.[2] (This also I think should be kept quiet because of his having to buy up rights.)

It should bring in some money.

Bob is running the papers at Marion. This seems to be one venture I have stumbled into that pays, however the people of the county are more comfortable with Bob running them than myself. I am a bit of white elephant on their hands.

Bob runs them well, likes it and the people like him. I shall sell him the papers, letting him pay not me but John and Marion. This should be a little start for all of them.

By the way, my second son, John, is in New York, at 100 E. 106th Street. He is spending some part of the winter there, copying in the Metropolitan. He wants to be a painter as you know. He is rather a nice boy and if you have an opportunity and can drop him a note and see him some afternoon or evening it would be nice.

I shall probably sell the farm—Ripshin—if I can. I am looking for someone who would like such a summer home. If you hear of anyone tell them about it.

So you see I intend to drift, letting what will happen to me. Already I am getting over the feeling of hurry built up in me when I was a man with a big house, a wife with a fondness for expensive antiques etc. It really takes very little for me to live thus.

And what a long letter. If you have a chance show it to Stieglitz. I owe him such another.

Perhaps, in the spring sometime, if I am drifting about in the warm south, you might come and drift with me for a few weeks.

Sherwood

Permanent address—Marion, Va.

MS. Yale

1. *New Republic* 61 (25 Dec. 1929): 143–44.
2. This project was not completed.

TO Burton Emmett

[c. 2 February 1930, Columbus, Ga.]

Dear Burton Emmett—

I have decided against the novel—"Beyond Desire"—manuscript of which I sent you—and would like to have you send the manuscript back to me. The novel is not fine enough. It is too broken.

If for any reason you want very much to keep it please attach this letter to it and please also make some arrangement that it shall not go out of your hands.

I do not want a patched crippled piece of work to bob up some time in the future, after you and I are perhaps gone.

I hardly know yet what was wrong. Perhaps I am through with the problem of men and women, sex etc.

I have been seeking a more complex interesting theme.

It has pretty near come to this . . . that I think the most interesting theme in America is modern industry.

This may be because I began life as a laborer.

And there is something else. I have at any rate been trying to do some thinking this year and I am pretty sure that nothing nowadays is affecting life like machinery. It is more and more recasting all life, throwing men out of work, making a few men rich, pretty much destroying craftsmanship.

But that it . . . that is to say machinery . . . is beautiful in itself.

So here I am, drifting about in Southern towns, going into mills . . . when I can get in . . . looking at machinery . . . looking at men working at machinery, trying to get the factory feel into me.

It is intoxicating. What I will get out of it I don't quite know yet.

I'm doing it anyway, living from hand to mouth at it. Bob is handling the papers and will earn out on them.

The novel wouldn't do. I would much rather you sent it back and took what came later.

Love to you both.
Sherwood Anderson

Written from Columbus, Ga.—address Marion.

MS. NL

TO Burton Emmett

17 April 1930, Helen, Ga.—a lumber camp

Dear Burton Emmett.

I am in receipt of your letter which reached me in North Georgia, in the mountains, in a lumber camp.[1]

It is a little difficult for me to say what I would want to say about the material. As you yourself know, the collector's impulse has always been a bit puzzling to me.

But never mind that.

This I do know . . . that you cannot possibly judge values in this field by immediate price set by dealers.

What must be considered, I dare say, is the ultimate place a man may hold in the development of the culture of his times.

I think it goes deeper than that. It will depend, in the last end, on how much of what I might call "major poetry" is in a man's work.

Is the poetry of existence in his time at all found and expressed in his work?

Contemporary judgment is not much good.

We are in a queer time, a queer civilization. Nothing apparently lasts. Do not however be fooled by that. Sound work stands up.

I have produced some of the really sound work of my day and I hope may produce more.

In our day a man is both promised too much at first and then an attempt is made to push him aside too rudely and abruptly.

The daily press, syndicated opinion, the desire of new men to push established men aside and set up new idols . . .

All of these impulses are intensified in our civilization.

It does not seem to me at all fair to treat the artist, the rise and fall of his values, as you would treat the stock market.

I know it is an unavoidable tendency.

Forgive me for mentioning it.

You say—"if you were to have a novel" etc.

Surely that would center attention on me again.

I do not want attention centered on me. If I could work the rest of my life unknown, unnoticed by those who make current opinion, I would be happier.

To work for the market kills everything finest in a man's life and work.

If I could do anything to center attention on myself now so that what we might call "my immediate values" would go up, it would be the last thing I would do.

Dear man—you can see surely why I have to keep alive my contempt for such valuations.

An artist should not have to figure on these things. To compel him to do so is destructive. There is too much of that sort of destruction.

Well, unfortunately, I did not inherit money. From time to time money has been offered me in order that I might be able to work in peace but always on conditions that have made acceptance impossible.

Your own offer is generous and fine.[2] You can't possibly get the values out of me in your life or mine. I tell myself that there is affection in it. I want affection. It is the only thing that seems to me to have value.

If you can do it . . . and I know you can . . . on that ground I can accept . . . just because it is bad business.

I like bad business so much better than good. I can't help that feeling.

I won't ask you to help me with the cigarette people.[3] Whether or not I'll get to them I don't know.

I'm aiming now to clear the papers as fast as I can in order that I may pass them on to my kids.

My plan for myself is to live as economically as I can so that I will not have to think much of markets.

You see, dear man, the very thing that sent my "values" up, a year or two ago, sickened me. My publishers hounded me for a new novel, in order to take advantage of "the market." The very fact stood in the way of my writing a novel. I couldn't do it.

It was like bringing "the markets" into a love affair.

There does still remain a kind of love between myself and the white sheets of paper on my desk here. I have had to fight to keep that love alive. I am fighting.

I say all this to explain to you what may seem only perverse in me sometimes.

I only mean, as you know, that all real values lie deeper than the surface.

I thank you for the assurance as regards the novel ms.[4] I want to be sure it is not published.

I shall send the new note[5] as soon as I get home to Marion, early in May.

My sincere affection to you and Mrs. Emmett.

Sherwood Anderson.

MS. NL

1. Anderson was visiting Mr. and Mrs. John Greear, formerly of Troutdale, Va., with whom he had stayed during the summer of 1925.

2. Emmett offered to place a value of $3,000 on the manuscripts Anderson had sent him, thus reducing the 1927 loan to $2,000.

3. Anderson had expressed interest in visiting cigarette factories as a part of his reporting on labor conditions in the South and suggested that Emmett's influence might be useful in carrying out this project. Emmett, however, declined.

4. Emmett had assured Anderson that the first "Beyond Desire" manuscript would not be published.

5. That is, the $2,000 note.

TO the Editors of *Scribner's*

18 May 1930, Ripshin Farm

Dear Sirs

Answering Mr. John Hall Wheelock's letter in regard to the article—"A Woman's Age."[1]

Although there is undoubted beauty in the machine we will only go half way if we do not admit that, at present, the machine is doing men harm.[2]

It is partly because men have not mastered the machine as yet. Why cannot we admit both things—that in making the machine what it has become we have done a marvelous thing and in the same breath admit that the machine is as yet too much for us.

My notion is, as you see, that woman stands up to this test better than men. This because she creates in the physical world and the machine cannot really touch her there.

In an article to follow this I want to develop the idea that eventually women will again begin to demand more maleness.

She will need it, needs it now.

She is only taking possessions as a substitute.

If, for example, we ever have a youth movement of any account it will have to take this form.

Why would it not be a master stroke for *Scribner's* to try to develop such a movement in America.

My quarrel with D.H. Lawrence, for example, was only that he utterly threw over the machine age. That's no good. We've got to face it. If you read *Lady Chatterley's Lover* or any of Lawrence's later books you find him proclaiming a return to the land as the solution.

That and sex.

I know I have been bracketed with Lawrence a good deal in this matter and I have felt close to him.

But I do not throw over the Industrial Age—the machine.

I am accepting it, taking it in to me all I can.

I want to tell you men that it is pretty terrific. I spent most of this last winter with the machine, actually in factories, and I can say to you that men like us, you editors at your desks and men like myself, also for the most part at a desk or walking about in streets or in the fields, do not quite know how terrific a thing an institution, say like the Ford plant, is.

It is hardest, of course, on the more sensitive men. I swear to you that, although I am a rather strong man, two or three hours in a modern factory was all I could stand.

It shook me to my very toes.

Let us admit I was consciously trying to give myself utterly to the rhythm of it.

That doesn't mean that the workmen are not affected as I was, if to a lesser degree.

I am trying to get at the theme of Mr. Wheelock's letter of May 7th to me. I think it is absurd not being serious about all this. There is no fun in life if you cannot be serious.

It is a matter of shifting of emphasis perhaps. We are not taking the machine seriously enough. We are taking it too seriously.

What is the way out then?

Let me return to Lawrence. He sought a new center for life in sex.

The matrix, eh.

That won't do.

Man has got to have his own world again.

It must mean a return to interest in government, to poetry, play for its own sake, most of all a new interest in life.

Man will not be destroyed by the machine if he does not expect salvation from it.

I have been told by a good many women that they do not marry because they cannot find men male enough for them.

They do not necessarily mean the liberty pole.

They do mean men who get the machine, possessions etc., into the proper relations.

What about a youth movement founded and based on an attempt at a return to this sort of real maleness.

I suppose you cannot start such a movement. It must spring up spontaneously. But it must come.

Personally I am sure not going to give up the machine to get it. We have talked damn big in America. Well, here is our test—to keep the machine, develop it, see and understand both its beauty and its danger and yet be men.

As to the notes on the manuscript. Page 1. I see you prefer not to break the sentences at x up into paragraphs.

It really doesn't matter.

As a matter of fact I know that I am essentially a poet. It just happens I don't want to be proclaimed one. It's too much like being proclaimed a lover. I'd much rather sneak poetry across.

I break up paragraphs like this sometimes because it seems to me to make a kind of rhythm in the reading that I want. I want the mind of the reader to be singing as it reads without quite knowing what has happened.

However surely I do not stand on it as a vital matter.

I have eliminated the bracketed sentence, page 3—as you suggested. It was not an important sentence.

The word "not" page 5—agreed.

First elimination—beginning page 9—I have left in a part of this page 10. Do you not agree with me?

Second elimination—beginning page 11 and running to the 4th line page 12—agreed.

Third elimination on page 12—agreed.

As for these suggestions I see no reason why you should not always make such suggestions regarding material of mine. Why indeed should not editors be editors?

Anyway I have a very grateful feeling that your suggestions have immensely strengthened this article.

Sometime ago, when I was worried a bit about financing the work I am now trying to do you suggested that you would send me $1000. If you feel like doing this now, taking the chances on my being able to work out something satisfactorily to you in the follow-up woman's article. Or in either "Lumber Camp" or "Sugar Mill"[3]—both in preparation—it would be rather nice to have this money. When I have been here on the farm for a month or two I expect to get into the car and go back to the factories again.

Address me directly at Troutdale, Virginia, for the present. My son is running the weekly newspapers at Marion, although I contribute to them.

Incidentally I wrote a long poem on the automobile, sold to a Western woman's magazine,[4] I would like you men to see when published, just for fun.

When it is published I will send it to you to see.

Sincerely,
Sherwood Anderson

TS. Princeton

1. "It's a Woman's Age" appeared in *Scribner's* 88 (Dec. 1930): 613–18. John Hall Wheelock, a *Scribner's* editor, had written Anderson to acknowledge receipt of the manuscript and to suggest a few revisions.

2. Wheelock had queried whether Anderson's themes of the beauty and the harmfulness of machines were consistent.

3. These essays were not published.

4. "Machine Song: Automobile," *Household Magazine* 30 (Oct. 1930): 3.

TO Burton Emmett

Sunday [25 May 1930, Ripshin Farm?]

Dear Emmett

Your fine sensitive letter came. What is involved is I dare say a question of values.[1] It is a subject over which the most learned scholars have struggled endlessly. Thank God we are friends. We can talk about it without hurting each other.

Who can question the want of value in money.

Who can question that, in the most real, the most precious things of life, money has no value.

A good many people have tried, from time to time, to help me with money. You are the only one who ever succeeded.

For God's sake, if I grow abrupt sometimes do not think that I do not know that you, Burton Emmett, have as fine a graciousness as any man living.

Only last year, when I wanted to tackle the industrial thing a rich woman wanted to give me money to work on and to pay my debts. As a matter of fact the $5000 I owed you was on my mind.

She couldn't do it.

Others have tried.

They failed in this—that, with the single exception of yourself, they all have tried—often in a subtile way—to direct my mind and feeling, as regards my work.

There has never been the slightest hint of this in you.

To return to values. Can you understand, dear man, that the insistence, on the part of publishers, that if I would write a new novel now it would place me out in front in American writing, etc., etc.

Make me money etc.

God knows I needed the money. This outside insistence spoiled the novel I tried to write. It may have sickened me finally with the idea of the novel.

You have got to put up with this queer contradiction in the artist's nature. That bad novel, ms. of which you have, you only have by accident. There was the copy you have in my secretary's hands.

One night in Chicago I thought I had destroyed it quite. I opened a hotel bedroom window and let the sheets blow away.

Why—bad or good—I could have got money by it.

Even if it were good I might have had keen pleasure in destroying it.

Even though I know you want originals of my stuff I have to remember each time not to burn them. I can't always remember.

There is this contradiction in us over this particular question of value.

I have got together a package of mss. today—have tried to annotate them carefully.

Suppose Wm. Shakespeare alive. He writes me a dull letter. I would throw it away, burn it.

A farm woman, utterly unknown, might send me a letter full of sense and feeling. I would preserve that.

These are my instincts. I have to fight to remember.

As a matter of fact I place absolutely no value at all on the things of mine you have. I consider the $3000 a gift. You will have to let me take it that way. I take it as a man who has money dividing a bit with a man friend who hasn't it, because he believes in him and his work.

I'll never get any sense of values at all in these scrawled pieces of paper—so much of it with only my failures scrawled on it. It is waste paper to me—nothing.

Your own spirit isn't. I take you as my friend. You have a right to your own values. What else can I say, dear man.

With love to Mrs. Emmett.
Sherwood

Would you like me to save letters, just from people who write me, having been moved perhaps by something I have written?[2]

MS. NL

1. Emmett had explained that he applied market rather than critical values in appraising at $3,000 the manuscripts Anderson had sent him.

2. Emmett replied that he would be glad to receive such letters, and Anderson later sent him some.

TO Burton Emmett

[7 June 1930, Black Mountain, N.C.]

Dear Burton Emmett.

I have the copy of the things marked so—that is to you—"To be worked on."

I am writing you from a little town over the line in N.C. I have a small car now. It is good to get away from my desk now and then, just wander through the hills, think without trying to work, stopping to talk to garage men, farmers etc., staying at little country hotels.

I have a real desire to have you and Mrs. Emmett see this country some day. Within a few hours drive of home you will see what Switzerland can no more than equal. There are mountain roads that take your breath away.

My days have been peculiarly crowded. So many things, impulses etc. that I have tried to work as a painter works . . .

I begin a canvas, that is to say a sketch or a story, and then a new thing comes. My desk nowadays is piled with little piles of unfinished things—like unfinished paintings.

To be worked on—carried along, I hope, another day.

That will account for the unfinished things I may send you from time to time. Many of the things thus begun never will be finished perhaps.

Or they will be done in another form later perhaps.

Often there are a dozen, two dozen attempts at one theme.

On some days you just get the prose music of a thing and cannot sustain it. Will you get it back. You have only hope.

Art is such a long long thing. If I could only have assurance of 200 years of life.

The Lawrence thing, in *New Republic*,[1] has brought letters from all over the country. I have felt for a long time that Lawrence in England and me in America—we two stand for something—the bringing back into prose art of the sensual. It gave us both the reputation of being nasty minded. That hurts of course.

It is the very heart of everything though. Are we to be ruled by the intellectuals—dry asses?

The conception of life—in art—must be kept warm and pulsating. Life cannot go anywhere on mind. You will find the whole heart of the struggle now going on, under the surface, right there. Lawrence was such a man.

By the way did you see the book written by the Englishman Wyndham Lewis last year.[2] He proved the decay of all western civilization by Lawrence and myself. There's mind for you—trying to make life seem decayed—dead.

You must understand, dear man, why I go back and back to working people, farmers etc. This poor farm woman, who is my neighbor, old and weak, trying nevertheless to work fourteen acres of corn this year, working it too, she is something. I would find, I do find, possibilities in her.

She is weary weary—physically. Perhaps, in her tired old body, as she comes home at night, the world of earth and sky does come in. It couldn't come in to Wyndham Lewis.

Or to editors of *New Republic*, alas.

I myself, when I am most tired, feeling too much, when all my body aches with emotions having passed through me, when it seems to me, as it does often, that I cannot live any more, am often most clear.

Whether Lawrence and myself are the men or not, it is nevertheless true that the road we have taken is the road.

There will be new difficulties but I'll not think about them now. I have a home and money for the summer's work. I'll see what that may produce.

Do not, dear man, think you have to answer my letters. I have felt lately a new relation to you—not just based on these words, scrawled on these sheets.

I mean as two men friends. You will find me often just writing, as I am doing here, to express my thoughts.

Sherwood A.

MS. NL

1. Anderson's review of Lawrence's *Assorted Articles*, "A Man's Mind," in *New Republic* 63 (21 May 1930): 22–23.
2. *Paleface: The Philosophy of the "Melting Pot"* (1929).

TO Frances Sage Bradley[1]

20 June 1930, Ripshin Farm

My dear Frances Sage Bradley

It was a queer sensation your letter gave me. There was, in particular, the money, $25.00. No one had ever done just that to me. Money is a queer thing isn't it. It is such filthy stuff. I have the artist's hunger to get hold of it. To such men as myself it means perhaps new shirts, bottles of wine, food etc.

I balanced the check in my hand. "Shall I keep it or not keep it?" You had been teaching school. Perhaps you had earned the money by hard work.

"But why has she been such a fool as to send it to me?" A pretty hard question that one. The very fact that you had sent it to me, an artist, proved, my dear, beyond the last shadow of a doubt that you are not an artist. Alas you do not know what an artist is.

Easy enough to tell you about the sketches. When the publishers tell you that they want only stuff signed by well-known names they are talking bunk. Most of these fellows, even the editors of the popular magazines, are pretty shrewd. They did not want to bother to tell you that your stuff was just plain bad.

It's bad because it's writey, dear woman. I dare say that, before you took that short story course,[2] you had an honest straight feeling about things you saw about you and so perhaps you put them down straight.

So you thought you would learn to write. Well, they have evidently pretty well fixed you.

My dear, every sentence you write is writey. It fairly stinks of writing. "The filmy fog wavering, fluttering, settling over the cove was an old story, and passed unseen like the intricate pattern of lace picked out by the fast-baring beeches and gums against the paling western sky." O, my dear. You were thinking of words weren't you. You thought, I'm afraid, "Well," you thought, "now watch me. Watch me throw some words at that fog."

So you threw them and the fog disappeared. There wasn't a sign of it left. There were only the words.

Words not laid against each other, not fitted together, meaningless words. But I won't scold you. I'll try to tell you something if I can. I'm going to keep your twenty-five and buy some shirts.[3] Think of me as wearing them next winter.

Now as to something about writing. Try first of all, if you must write, if it gets something out of you that you feel rather stops you up, try first of all to forget all magazines, all editors, all that business. If you just want to get your name in the magazines, or make money, you will get there faster by getting into a scandal or something of that sort, or, if it's a question of money, you'll make more writing advertisements.

This sounds harsh. It's true enough. Begin again to try to be as you were before you fooled with the short story people. They never could teach anyone anything but tricks.

Try, my dear woman, to feel rains on you. Let the sun shine on you. If you are a real woman love some man, if you can find one worth loving.

Try to let life flow through you a little. Above all forget words for a long long time. Keep silent a lot. Don't even say too many words. Remember that words are very tender little things and that these goddam people have tricked you into an almost unforgivable rudeness with them.

Keep this in mind also. The magazines are full of trick stories. The popular writers have no real feeling for words, any more than they have for the people they write about, but they are foxy. They know how to seem to be tender with words just as there must be thousands of women who know how to seem to love. Skillful whores can do that and the popular writers are some of them very skillful whores.

It is much nicer to be a nice woman and something tells me you are that. If you weren't I wouldn't take your twenty-five. If you weren't I wouldn't have thought about you for hours last night after I went to bed, if you weren't I wouldn't be writing to you now, I would have sent your money back and would have forgotten the incident at once.

I don't, as a matter of fact, hold you responsible. You have been caught by the same cheap shoddiness that is in almost all departments of life now. You have been made to think you want success, fame, recognition when what you want is love of life, to come into you, to go out of you.

Get this back, dear, fight for it.

When you get it back perhaps the little words will be tender and real in you again, like children wanting to come out of you. You may write then but, if you don't, it won't much matter to you. You'll have something worth more to you [than] all the fame and recognition in the world.

Fame is no good my dear. Take it from me. I know.

Sincerely
Sherwood Anderson

TS. NL

1. A school teacher and aspiring author from Washington, D.C., who had sent Anderson a check for $25 and two specimens of her writing for him to criticize. Anderson apparently planned to use his correspondence with Mrs. Bradley in his autobiographical writings, changing her name to "Luella Williams Grace, M.D."

2. Bradley complained that, after taking a writing course, she had been unable to place her work.

3. Actually, Anderson later returned the check.

TO Burton Emmett

[26 June 1930, Ripshin Farm]

Dear Emmett

I got your fine letter. I am accumulating some more stuff to send along—won't just piddle it into you.

I have been working on a book—to be called *Perhaps Women*, if I can get through it.

The idea is that we Americans are already in a matriarchy. I got through some 30000 words of it but found then that it was too scattered. I've put it aside to let it harden a bit in my mind. Next month I hope I may go back to it. The first section of this proposed book will appear in *Scribner's*, under the title "It's a Woman's Age." I think you'll like it. I think you have the ms. of that.

Some of the later part I did straight off—on the typewriter. It will have to be revised a lot. I'll save it all.

I did, this week, a nice short story—to be called "The Flood."[1] It is being typed. My typewriter ribbon went to shreds. I have to order new ones by mail.

I do want you and Mrs. Emmett to see the place here, as soon as you can. You'd both love it.

I'm glad you liked the "Cotton Mill."[2] It didn't just suit me. What I liked best in it was the feel of machinery. I think I did get that a little. Originally it was a direct attack on Sinclair Lewis. I deleted that.

I dare say you are right about the cigarette people.[3] They would balk or make conditions. Some of them are so like ostriches with their heads in the sand. They think they can hide everything back of factory walls.

They can't do it in the end. The whole age, of money making as an end in life, will have to end or it will all end in impotence. They should be willing to let men like myself look and listen all we want to but they won't. The result will be that they will get, someday, revolution—as ugly a thing as war.

By all means, if you haven't done it, get and read Lawrence—*Lady Chatterley's Lover*. It is a revolutionary book.

Here are so-called "filthy words" made clean and nice. I keep getting echoes of the Lawrence article. Do write *New Republic* and get them to send you a copy of that issue.

Just the same, Emmett, if you don't want to write the letters to people,[4] as suggested, we could do this.

Keep these in a separate envelope, or folder. If I keep them here they will get lost.

Then some day we might get together and edit them, see what we have.

Never mind *Plots and Personalities*.[5] Sounds like bunk.

It might be an adventure anyway to pass "Cotton Mill" on to the Liggett and Myers people—not involving yourself, your telling them about my having asked you to help me get free access to their factories, that you had thought at the time you had better not etc.

Just to smoke them out—always without their getting you mixed in it beyond the fact that you are my friend.

Just to see what they would say.

As always.
Sherwood Anderson

Will return your letter later.

MS. NL

1. Published in *Death in the Woods*, 243–56.
2. Published in *Scribner's* 88 (July 1930): 1–11.
3. Although Emmett had earlier declined to use his influence to help Anderson get inside a cigarette factory to gather material for an article, he wrote that, after reading "Cotton Mill," he was willing to do what he could to help with the project.
4. Anderson had suggested that they collaborate on a book of letters to young people who were searching for values in modern-day life.
5. *Plots and Personalities: A New Method of Testing and Training the Creative Imagination* (New York: Century, 1922), by Edwin E. Slosson and June E. Downey, a book which Emmett had previously offered to send to Anderson.

TO Thomas R. Smith

16 August 1930, Marion

Dear Tom:

I think I had better write a little something about the book on which I am at work and which I sincerely hope I will have ready for you people to see by the first of the year.

You might send this letter to Horace [Liveright]. I hesitate about writing him directly as I expect he is pretty much occupied out West. Last year I had what I thought was a fine novel going, but perhaps because of financial worries I rather hurried it and I believe altogether spoiled it.

Anyway I chucked it out of the hotel window one night. I spent most of last winter in the [factories] as I have had a conviction that what is going on in factories in America is the most vital story in American life, and I think I got hold of something.

What I am working on now is a book not like the *Story Teller's Story* but rather in something of the same manner. It is an attempt to tell in dramatic form my notion of present day American civilization, what it is doing to people etc.

Out of this I have got what seems to me a rather startling and true statement. It is that America already has begun a matriarchy. Women are in control and should be. The result of the Machine Age has been a growth of spiritual impotence in men, a thing that does not touch women so closely. Women are surviving it better. The spiritual impotence, inevitable to men in a Machine Age, will lead inevitably to physical impotence. Women are beginning to find this out. In every factory I have gone into I have found the women standing up to it better than the men. Every woman has within her something the machine cannot touch.

The argument of my book which I want to call *Perhaps Women* is that if the present Machine Age is ever brought down it may be brought down by the women demanding the men back.

I believe, Tom, I am getting this startling story worked out in fine dramatic form, almost like a novel. I want to take my time and do the book the very best I can as it is a big subject. I believe if properly handled it can arouse an immense amount of controversy. At any rate it is a true challenge that the American race is becoming impotent and there is plenty there to stir them up. I have a great deal of hope for this book and am anxious to have Horace, you and others see it as soon as I get it into form.

My love to everyone.
Sherwood Anderson

TS. PC (cc)

TO Burton Emmett

[10 November 1930, Marion]

Dear Burton Emmett . . .

I have been intending to write you for a long time but haven't. First because you have been away. I did not know that my letter would reach you.

I haven't been to New York but have stayed on here. I have done quite a lot on my machinery book. It wants something yet and I am merely waiting for it to come.

As you may suppose the tight times have hit us here, on the papers, but we did pay off the last of the notes, given the former owner, Nov. 1st, so that besides what little we owe in the bank here, that should be paid off in another year, and what I owe you, I am about clear on that.

Bob my son has worked hard to get me clear. I want to make over the papers to him as soon as they are clear. He will buy them, of course, at a reduced price and what he pays will not come to me but to the other two children.

There is a daughter in the University of Chicago and a son who is a young painter. The boy can hardly be expected to make a cent for several years and I want the money that he gets from the papers to bridge him over. He is the kind that can live on almost nothing, thank God.

I haven't earned much myself. Perhaps I am becoming too radical although, God knows, I am not a communist. Several magazines have asked me to do articles, in fact hardly a week passes that some one of them doesn't ask but what articles I write nearly all seem to say something too strong for them. Perhaps my weeks in the factories last winter awoke in me anew a sympathy for the under-dog that now begins to show.

I think too, dear friend, that I have suffered constantly, these last two years, from a sense of defeat, because of the failure of my marriage. I have spent so much time blaming myself. . . If I had done so and so etc.

I seem to need to love and be loved by a woman but I do badly at the job, or have in the past at least.

Why I seem to be giving you a sort of analysis of my state of mind. Well, I feel you my friend. I feel a sort of responsibility to you to work, to do good work.

It has been a time of general depression in ways not financial. I get the note of it from all sides. I think all artists feel it now. I get the note from all. There is, I think, a kind of general feeling that in some sense our modern industrial civilization has failed to feed men spiritually. Everyone wants something back that seems lost.

"I can't feel the earth. I can't feel the sun," one painter wrote me last week.

My plans for the winter are vague. Bob my son and I live here together in a little apartment above the print shop. I should get some books ready. I want, if possible, to say my say about the machinery thing in a book, do a new book of notes on life and perhaps get ready a new book of short stories. These things will bring me in no money for a long time but I have a few hundred dollars so I think I had better stay put here. For that matter, except for loneliness for a somewhat more intense intellectual life, I am happy enough here.

I keep trying to sell my farm and have offered it for as low as five thousand. It is a beautiful place. You don't happen to know a rich man who wants a hunting lodge do you . . . or a group of them. It is a beautiful place and I spent on it all of the money I made, in the one year of money making I ever had, the year of *Dark Laughter*, and there is fine quail and pheasant hunting.

The Lewis thing[1] was very depressing to me as it must be to all thoughtful men. The man has never touched American life, except to make it uglier by his touch, and now he is given this honor that should, if it were to go to an American, have gone to Dreiser. Dreiser has had real tenderness in him, Lewis never. It seems to me that Lewis must have got it rather out of European dislike of America rather than liking.

I hope you are both well. I know you must have had a happy time. Bless you both for being the nice people you are.

Sherwood

TS. NL

1. Sinclair Lewis became in 1930 the first American to receive the Nobel Prize in Literature.

TO Karl Anderson

[late November 1930, Marion]

Dear Karl . . .

It is queer how these things work out . . . here I have been thinking of you pretty steadily for weeks, feeling that it is a shame we are so out of touch, something missing in both our lives that might better have been held onto, and then your letter comes.

I haven't been in New York I believe since I saw you. Like you I passed through a bad time. It may be an inevitable part of getting through a certain place in life. You hope for so much, dream such dreams and then, suddenly, you realize that your dreams are not going to materialize. What you will do is so little. You have to face life in a new way, as a beaten man but determined not to bellyache. It takes time to adjust. Youth goes on so long in America. Very few men ever get grown in the European sense.

You know I made some money out of *Dark Laughter* and it near ruined me. It spoiled my relations with Elizabeth. She got it into her head, I'm afraid, that we were going to settle down, that I was to be a country gentleman. In one year I made almost thirty thousand which all went into Ripshin, furniture etc.

Then I quit producing. Fortunately I bought the newspapers here, the most sensible thing I ever did. I have got no money out of them but they have made a place for my son Bob and I am about to sell them to him. They have already about paid for themselves out of earnings. I'll sell them to Bob at two-thirds of what I paid and let him pay not me but John and Mimi. John is going to be a slow comer. He will make a painter though, Karl, and I'd like him not to have to go through what you did to get a start. It is lucky that he is a frugal kid. I paid 15000 for the papers and will sell them to Bob at 10000 so that he can gradually pay off the other two giving them 5000 each to go on. Bob can make a living as he does it.

Now I shall sell Ripshin as I do not want to be a country gentleman. I am offering it as low as 5000 so if you know of anyone who wants a country place for the summer at almost nothing tell them of it.

I'm broke but that doesn't seem to make any difference.

As for my personal life I had an affair with that woman you met, sister-in-law of the young painter, but broke it off. I retained him. He is a real painter I'm sure but has had a bad time making a living. However his father-in-law gave him a house to live in this year and I got him together enough money to live and work another year.

It is rather strange how much I am influenced by women. They are such an important and necessary part of my life. Another woman[1] came along and got at me in a new way. This wasn't an amorous matter. She felt, I think, that I was wasting myself so she got ahold of me rather for a purpose of her own. She felt, being a woman of brains and purpose, that the writers here in America were overlooking one of the biggest phases of American life, the factories. No one was going into the factories, seeing the life inside factories, seeing modern machinery at first hand, noting its effect on men etc. and she got me interested.

I turned the papers here over to Bob and went South, to the cotton mills. I had rather a bad time, that is to say getting into the factories, the owners being suspicious, but by persuasion and some bluffing I did get in. I also spent a good deal of time with workers in their homes etc. It gave me a new grip on life and out of it all I got new loves, not primarily amorous, as so many of my loves have been, but all involved with things I'd like yet to do. The woman is a part of it, a tremendously important part, but not quite in the way other women have got at me. I see little enough of her as she works terribly and constantly but I feel her as essential in what I am doing and hope yet to do.

Tell Helen about the place. She might sell it. Anything she could get over 5000 she should keep as a commission. With 5000 I could go on for two years yet with this factory thing.

You see, Karl, I do think there is something wrong here. I have felt it in you too. The depression here is not all financial. It is spiritual. The whole atmosphere of an industrial age is bad for artists. You know how I have always felt about money and success. I was at Danville at a strike there last week and incidentally went out to Laurence Stallings.[2] He has made a half million I suppose and it has raised hell with him. He started to be nice, I'm sure, but the simple fact is that he isn't nice now. He's just one. What I want to do is not propaganda, against industrialism and the things it throws up in men, but I do want to do my share toward starting a back fire. I'd like to devote the rest of my life to it. I guess, Karl, that in an age like this you have to help build the nest for the younger men, like Charles Bockler, John and a thousand others, before many eggs can be laid.

There is a way, Karl, in which I think I can have a certain influence. I have muddled personal life pretty successfully, have been arrogant and terrible in many ways, rather I am afraid as you painted me in that portrait of the three brothers (I felt the reproach in that and it was earned) but I have kept a kind of faith. In a queer way there is power in my position, the more power perhaps because, after all the publicity I have had, after occupying the position I have for so long I haven't a cent. Young men do feel that and I think I should use what power I have got in that way to try to press home the lesson. If for example you and I could have simply been artists, with no success bug at all, how much more pure and real we might have been. I hardly know what I can teach except anti-success. I suppose that is what I mean by a cultural back fire to the America thing.

I do get some opportunities. Last week for example I went to Richmond and delivered a speech before 3500 people from all over the state, the governor on the platform and a lot of big bankers, chamber of commerce men, college professors etc. on the platform. I'll just send you the manuscript of what I said. I was simply introducing two college men who afterwards conducted a debate.[3]

Out of the whole ruck of these two years of readjustment and depression and poverty really there have been a few good things. I did a thing for *Scribner's* called "Cotton Mills," some good things in *New Republic* . . . one on Lawrence when he died (really fine I think) and some things in *Nation*.

Best of all I feel that I am rather changed, much more humble really. I'm really all right. The whole background of what I want to do now, at any rate, has less of me in it and has in it some real feeling of a kind of bed I'd like to help lay down for young writers and painters who may come on here. I'd like to devote the rest of my days to that.

Sherwood

I fancy you would be interested in reading the book of the young Southern group *I'll Take My Stand*.[4]

Painting by Karl Anderson of Three Anderson Brothers:
(left to right) Earl, Sherwood, and Irwin
COURTESY OF YALE UNIVERSITY ART GALLERY

Have you read the letters of Vincent Van Gogh—published by Houghton Mifflin Co.[5] I only got ahold of one volume. I fancy they cost too much to buy and we have no library here.

TS. NL

1. Eleanor Copenhaver, who in 1933 became Anderson's fourth wife.
2. Playwright and journalist, then living in North Carolina.
3. On 14 Nov. Anderson introduced Stringfellow Barr, editor of *Virginia Quarterly Review*, and John Crowe Ransom, poet and English professor at Vanderbilt University, who debated the issue of southern industrialism.
4. A collection of essays published in 1930 by the Fugitive group at Vanderbilt University, including Ransom.
5. *Further Letters of Vincent Van Gogh to His Brother, 1886–1889* (1930), published in two volumes.

TO Burton Emmett

[21 January 1931], Marion

Dear Burton Emmett . . .

I have been intending to write to you for days but things have been rather in a jam here. Bob has been sick and I have had to help a lot on the papers. I have done recently quite a lot of running about. I have been in a writing mood. There are two things you will be interested in. *Forum* has taken an article on country newspapers I want you to see when it comes out.[1] This week there was an article on Danville, Virginia in *New Republic*.[2]

I feel as I believe a good many other men of the artist class do now. In some moods, Burton, I feel that our whole American Civilization is on test. The next twenty-five years may be the most critical years we will ever have to live through. It may be that capitalism is having its real test now.

Last week[3] I went down to Danville and spoke for an hour and a half to two or three thousand striking cotton mill workers there. I did not think they had a chance to win. I don't believe they can win. I went there because I felt that perhaps I could say something that these poor people can a little hang onto when they realize they are whipped.

So I went and tried to give their particular struggle something of its historic setting. I spent a good deal of time on the speech and before preparing it studied the speeches of Lincoln. I tried to get it all into simple words. The thought back of it was that the struggle in England, a long time ago, for Magna Carta, the French Revolution and the American Revolution were all nothing but strikes, the strike that we call the American Revolution being nothing but a strike, as is the one at Danville, for recognition of the Union. Really, dear friend, there is something very pathetic and touching in the attitude of workers toward any man who is willing to give to them a little of himself. I don't know how you feel on such matters but I was a factory man myself once. The system had me once and I have always thought my escape was just a kind of accident. I remember a year in Chicago when I was a laborer there. I had no education. I tried to go to night school. Each night, when I arrived at the school, I fell over on the desk dead with weariness and slept. It seemed pretty hopeless.

I have a kind of fear that, if we do not have a bit more intelligence in handling things and if we do not do something in government to take up the slack in employment . . . the machine continuing to replace men . . . we will soon have one grand mess on our hands.

Really I have four books that should be coming along in the next year. There is a crazy kind of novel, perhaps half done.[4] Then there is a book on women in factories,[5] a book of essays and a new book of short stories. I am trying to gather the threads of all these together.

We get along pretty well here. I think I told you that we succeeded in paying off the last of the seventy-five hundred we owed the former owner of the paper. We owe yet about three thousand at the bank here. Until the last two months advertising has held up pretty well but now it has dropped pretty low. There is practically no general advertising. If we hold even and pay our pay roll the rest of the winter I think we will do well enough, don't you?

There is another thing I am interested in. It is the country weekly as an institution. I believe now, after three years of this experiment, that the country weeklies could be made into a real cultural force in the country. I rather had this in mind in writing the article for *Forum*. I have arranged to go out to Chicago, to Northwestern University, to the Journalistic Dept. of the University, to deliver a series of three lectures on the subject.

My thought is that perhaps I can have some influence in directing some of the brighter young men and women into country weekly work. The weeklies need better people. So often now they are merely little commercial institutions with no courage and no force to them. I think later a real effort should perhaps be made to organize the best of the weekly editors along cultural lines but that is no doubt a job for some other man. I think I will be doing my share if I stir the matter up.

At any rate I have arranged with a lecture man to book me up on this subject with a lot of the schools and universities for next winter. I will also lecture on the machine and on women in industry.

I have a kind of notion, have you, that we are about to come into a time of pretty wide discussion. There has been a kind of mental deadness to life, an acceptance, that I think will pass. There will be an effort to find new leadership.

I can't well resist the temptation to give myself partly at least to this effort. I think all I can do is to help stir things up a bit.

The other day in going through my stuff I sorted out a great pile of mss. It is a bit of everything, beginnings of novels, short stories, articles etc. that did not come off. Such a lot of waste there is, man. I have made a bundle of all this. I don't know whether you want it or not. It seems foolish for you to clutter yourself up with it.

I would like to see you and Mrs. Emmett. I seem never to go to New York anymore. It has been a long time since I have been there but, as there is no business to call me now and as I want to make every cent of my own income count, I do not go.

Lots of love and good
health to you both.
Sherwood Anderson

TS. NL

1. "The Country Weekly," *Forum* 85 (Apr. 1931): 208–13.
2. "Danville, Virginia," *New Republic* 65 (21 Jan. 1931): 266–68.
3. On 13 Jan.
4. An experimental work called "Crazy Book," not completed.
5. *Perhaps Women*, the only book Anderson actually published in 1931.

TO Charles Bockler

[2 February 1931], Marion

Dear Charles.

I have been in a dead blank place again. They are like bad air pockets. Down and down you sink. I've never been able to figure them out. There is a kind of flight you try to maintain. How difficult it is.

I had a letter from my older brother Karl. He has written a book.[1] He may come to see me. It was warmer, more friendly than his letters usually are.

He spoke a good deal about women. He has a wife. I think he and she have hated each other a good deal. They have however stuck together. I can't make out whether he is glad or sad about that.

There have been grand days here, the sun shining every day, the air crisp and cool and the moon shining at night. There have been unusual and lovely cloud formations.

It has been lonely—I have no close friend here except Eleanor Copenhaver and she is rarely here. She has been working terribly hard at her job in New York this year and has, in addition, been working at Columbia for her Ph.D.[2] That is absurd but it is still true that a Ph.D. helps such a woman wonderfully in getting paid for her work. In a sense, perhaps a good deal, Eleanor has made me what I seem to be now, partly at least a man of action. She did make me feel working people a good deal more than I had for a long time. She is small and strong and dark with black hair and alive eyes. Well, I love her. It doesn't mean I do not love others too but I love her.

I seem always, Charles, to need these doorways out into life. Women are vital, necessary to me. Am I just an egotist, using them. I don't know.

It is hard for me to live with anyone. I came nearest it with Tennessee Mitchell. We almost did it.

There was a brooding silent quality in her. I worked around that, watched it, was fed by it. It constantly broke up. She said . . . "I could make it with you but to do so would have to make some kind of absolute inner surrender."

She couldn't.

I thought . . . "If she does that something will break in me too."

I don't know how it will come out with Eleanor. I think we both feel about the same. I think we are both in a mood to take what we can get. She works terribly hard and is quiet, doesn't talk much. Things are comprehended, in her brain, quickly and rather instinctively. I have your still life of the blue stone jars with apples in the living room of their house there.

Bob got into trouble—driving a car drunk. I shall, I think, get him off without a jail sentence but to do so will have to use my influence here. It puts me in a queer position. I hate driving people and would not do it for myself.

I need man's friendship too, of a kind I can't get here and that I imagine you can't get there. It leaves a deep hole, not having it. I keep planning not to spend so much time here but, to date, every time I've left Bob has got into some sort of mess out of which I have to help extricate him. I hardly know whether he will pull this off or not. He has plenty of talent and energy but wants balance.

I am going to send you later, when I have copies, copy of my long speech at Danville.[3] I tried to make it as simple as I could, to reach working men's minds. I think the labor people will make a little booklet of it.

I have decided I will speak, perhaps a good deal next year. It seems to me that, if I am not compelled to speak of art, or writing, but can speak of labor, machinery etc., I'll be all right. Speaking of writing publicly is too much like talking of a man or woman you love. You shy off.

There is a lawyer[4] here with whom I work some. I like him. He has read little nor has he thought much but he is beginning. I can see his mind rather unfolding. In his nature he is a generous man.

I must stop writing. I wish of course you were here so we could walk and talk. The workers at Danville have given up. It was wise. I can't help feeling however that they got a good deal.

MS. NL

1. Karl Anderson's novel, "One Was a Celibate," was never published.
2. She was actually working on her master's degree in economics, which she received in 1933.
3. The text of the speech was mimeographed.
4. Charles H. ("Andy") Funk.

TO J.J. Lankes[1]

[5 March 1931, Macon, Ga.]

Dear Lankes

I am thinking of publishing a book which I want to call *Perhaps Women*. It is [a] queer book. It describes, I must say in a rather broken way, a night visit of a man to a cotton mill in the South. The idea of the book is that modern man, because of his enforced relationship to the machine, is being made impotent. You will get the notion that man has accepted the vicarious power, got from the machine, as his own. Having accepted as his own a power outside himself he has lost the ability to develop his own power . . . or is losing it.

My theme also is that women are less affected by all this . . . that woman escapes man's danger in a machine age because her relationship with nature is more direct and personal.

I believe, as you must, that the artist is the ultimate male but that all men have something of the artist in them. They are therefore being destroyed by the machine by being made impotent. I want to put the book out largely as a statement to arouse discussion.

I wonder if I could interest you and Burchfield[2] in something. I'd like to have something from both of you in the book because I feel you both as such distinctive American artists. I have cut out a reproduction of a thing of Gauguin. It in an odd way suggests the impotence of so much of modern manhood compared with the potence of womanhood. Suppose you did a thing, in your own way, after this, giving it a Lankes touch, and letting me introduce it in one of the opening pages of the book.

In the pages of the book itself, in one place,[3] I have said . . .

> If I should ever finish my book, containing as I hope my statement of the inner meaning of life here now, and the book is ever published, I would like the publisher to put a picture upon the paper jacket it will bear.
>
> I would like a drawing by Charles Burchfield, of my native state Ohio, or a wood-cut by Julius Lankes of my adopted state Virginia.

The picture would show a cotton mill looming huge in the night before me (Sherwood Anderson). I would be half buried in shadows and in darkness. The building before me would be, as I say, dark and huge but lights would shine out from its thousand eyes.

It would be a fact, that building, as the machine is a fact in American life, as the factory is a fact, as the radio and the automobile are facts.

Do not make me, an American artist, striving to be of his day and time, a bold strong figure as has been done on the paper jackets of some of the books I have published. If my book is ever finished and one of you men consent to do this job, make me small and shrinking before the fact.

I beg of you to put in the heavy iron fence surrounding the mill yard and the equally heavy iron mill gate.

Let me stand there, small and shrinking, a kind of Chaplin striving to rub red South Carolina clay off his clothes. (I had just fallen in the mud.)

Do not hesitate to make me a rather impotent figure. Modern male impotence in the face of the machine is that statement I am trying to make in this book.

Why, Lankes, I do not know that I have right to ask Burchfield or you to be interested in this statement I am trying to make. I am trying to arouse real fear of the machine in both men and women. Suppose you send this letter on to Burchfield and ask him to write me. I do think the statement, put into dramatic form, is worth making.

Sincerely
Sherwood Anderson

Write me at Marion.

TS. NL

1. Virginia woodcut artist.

2. Charles Burchfield, painter of rural and small-town scenes. He declined Anderson's proposal.

3. The section of *Perhaps Women* to which Anderson refers is "Ghosts" (89–97). Most of the passage he quotes, however, was cut out prior to publication.

TO Charles Bockler

[30 March 1931, Marion]

Dear Charles

It is a day when I feel very small. There are days when I am afraid of people. This is one of them. It is cold and bleak outside. I went to the

P.O. hoping no one would speak to me. The sky seemed big and the buildings and all the people.

I suppose that is why we want women, days like this. We become frightened children again. Women should learn more from their lovers than they do. They should learn from their lovers what children are like.

Yesterday was cold and bleak. I went walking with a man here. It was bitter cold. We came to an old brick yard. They had taken the fire from a kiln the day before but it was still hot. We huddled against it out of the cold.

A man came along the road, chewing tobacco and spitting. The man told me about him. He is a white man and some years ago married a young white girl of sixteen. Then he went about selling her to Negroes and whites. He lived by selling her. They were both arrested.

In court she began pointing out this man and that man. "He sold me to that one, and that one, and that one."

All the men in the court room got scared. "She might point at me," they thought, even though they had not been with her. They remembered things they had done.

I am going to speak on April 21, 22 and 24th at Northwestern University, and then, during the following week, at Chicago University. I am not sure about the lecture at Chicago University being open to the public but at least some of them at Northwestern will be. I do not know the exact dates at Chicago University but as soon as I know will tell you. If your sister comes to any of the lectures ask her to come and speak to me.

I wish I could be at the show. Try not to expect anything.

I have worked and worked at the lectures. The only way I can justify doing it to myself is to put into them the best I have.

I hope you do not have queer lost days like this but I guess you do have. It is a good thing I guess that women do not get onto us. We are not brave. We are only sometimes bold.

I am sure you are like me in that you have such times when you feel yourself just a lost thing floating in some queer kind of emptiness.

S.A.

TS. NL

TO Laura Copenhaver[1]

[July? 1931, Marion?]

Dear Woman . . .

I have been hurt and frightened thinking of what I wrote you the other day about the Daughters of the Revolution.[2] What happened was what is always happening. I took one thing and struck at it. It obviously is a comparatively innocent thing when put against the evils everywhere.

I am trying for example to keep my love for Eleanor a mature love. I am trying not to be just a boy, like Bob for example, seeking just a woman to love because I need love in my own life. It is all right for Bob to be so because he is a boy in years. I myself have perhaps but a few years to be a mature man if I am to be one before I die. It is the challenge for me.

There is a challenge in the fact that Eleanor is a woman and has other people who love her. If, because of my life, the history of my life, it hurts the others too much, then I am not to ask for her personally. I mean there is a life there, within your family. My bringing myself in brings in an extraneous thing. Does it help or hurt. It has to be balanced. I can't love Eleanor as a boy would love. I have to take the responsibility of it and all the things affected by it.

I write these things to you and Mr. Copenhaver because I say things more clearly in words written than in words spoken. It is because I am a writer, have been one for years.

I have been thinking of something you said to me when I spoke to you of the book on which I am at work. You said, "The idea is too subtile. Can you get it across."

I wanted to explain my attitude toward that. I think everything at all worthwhile is subtile. Nothing not subtile and very difficult is at all worthwhile. It was, I think, in trying to simplify the ideas of Christ that the world lost Christ. We say to ourselves . . . "But if we do not make it all plain and simple it will not be understood," and then in making it plain and simple we lose what we were trying to say.

I have been writing to Eleanor about all this in connection with the thing in which we are both interested. I tried to say to her how that a man like Rockefeller or Ford might be no more harmful than say a Tom Tippett.[3] A Ford thinking that if he gives people automobiles to ride in at a low price he has served the idea of progress, a Tom thinking that if he can start a revolution, start men shouting and screaming through streets and tearing down buildings, he also will be serving progress.

The danger lying always in thinking that anything worth anything is simple.

Everything is subtile and difficult.

Of course I am unconsciously pleading with you in all this. I want you to realize, as Eleanor does, how subtile and difficult my own road as an artist is. I wasn't frank with you. I said that I did not know whether or not Eleanor loved me. Of course she does. That is to say she loves what is fine in me. No one can love the rest, least of all myself. Whether she wants to marry me, or should marry me, is of course another matter.

With love
Sherwood

TS. NL

1. Prominent Marion resident and Lutheran churchwoman, later Anderson's mother-in-law.

2. In discussions with Mrs. Copenhaver, Anderson often criticized the Daughters of the American Revolution, to which she belonged, for its hereditary requirements for membership.

3. Author of *When Southern Labor Stirs* (1931), a report on his investigations of strikes in southern textile mills.

TO John Anderson

[July 1931, Marion]

Dear John.

I guess those apparently loose unorganized thoughts and even visions that come have some purpose after all. It takes time, I guess, to find out. I get a long story started and sometimes it breaks in two. Some minor character comes in, as though a stranger had suddenly walked into a house. That changes everything. The new person may be absorbingly interesting.

You try to bend the new one into what ever you are doing and pretty often it spoils all.

Just the same it is something. There is the new one also wanting his, or her, story really told.

Life is like that too. You love someone, a woman say. So you think you are all fixed. Then suddenly you see a new woman you love more.

I imagine that in painting also one impression often overlaps another that way. You are lucky when you get an impression so strong that, in spite of everything, it comes back and back, so you can work steadily a long time.

I guess it's better to keep on working loosely. I know with me, for two or three years now, all has been too loose. I have written most of several novels that have to be thrown aside. There was a reaching after something I wasn't getting. I begin to get it now a little I think so I work more steadily.

I sent off *Perhaps Women*, to be printed, and Lankes made a wood block for it.[1] The clay hasn't come yet. I don't know that it matters as I write every day until I am exhausted. Next month Eleanor will be here for the whole month. Pretty often I go out along the river now in the late afternoon, taking a fly rod. I wade in the river and cast for bass. I don't get many but it is nice to be out like that. Bob is still too restless for steady company. I want to be alone and think out my own problem.

It's a bit different than painting and must tremendously take people in. That's why it must have something that is NOW in people's feelings . . . maybe they haven't found out about themselves. You have to feel for that.

I become perhaps revolutionary. It is partly because I am trying to find out what happened to a young revolutionist who got killed, about whom I am writing, how he got that way, what it meant to him, etc.[2]

You give yourself more and more to that mood.

Often it happens that these side visions, of which you speak, are something. It may be with painting as with writing. There is something you thought you have got hold of but hadn't. The sub-conscious or, anyway, something in you, is trying in this way to tell you. It is often that way with me.

I had to have two teeth out and have few enough as it is. I'm well and so is Bob. He is working like a nailer. Love to Charles[3] and all the house there.

S.A.

TS. NL (ph)

1. Lankes's woodcut of a man and woman on horseback appears on the frontispiece and dust jacket of *Perhaps Women*.
2. Red Oliver, protagonist in Anderson's novel *Beyond Desire*.
3. Charles Bockler, with whom John Anderson was spending the summer.

TO Charles Bockler

[July 1931, Marion?]

Dear Charles . . .

I am delighted to have the word about John and also about your own work. Evidently you are both having a good summer. I have been going pretty steadily, with lapses as usual.

Here it has been a summer of constant heavy rains, much different from the last one. For the last two or three weeks there have been heavy thunder showers every day and the farmers cannot get into the fields to harvest the ripe grain. The binding machines sink too deeply into the ground, even when for a few hours the sun shines.

Mrs. Copenhaver has been very ill, at the point of death. She is sixty-three. There are some of your things up there and also a thing of John's, a very delicate little flower thing. When the woman got a bit better, at the end of last week, she asked to have three or four of these things brought into her sick room.

I did not know what to do about the young painter so I sent him to you and John. I liked him particularly perhaps because he was a painter. I have a soft spot for all young painters. Perhaps I have seen too many young writers.

The woman you saw in the woods in her bare feet sounds nice.

The country here is very rich this year. It has been such a year of growth. Last year everything went dead in the heat and drought. The vines growing by my window here that were last year dead looking things with shrivelled leaves are this year broad of leaf and rich with juices.

It would be I fancy, in France, a good wine year. What a crime that Americans have so lost sense of earth. I tried to talk to that young man about something of the kind. There was a man I saw yesterday in a field. He was picking up bundles of wheat and making shocks. How nice he was against the hills. If every community could have a few painters, making people feel the niceness of the fields and hills . . . themselves a part of the niceness of everything . . . like trees for example . . . then perhaps they wouldn't go away to cities because farms no longer pay. They would stay because they loved the ground.

I went out yesterday and waded in the river. I had my bass fly rod. It was great fun although I didn't catch anything.

Bob said, rather wistfully, "I hope someday John will want to paint down here."

I am wondering about you & Kack. I pay a man $25 a month to live in my place. There is a cow there. I wish things could get cleared up so you and Kack could come & live there. Perhaps by next spring they will.

Love to all.

TS. NL

TO John Lineaweaver [1]

[28 December 1931, Marion]

Dear John

How lovely & decent of you to write—about "Mill Girls."[2] I had thought it did something I wanted it to do.

A low tone—music buried in the prose—like a slow dance—

I am trying to make a long novel[3] that way—in different keys—things beating on the consciousness of a young man—

Sharp—slow—fast. To make the prose express the whole movement. It's a nice challenge.

I think Faulkner's difficulty is ahead. I saw him at Charlottesville[4] &

told him that. They'll make an ass of him if they can, prying into him, boosting him—

Then dropping him for another new man.

There's the difficulty—to ride through that & forget it.

Bob has taken over the apt. with his new wife.[5] John has a room in Iron Alley and I have a nice room that looks out on our lovely hills. I'll not be here much. I plan to go to Europe this summer.

As always
Sherwood Anderson

MS. NL

1. A Lebanon, Pa., businessman and former college classmate of Robert Anderson.

2. Published in *Scribner's Magazine* 91 (Jan. 1932): 8–12; incorporated into *Beyond Desire*, 69–102.

3. *Beyond Desire*.

4. Anderson and Faulkner had attended the Southern Writers' Meeting at the University of Virginia, 23–24 Oct.

5. Mary Chryst Anderson, an English professor at Marion College.

TO Charles Bockler

Sunday [c. Feb. 1932, Marion]

Dear Charles . . .

I am writing you, as you see, on stolen stationery. For a long time I have been thinking—of the shame in it that our communications have grown so thin—

Knowing well enough, Charles, that it is my own fault.

My own crowded life—my effort to get work done—doing so little.

There have been times when I might have come to see you. I did not like to ask you to come to Baltimore, perhaps just for a brief hour of talk.

Your presence is felt of course constantly in your work I have. There was the painting over the mantle in the living room—at Maurice's house before he died.[1] His son has it now.

Perhaps you never heard the story of that house—after he died—of the mysterious murder done in the house. The story is too long and strange to tell here. I'll tell you sometime.

There was a room in the Copenhaver house here. For some reason no one could go and sit in it. There it was a room on the ground floor—the walls covered with old family photographs. There was an old unused piano in there.

I got them to do it all in light yellow. Eleanor had one of your paintings and I loaned another—for a time. You should have seen the difference—how the room began to call to you—invite you.

I'm becoming more and more a communist. I think it must be coming nearer—an inevitable thing. I guess this time is good for all of us. If you can, eventually, get that mail carrier's job. It seems to me the right thing—taking letters and packages to people.

There should be hours every day out on roads—an inevitable contact with people. It should give you a kind of hold on something—on people—a countryside perhaps in the organization of which you have a part. After all we are pretty lucky—those of us who paint and write and make songs.

I'm pretty sure money is the great evil. You get it and it separates you—at once—from life.

We are all cramped, hurt, all the time, by what goes on.

How can art flourish. I'll tell you, Charles, if the Russians pull it off—you'll see—someday—a flowering there.

Think of a whole nation of people who can be sure of work—the old and the sick and the weary decently taken care of—

The land belonging to the state—the factories belonging to the state.

Here you are—you and John and a thousand others. How terribly houses, in which people live, need living pictures. The work you would all have to do would be inexhaustible.

It's worth fighting for—the beginning of it. It's worth any price. I guess all of us, in every part of the world, ought to pray, every day and every night, for the success of Russia . . . for their keeping clean . . . making perhaps an example for the rest of us, someday.

John seems pretty healthy. He has made some friends of his own. He's painting people more and more. He has one now—a little tough looking girl—in red—terrifically alive. It's gorgeous I think.

I'm going on my long journey soon—first to California—to lecture—to get money for the trip to Russia. "Seeing," as J.J. Lankes said—first the tin can civilization of the American west coast, a flapper necking in a car, and then Russia—a strong woman in the throes of giving birth.

Love,
S.A.

MS. NL

1. Maurice Long died on 18 Oct. 1931. Anderson eulogizes him in "Two Irishmen," a chapter of *No Swank*, 31–34.

TO Edmund Wilson[1]

[22 April 1932], San Francisco

Dear Wilson.

I wired you yesterday from here. The manifesto sounds grand to me. I do not see what else we can do.

I think one of the signs that it is time for the writers etc. to line up definitely is the general attention your own recent work has got.

Everywhere I hear of it. Although apparently, Wilson, there are few enough intellectuals who are ready yet to take a bold stand, they all want someone to do it.

The lecturing hasn't bothered me very much. I haven't been talking about writing but about machinery and newspapers. I guess I have something of the ham in me. I don't seem to mind strutting before an audience.

I am staying here for a week or ten days longer because I have got to work again on the finish of my novel[2]—the last section of it. Will perhaps not get off to Russia before July.[3] Are you going.

I wouldn't mind saying, Wilson, to you that if at any time anything comes up like this manifesto and my name added has any value you are at liberty to use it. Where you are willing to go I'll go.

Sincerely
Sherwood A.

MS. NL (ph)

1. Wilson had recently published *The American Jitters* and had asked Anderson for his endorsement of a statement of support for the communist movement in America. This "manifesto" later evolved into a pamphlet, *Culture and Crisis* (1932), signed by fifty-three writers and artists, including Anderson.

2. *Beyond Desire*.

3. Anderson did not make this trip.

TO Van Wyck Brooks

[c. 26 May 1932], Marion

Dear Van Wyck

I can't think of any other life that could have been written as you have written the Emerson[1]—in some queer way always consciousness of earth, trees, grass, water, etc. but it, just the same, never getting into the man.

No soiling, lust, sin—

I always felt that about him.

It comes out of this book too. You feel you have been in the presence of the man, walking with him, dining with him, thinking with him.

I just got home from California with a queer new novel almost written but was struck down by a rotten cold, so at once I went to bed and have been lying there, not minding the tight head and throat as I read.

It's a simply charming book I think and I am very happy about it.

Affectionately
Sherwood

MS. Penn.

1. *The Life of Emerson* (1932).

TO Roger Sergel

11 June 1932, Marion

Dear Roger:

Viking Press wrote me that they were going to accept your proposition about the play[1] which they will do, I suppose, shortly, and incidentally, of course, steal from me half the money you pay them, but so the world wags.

Gin or more gin I was tremendously interested in your letter to me and understood just your state of feeling when you wrote it. The same thing happened to me a couple years ago. We are getting religion, like Holy Rollers. Personally, I can't go the socialists because in the end and when the rub comes they always cave in. There is too much sweetness in that crowd.

Of course, the Russian crowd here are pretty wrapped up in the Russian technique. They are pretty narrow and technical, but after all they seem to be about the only crowd in America just now who have any guts. They do seem to have stomachs.

I think you must feel as I do that some of these days the smash has got to come. Men and the individuality, so much talked about, and expressed largely in the possession of money, is, I am sure, at the bottom of our present mess. It makes half at least of the brutality and ugliness of life.

Have you read Darrow's book?[2] If not, you and Ruth should read it. The man expresses, it seems to me, all the best of the passing generation. You have a feeling of a fine gentle straightforward man, but something always seems to stop him dead. After all he is a man without faith and we have got to have faith and a religion. It seems to me that not having it is what is the matter with us and so we will have to fight to get it. The old protestant idea that "God is in his heaven and that all is right with the world" won't do. We can't go on the promise of some future heaven at all. It's too much of a bargain and we don't want a bargain. We want to serve without a bargain.

I think it is rather silly for you and Ruth not to come on down here for a week with me in these hills. To the devil with the Republican Convention. We should have a talk. It would do us all good. I won't go to Russia, at least, before fall now. I must finish this novel I am on[3] and besides while I was out in San Francisco I wrote most of another book,[4] addressed to writers and artists—young ones in America especially—saying something to them of what you have just said to me in your letter. I think we all want and need now a life of activity—a going toward something. It just happened that when your note came to me—and it stirred me—I was working on a chapter of my novel called "In a Cotton Mill at Night."[5] What I'd like is this—why don't we go on a pilgrimage to American industry. Let's float from town to town and from factory to factory—go to the mines—go where the workers are—go to their houses—try to connect ourselves again with the reality of life. It's the road I'm sure. I would like a chance to talk it over with you and Ruth. I hate to think of you going on there too long, wearing yourselves out at that game. You are too valuable.

Why don't you both come on down here and let's have a talk about it. Remember I have got an empty house here in the hills all furnished ready for you to move into. If you want to bring the boys down and leave them here for a month or two, you can. They could have horseback riding and fishing and mountain climbing to their hearts' content.

With love,
Sherwood

TS. NL

1. *The Triumph of the Egg*, Raymond O'Neil's dramatization of "The Egg," was published by Sergel's Dramatic Publishing Company in 1932.
2. *The Story of My Life.*
3. *Beyond Desire.*
4. "J'Accuse," never completed.
5. *Beyond Desire*, 382–89.

TO Burton and Mary Emmett
[18 August 1932], on board ship

Dear Burt & Mary.

I am writing this note on Tuesday—2nd day at sea.[1] The last few days ashore were terribly strenuous. There was the excitement of the trip to Washington.[2] Then I drove alone 425 miles in 10 hours to get home. Then at home—everything to do in 2 days—a hot night trip on the train. All day in N.Y. I saw reporters—was broadcasting etc. I had kept going on whiskey. I'm glad it's over and I can relax.

Burt—I was terribly ashamed not having the change to pay that big taxi bill.

Mary—the flowers are lovely. I've put them on the dining room table so the others can share them. I also shared the whiskey.

I am 3rd class—and very comfortable. They had provided a first class room for me but I didn't want it. The delegation is largely working class and students. I often wish it were possible to take you two with me on some such jaunt as this. There is one man out of the old Dana family of Boston[3] but the rest represent protesting groups of students, mill girls, ex soldiers, factory workers, etc. protesting against war. They are nearly all young—the young dreamers. There is a gentleness and sweetness in them that is amazing—a kind of inner decency and goodness that is charming.

That these people should be counted the dangerous ones—it is such an upside-down affair. I am so sorry I was so tired and I'm afraid 1/2 drunk the last night when you were both so nice to me.

Sherwood

MS. NL

1. Anderson apparently should have written "Thursday," having boarded ship on Wednesday, 17 Aug. He was en route to Amsterdam to attend the World's Congress Against War on 27–29 Aug.

2. The trip to Washington was an unsuccessful effort to meet with President Hoover in support of the Bonus Army.

3. Henry Wadsworth Longfellow Dana, educator and active pacifist.

TO Karl Anderson

21 September 1932, Marion

Dear Karl:

I am ashamed that I have not either come to see you or written you. Life has been rather a whirl-wind for me for the last two or three months. After I saw you the novel[1] about which I had been thinking for the last two or three years, and on which I had done a lot of work that had to be destroyed, suddenly came alive in me. I finished it and it is being published this week.

I think it is a disturbing book and I have no idea what kind of a reception it will get, but on the other hand I feel it a very solid piece of work and I am satisfied to stand on it.

There are so many things about which I would like to talk to you that it is almost impossible to get them into a letter.

I came through Westport less than a week ago on a hurried trip from Boston, having got off a ship up there, and I was ashamed that I could not stop. I did call your house but got no response. This after I had got to New York. I only stayed in New York a few hours, seeing newspaper men, and then hurried on to Marion.

I had gone suddenly to Amsterdam to a World's Conference Against War, my expenses for the trip having been paid by a rich New York woman.[2] It was an attempt on the part of the intellectuals to get together with the workers of thirty-five nations for direct action against war and was very exciting. Now I am at home trying to gather together another book[3] for spring publication and will be here, I am sure, until the middle of October. Then I plan to go to Russia for the winter.

There are many things about which I would like to talk to you and I

Mary Emmett
COURTESY OF ELEANOR ANDERSON

wish you could run down here. You have never been here for a visit with me since I have lived in town. Now that Bob is married I do not live in the apartment over the print shop, having turned that over to him, but I have a room in a house nearby and there is a vacant room beside mine you could use.

The country is very beautiful now and I have a car so that we could get outdoors in the afternoons.

I do not think we ought to miss this opportunity. There are things in the wind that are bound to make a definite change in my life and I really need to have you come and see me and have a visit with me.

Please tell me you can do it.

With love to Helen and the children,
Sherwood

TS. NL

1. *Beyond Desire*.
2. Probably Mrs. Edith Cram, active in pacifist causes.
3. "Book of Days," an autobiographical work never completed.

TO Ruth Sergel

14 November 1932, Marion

Dear Ruth:

I had a letter from Adelaide Walker[1] in New York and they are organizing down there a workers' theatre.[2] I think Adelaide Walker has some money. Their plan is to scale admission prices down to 25, 50 and 75¢. The people who wrote *The Merry-Go-Round*[3] and made quite a success of it last year in New York are doing a play for them and Edmund Wilson is also doing one. I speak of this because it might just happen that these people might write you about using the little play *The Triumph of the Egg* and if they want to use it at any time I would be very glad to give up my share of the royalty. I expect it might help some if they did the play.

I came home part of the way through a snow storm and it has been cold and blustery here since I arrived but it is grand to get out of doors again and into the hills. Last night I was one of three men selected to be judges in a horn blowing contest. I'll bet you don't know what that is. This is quite a fox hunting country although they do not ride to hounds as they do in the fashionable part of Virginia. Here the hounds are likely to be owned by small farmers, country doctors, etc. and they all go out together afoot for a hunt, and the grand thing is to get on some hill and hear the hounds giving cry in the distance. The hounds are recalled when the fun is over by blowing a horn made of a cow's horn. It is quite a delicate and nice thing to do and do well and the other night there were nine men who stood in a little valley while three of us went off to a distant hill to listen. It was a clear cold moonlit night and the sounds of the horns were charming.

I am sending Roger a Currier and Ives—a print of Maude S. when she was the champion trotter of the world. This was when I was a boy. I have always loved this print and that is the reason I want Roger to have it.

As a matter of fact, Ruth, with a son and brother as a painter and with two or three young men friends who are painters, my room is always splashed with color anyway and I have paintings loaned out in a half dozen houses here in town.

I find that the mushroom book that I intended to send to you is packed away with some other books of mine but I will be going through these boxes some in the next week or two and will send it on to you immediately. I suggest also that you go into McClurg's some day and get a little book called *The Common Mushroom* which is one of the best. It costs about $3.00. Then I suggest that you write a note to the Hon. W.R. Motherwell, Minister of Agriculture, Ottawa, Canada, putting a dollar in the envelope and asking them to send you their book called *Mushrooms and Toadstools*. This ought to give you a good library.

I never did talk to you and Roger while I was there about a dream that has been in the back of my mind for a long time. I love this country down here so much that I have the idea that if you two ever came here and got the tone of it you would come back again and again.

Sometimes I wonder about the advisability of you staying on and on in that cramped city life. After all aren't you both losing more than you gain? Life gets so intensive. There you are both in that office all day every day, then home together on the train and together in the evening. Of course, I dare say there is a certain economic gain about keeping a business like yours in the city but after all couldn't it be run in a small town and even though it didn't make so much money it would be bound to give you a living and after a few years might grow on as fast as in the city.

On the very night when I came home I went out to Bob's little place here and there was Bob and one of the young boys from the shop riding half-wild colts up and down over the hills, and I began thinking of your boys and all this possible contact with animal life and growing things that we are all so much missing in America now. It may be at the bottom what is wrong with all of us.

I know this will sound to you and Roger very much like a real-estate man talking but I wish I could induce you when you go to Pittsburgh to come around this way and see what I mean.

Anyway why can't you plan to come here next summer? There's my house over there and there's no one living in it.

Please do think of this sincerely, dear Ruth. I don't see why you couldn't let the little favor you and Roger did for me[4] stand for the rent next summer. It would make me feel so grand.

With lots of love,
Sherwood

TS. NL

1. Labor activist and wife of Charles Rumford Walker, author and editor.
2. Later the Theatre Union.
3. Albert Maltz and George Sklar, who also wrote *Peace on Earth*, first produced on 29 Nov. 1933 and published in 1934 with a foreword by Anderson.
4. The Sergels had sent Anderson the money to visit them.

TO Arthur Barton[1]

26 November 1932, [Marion]

Dear Arthur Barton:

I got your letter and the first synopsis of the play *Winesburg* yesterday and have been excited about it ever since. I took a drive in the afternoon and at night went to bed, not to sleep, but to live through possible scenes in the play.

I might as well tell you frankly that I opened the synopsis to read it with fear. Before now attempts have been made to get at plays in some of my stories and novels but always I have found something in the attempts so utterly aside from the spirits of the stories that I felt they were hopeless. On the contrary, my dear Barton, I read your first synopsis, as I have suggested, with a good deal of inner excitement. "It can be done," I found myself saying to myself. Now do not be surprised if I write you two or three letters within the next few days giving you my ideas. I think what I will do is to take your synopsis up, scene by scene, and give you my suggestions and it will take a few days to do this, partly because I want them to develop in my own mind. I have to grow used to the idea of thinking of *Winesburg* as a play.

What I expect you want of me now is a general impression, got from what you have already put down and this is what I will try to give you today.

As to all such matters as the number of scenes in the play, etc., the practical matter of producing it in a theatre—all that I will leave to you.

Now as to the synopsis—pardon me for beginning at the end. You will realize that to make the end effective—the boy leaving the town where he has been raised to go out into the world—we will have to build up this feeling of George's departure to give it significance.

To do that we will have to build all through the play to that one end and this will naturally affect all the characters throughout the play. The feeling will have to be given that George's departure from the town is also a beginning—the beginning of manhood—a thing keenly felt in that way in him at least by the girl Helen.

To do that I believe it will be necessary for you and myself to go over the actual theme of the book which should be the theme of the play.

Now to me it seems that the theme of the *Winesburg* book, the thing that really makes it a book—curiously holding together from story to story as it does—is just that there is a central theme. The theme is the making of a man out of the actual stuff of life.

An American boy as you see growing up in an American village. It is an ordinary American town. There are all sorts of influences playing over him and around him. These influences are presented in the form of characters, playing on his own character, forming it, warning him, educating him. I do not know whether or not you, Barton, were raised in a small town but that does not matter. The same sort of influences would be at work on any boy in American life whether he were raised in a small town or a city. In the midst of the confusion of life the boy is always accepting or rejecting the suggestions thrown out to him by other people, directly and indirectly. In this play we will have to get from the beginning a feeling of growth in the boy.

To go back again for a moment let me tell you something that may amuse you. These stories of the *Winesburg* book were really written in a Chicago tenement, not in a village, and the truth is that I got the substance of every character in the book not from an Ohio village but from other people living around me in the Chicago tenement. I simply transferred them to a small town and gave them small town surroundings.

Now in all my suggestions you must remember, Barton, that I have no experience with the theatre. But this attempt to work with you to make a play and the reading of this synopsis has certainly given me, as I never had it before, a sharp sense of how much we will have to depend upon the players.

Now let me go back a moment to the theme of *Winesburg*. There are these queer, interesting, sometimes essentially fine, often essentially vulgar figures of a town. Think, Barton, what a great percentage of American men and women who come into the theatre were raised either in small towns or on farms. They got their early impressions of life there. Just as our boy George Willard did and then they went away to live in the city as he did. You have heard the saying attributed to the

Catholics—"Give me the child until he is ten and you may have him afterwards. I will not lose him." It seems to me that what is notable about *Winesburg* is that it does treat those American villagers, twisted as they may be—"queer hopping figures" a critic once called them—it does treat their lives with respect. That also we will want to do. What the book says to people is this—"Here it is. It is like this. This is what the life in America out of which men and women come is like."

"But out of this life does come real men and women."

That it seems to me is the essence of the theme of the book and the thing we have to put across.

What your first synopsis has suggested to me is the possibilities that lie in four characters of the book. They are

the boy, George Willard
his mother
his father
the girl, Helen White.

These should be the dominant characters in the play because they will all affect most deeply the development of the boy George.

But before discussing them let me discuss also for a minute the young man Seth Richmond. This is what I think about Seth. There is nothing especially evil in him. He is simply a boy who sees life absolutely in terms of himself. He wants the girl Helen White for two reasons. She belongs to a respectable and well-to-do family—is you remember the only daughter of the town banker—and is also to Seth's mind beautiful.

But he will not be thinking of Helen's beauty as a thing worthwhile in itself—aside from himself. He wants to succeed in life, make money, be a big man, and he would like to have Helen to decorate his own successful life.

GEORGE WILLARD

George Willard is not like this. In the first place he is capable of even more brutality than Seth because he is essentially a dreamer. He does not figure out his own acts with the general scheme of his own life in mind. He dreams of becoming a writer but that is only because almost everything in his own life goes wrong and he has a vague feeling that in some novel or story he may write he may be able to build up an ordered fine life. George should be of the rather poetic brooding dreaming type. Always saying things he does not mean and yet in some queer way holding on to some idea of decent manhood and respect for other people and their lives.

The father is a man who began life as a hotel clerk in a shabby hotel in a little village. There was quite a remarkable and spirited girl there, the daughter of the hotel keeper. This could be one of the grand characters of the play and could give some actress a gorgeous opportunity. She is of the kind of girl and woman not so beautiful on the outside but having in her a lot of inner fire. As a young girl living in her father's little shabby hotel she meets all kinds of rather second-rate men, travelling men and others, and goes about with them. Several of them make love to her and she lets them but all the time there is something in her that is seeking a finer type of man who may give her real womanhood. This she never finds and she takes as husband the hotel clerk who becomes ostensibly George Willard's father. As to whether or not he is really the boy's father might very well be false and I have imagined a scene in the play between the husband and wife when she, angered by his attitude toward the boy, tells him, to his teeth, that she doesn't know whether he is the boy's father or not.

Now, Barton, in the book I made this woman a rather drab figure but we will have to be a little careful about her in the play. How about having her a prematurely grey woman of about thirty-five or forty, tall and slight, with tired eyes—rather pale, but still with the same spirit in her that attracted men when she was a girl, when excited or angry her form straightens and she becomes again a living thing capable still of attracting men. And then when the excitement is past swings again into this rather tired defeated woman. I believe there are actresses who could put this across.

I said a moment ago that this woman, when she was a young girl, had a dream of a certain kind of man who might be her lover that she never got. The dream transfers itself to the boy George and she is determined that he shall hang on to some sort of fine manliness she never succeeded in finding in the men who have been her lovers.

THE FATHER

The father, or at least the man who thinks he is George Willard's father, is the typical minded, small town man of the rather mean spirited sort. When he was young he would have been rather good looking. His ambition in life was to be a rich man. He is the boy Seth Richmond beginning to grow old.

Now he is a defeated man and knows he never will be a rich or a big man and like the mother he has transferred his dream of what he would have liked to be to his son but the dream is essentially a cheap dream.

The mother knows this and is afraid of his influence on the boy, thinking that if the boy became what the father wanted, or thought he wanted, he would be a cheap tricky man at bottom only out after some kind of showy success.

HELEN WHITE

I think we should take the girl Helen White as a figure very much like George's mother when she was a young girl.

There is this difference. Helen White belongs to one of the most prosperous families in the town. She is the only daughter. She is not exactly a beauty but is full of fire and spirit. Unlike the mother of George Willard when she was a young girl, Helen White is protected by all the forces of conservative society but like George's mother she is ready to break through conventions whenever she thinks she has found what she wants in a man.

I think of her, Barton, as a pretty shrewd girl really onto Seth Richmond and is in love with George Willard from the beginning but just the same she is not going to take George unless he can make a man of himself.

I've gone into all these details regarding the characters and the theme of the play because I think we should first of all get the various forces around this boy George Willard pulling him this way and that way so that the audience may also have a notion of the forces at work on him and become absorbed in the real theme of the play which is as I see it the simple story of what happens to a boy with these ordinary forces of life playing around him, how he handles them, and what the audience feels he becomes.

I will write you again in a day or two taking up each scene of the play as you have outlined it, suggesting what changes come into my mind and how I think the various forces I have outlined here should find their expression.

In the meantime I will send this letter off to you so that you may be thinking of the play in these terms and also so you may write me and tell me whether or not this general outline will fall in with what you think the play should be. What I think we want to do is to get away from the idea of making the small town ridiculous or too dreary or sentimental—in other words to make people feel that a cross-section taken thus from a life in a small town would not differ from a cross-section of life taken from anywhere and that the forces over this boy George Willard are the same kind of forces that play over all American boys. If we can do that we will have a real play.

Sincerely,
Sherwood Anderson

TS. PC (cc)

1. A New York playwright who had approached Anderson about their collaboration on a dramatic adaptation of *Winesburg, Ohio*.

TO Arthur Barton

3 December 1932, Marion

Dear Arthur Barton:

I have sent you some more scenes of the play and am about finished with my layout of the last scene in Act I. As you suggested I will go right on with it and I hope that by the time you have got your new play[1] produced we may have this one in such working shape that you can come on down here and we can thresh it out, scene by scene. It does not seem to me that we need worry about following the exact details of the lives of Winesburg.

I do not believe it makes much difference what becomes of characters that do not carry through such as Dr. Parcival or whether Seth Richmond's father is dead or alive.[2]

As I conceive of the play, there is as the central theme the two boys, Seth and George, and the wholly different outlook on life—Seth the careful shrewd self-centered boy and George the imaginative lovable one.

Then there is the point of view of father and mother and the intense struggle going on between them for the boys' minds and affections. This I think of as the central theme of the play.

Then there is the struggle of the two boys for Helen White.

I believe you will agree with me that we cannot pack Winesburg into a neat hard package but will rather have to let it create its own form. For example the whole question of the introduction of characters like Dr. Parcival, Joe Welling and others is primarily a question as to whether they help develop the whole central feeling of the play.

We will not want a hard sharp smooth story and I believe we can get plenty of intensity and feeling without it. This will be a matter for us to thresh out when you come here.

For the present I will plough right on and hope to be ready for you when you are ready.

Sincerely,
Sherwood Anderson

P.S. It has occurred to me since writing the above that you may prefer that I do not send the scenes to you as I go through them—that you would prefer for your own mind to be clear for your own conception. I suggest that you write and advise me about this.

TS. PC (cc)

1. *Man Bites Dog*, co-authored by Barton and Don Lochbiler, opened in New York on 25 Apr. 1933.

2. Barton had inquired about the fates of these characters in the play.

TO Arthur Barton
7 December 1932, [Marion]

Dear Mr. Barton:

I have your nice letter of this morning and will be able to send you, today or tomorrow, the last scene of Act 1.

There is something in your letter of today that so pleases me that I am making bold to write you this morning, quite frankly, about some things I feel.

You see, Barton, these characters of *Winesburg* are so familiar to me—they have lived so long in my imagination—that they seem to me almost like people of my own family, or people with whom I have lived in a house. This, as you will be quick to understand, has had a certain effect on me. If I acted at first a bit skittish and queer about your proposal for the play it was because I never in my life attempted to work with another man and, to tell the truth, felt afraid of the attempt.

Then when I got to work on the play I had doubts again. I was afraid you might be one of the sort of men who would feel, when he saw me rushing ahead, inventing dialogue, recreating the scenes, etc., that you might be one of the sort who would feel resentful—saying to himself . . . "This man is trying to do everything. He is taking over, too much, my own part of the job, etc."

You see, Barton, it is a special situation. All of this material is so familiar to me. As you must realize, in running through the *Winesburg* stories, the stories themselves are tremendously condensed. My own imagination, playing over the material of the stories, both before writing the book and afterwards, my mind playing with these people has often cast them into situations not contained in the book . . . all sorts of situations, speeches from their lips, etc.

So there is in me this rather intense familiarity that makes me bold to ask of you what I do ask. It is that, in attempting to make this play, you be generous enough not to be offended if I sometimes take a somewhat dominant tone. It is enough, of tremendous importance for you to do in letting your mind play over the scenes as created as a sharp critic, getting the play accepted in the right quarters, if it is accepted, and seeing that it gets a decent stage presentation.

The whole situation as you know is peculiar and the reason that I write in this way is that I know a great many men might be offended, thinking it a reflection of their own craftsmanship seeing another apparently inclined to rush ahead independently, like some fool actor wanting to hog the spotlights on the stage.

What I am trying to say, Barton, is that this is not my impulse. I think I may say, without undue egotism, that, as you know, *Winesburg* is already an American classic. I happen to be the father of the child. I am an older man.

As I have already written you, your synopsis has jerked open a door for me. You did this for me quickly and sharply. It has been your idea, your quickly casting of the material into a workable story, that has already thrown this material for me into a new life. If there is any credit to be got from our efforts together it will be as much yours as it will be mine and I am only trying to say that, although I am not a colt in years, I am a good deal of an unbroken colt. Or better perhaps a lone wolf.

What I am getting at is that I am suggesting to you that you be generous enough to take the scenes as I send them to you and work on them, letting your own imagination play over them in relation to the stage. I believe we will work faster and better in this way.

With this thought in mind I believe I will attempt to give you this morning a sort of quick short outline of the entire play as I see it in my own mind. Scene 4 Act 1, that I will send you today or tomorrow, will give you an idea of how I have used Joe Welling in this scene.

As for Act 2 I have already made the draft for Scene 1 which takes place before Helen White's house. You have already made an outline for this scene and I believe that we must at the beginning of Act 2 introduce Helen White and her figure and character in the minds of the audience. As already suggested I have written this scene but want to hold it for a few days and go over it carefully before sending it to you.

I believe we can handle Act 2 with three scenes, one in front of Helen White's house, one before Louise Trunion's[1] house and finally a big scene between the father and mother in the hotel. This would eliminate the scene in the newspaper office and the pool room. The effect of which scenes I believe can be condensed into the three scenes suggested.

The big scene at the end of Act 2 would be an intensive struggle between the father and mother, the father having worked himself up to a final effort to become the dominant figure in the little family. He insults the mother through his talk of the son. I believe I will change this scene. In your quick synopsis you had the mother kill the father but I have changed this. As you will see from the scene in Act 1 in the doctor's office Elizabeth Willard is in no shape to stand a shock. As I have this scene in my mind the mother with the scissors rushes at the father intending to stab him and does wound him slightly in the shoulder but at the critical moment, when she raises the scissors to stab him, she herself falls dead at his feet. This would be the big scene at the end of Act 2.

In the final act, Act 3, there would also be three scenes. I am wondering if the scene where George Willard comes into the room and tries unsuccessfully to look at the body of his dead mother wouldn't be bad. I am afraid this would be pretty hard to put across and so instead I would open Act 3 with another scene between George and his father in which the father tries to get out of the responsibility for the mother's death and to do so tries to make her look cheap to the son.

This would give an opportunity for George Willard's final rejection of his father and his father's philosophy. It can be the scene that brings out the growing manhood in George.

Then the second scene of Act 3 would be the fairground scene with Helen White and George Willard together and their getting at an understanding of each other. And the play would close with the last scene at the railroad station.

For this last scene I've a good plan for reintroducing, after a passing moment, Joe Welling, Ray Pearson, Dr. Parcival, Dr. Reefy and the father. I've already made a good many notes on this final scene and believe that working together we can make it very effective. I believe the note we want to give at the end is that George's departure from Winesburg is also a beginning and the feeling in the audience that there is in him the making of a man.

With luck, Barton, I should be through these last two acts in two or three weeks and then, if you will come down here for a few days, we can go over it scene by scene and you can take it back to New York and begin what will be your struggle, to get it placed right and produced right.

With sincere regards,
Sherwood Anderson

TS. PC (cc)

1. The name was spelled "Trunnion" in the original *Winesburg* but changed to "Trunion" in the dramatic version.

TO Roger Sergel

[mid-December? 1932, Marion]

Dear Roger—

Truth—where are you?

Are you under the bed—on the roof—have you climbed a tree—

Have I not said that, time and again, with whatever trumpet blast I could get hold of? Ruth, I know, used to love a poem of mine called "Man with the Trumpet."[1]

I do not believe I ever wrote a book without saying it.

I joined with Dreiser, Elmer Rice[2] & Waldo Frank in giving out a statement for the Communist ticket in the last election.

Did you read my open letter to President Hoover.[3] I had about $2000 of lecture engagements for this winter and at the time less than $500 between myself & nothing and the Communist declaration, with the Hoover letter, cancelled them all.

I am at present living on advance royalties on books not yet published.

All very well to speak of trumpet blasts, Roger, but who owns and controls the radio, the newspaper—all the channels of public expression.

And there is something else. I admit I can't help letting it control me. Elizabeth Willard was a woman living in the day of Wm. McKinley. I have some difficulty seeing her as quite clear on what she wanted in her son. No matter what I feel or believe, I can't help letting the character control—rather than taking over control from the character.

Your criticism of me in this is one that has been thrown at me time and again—

Be clear. Be clear.

But I am also an American artist writing in a time and out of a civilization in which there is no clearness and trying—stupidly perhaps—also to reflect the terrible vagueness and uncertainty of my civilization.

As regards all the others, Roger—hell let them keep all the money if they will only give the play a hearing—

I am glad for your letter just the same and the producer shall see it. I dare say the thing may be a matter of emphasis by the actors.

Love to you both.
S.A.

MS. NL

1. Published in *The Triumph of the Egg*, 268–69, and *A New Testament*, 22–23.
2. Prominent New York playwright and political liberal.
3. "Listen, Mr. President," *Nation* 135 (31 Aug. 1932): 191–93.

TO Roger Sergel

23 December [1932, Marion]

Dear Roger—

I have been walking around in the sun—in a melting world, thinking . . .

About this matter of statement again—seeming necessity for statement now—

Thinking I would speak to you of an odd experience.

Has it been so with you?

Every time I have gone warmly toward an American man—Van Wyck Brooks—Waldo Frank—Paul Rosenfeld—I could name a dozen others—my very going toward them has frightened them—

Is it thinness in us now—is there something in the American air.

I quarreled with you the other day—in my mind—when, after your illness, you wrote a sort of exaltation.

Was it by accident that you said—"as though a beautiful woman had come into the room."

Whitman sensed death so too. "Dark mother—always drawing near with soft feet."[1]

But, Roger man, we can't have that—

We don't deserve it.

There is something else for us now.

I never had said what I wanted to say about your novel[2]—that it was as beautiful a thing you, or any man, could do, on its plane—

The plane being the individual struggle of one man and one woman to live within the walls of one house in peace.

However my own belief now being that our struggle—as workmen and men—in America—is now beyond that—

It has some relation to God—refound—among men.

It in some way carried from man to man.

There is somewhere a banner to be carried and, when we can carry, can, as men, help one another carry it—then—and, I'm pretty sure, not 'til then—

Carrying it in life, in a breathing living world again—

Then only can we come back to our women with something real for them.

MS. NL

1. Slightly misquoted from Walt Whitman's "When Lilacs Last in the Dooryard Bloom'd": "Dark mother always gliding near with soft feet . . . ."
2. "Ben and Joan," not published.

TO Laura Copenhaver

[late January? 1933, Kansas City]

Dear Friend—

Worse luck—I've been ill most of the time since I got out here. I got a flu I think and, as yet, it won't let go. I get better for a day or two and then, bang—down I go again.

I think Eleanor gets on pretty well with her job[1] but K.C. isn't San Francisco.

Out there—well the town had a flair—a lift to it. You felt the sea near and there was that thing you always feel in a port town—the smell and taste of other worlds always coming in to make people always a bit more cosmopolitan.

I can't see where K.C. has a thing. It's so American it hurts. You see New York, Chicago, New Orleans, San Francisco—even Cleveland & Detroit—there are the eager, radical Jews—or the Negroes or the orientals. There are a lot of Negroes out here, workers in the stock yards, but they've Americanized them too. O to see a big, wicked, crapshooting, razor toting New Orleans buck nigger.

Do you know, my dear, it would be amusing if your sometimes ill-conceived contempt for the Middle West were more or less sound after all . . . the Middle West of my own boyhood quite gone.

I mean that our Eleanor is not so likely to shine out here. It needs rather someone who can spout endlessly about love and internationalism and working for world peace—I mean large loose sweet sounding generalities that don't mean a thing. O Eleanor will do her job here O.K. but she won't be a star in this atmosphere . . . not mushy enough.

It's the sort of thing that makes all your own philosophy, about slowly educating people into a socialized life, seem so N.G. What's needed out here is fire and revolution and dynamite—these unspeakably dumb thousands . . . to depend on them—baugh!

I'm not seeing so much of my lady—an occasional lunch or dinner and then she rushes away to a meeting but on Saturday night we went to a big gaudy dance hall and danced until midnight and on Sunday we had 3 or 4 hours in the car—out on the Kansas plains. [wavy sketch]

They aren't flat you see—the country almost bare of trees—except those you feel were artificially planted about farm houses. The city is a great sprawling work place but the air is good when it isn't too dirty with smoke.

As for Eleanor—I must say she looks pretty well. She is getting to bed at night and up to date not letting the thing out here get on her nerves.

Tremendous lot of unemployment—

Many poor prostitutes in the streets.

I shall get to work myself as soon as I shake off this flu.

S.A.

MS. NL

1. Eleanor Copenhaver was working on a YWCA survey of community needs of women.

TO Burton and Mary Emmett

[19 January 1933, Kansas City]

Dear Burt & Mary—

I don't know exactly where you are but have been thinking about you both and so write to say "hello." I do so hope Burt is on his feet again and I am sincerely glad he is out of business.

I dare say the cream is off the cigarette advertising and I'm glad Burt got it when he did. I am writing from Kansas City and out here Chesterfields are being advertised by the stores at 10¢—so I don't see where there can be much left for advertising.

Nor do I think it will ever come back. That phase of America is gone.

I got off a new book of short stories—to be published in February and called *Death in the Woods*.[1] They are the short stories of the last few years gathered into a book. Some at least are fine.

Beyond Desire—after a stormy start—is doing better. I get amazingly fine letters from it but it won't sell much. It's a bit too close to real life and people hate life now. It hurts too much to look at it.

I went clear daft on the play—worked night and day for three weeks. Then the man—Arthur Barton (he wrote a play called *Wonder Boy*[2]) came to Marion and we worked together for two weeks.

I was afraid of him but he turned out fine. I was afraid he might want to New York smart my characters but he didn't.

So last weekend he took the play off to New York—to be submitted to the Guild and others and I lit out.

I am in Kansas City—in a cheap little hotel called the Puritan—which is funny—as it is as tough a place as I was ever in—but full of grand color. I think I'll stay here and work on the new novel.[3] Eleanor is out here, helping to do an industrial survey, and I'm interested. Would you believe it—I have a nice comfortable room—with bath—quite clean and nice for $5.50 a week. That suits me as, along with everyone else, I'm quite broke. I'd be in a mess if Burt hadn't started me with the newspapers, which keep the children busy & they can live.

Eleanor would have come to see Mary during her two weeks in New York but was still weak from the operation and very busy.

The drive out here was superb. Boy—if we ever do start to make this country what it can be and stop gouging each other to death instead.

I drove through the Tennessee Valley and over the Cumberland Mountains, and crossed the Cumberland, Tennessee, Ohio, Mississippi and Missouri Rivers. I do love this country. God, what we could make of it.

This hotel would remind you & Burt of your trouper days. It's full of little ham actors, prize fighters, ball players, whores and auto salesmen on their uppers. Lord God what gaudy people. I love them.

I think the play—*Winesburg*—has got drive to it and pretty tense drama and some fun and charm. It is built about the character of Elizabeth Willard and the drama is the struggle between the father and the mother for the soul of the son.

I hope you are both well. Little Eleanor is, as usual, working too hard—she having the same kind of tireless drive Mary has—but Lordy she is a peach of a person.

Lots of love,
Sherwood

Address me Marion.

MS. NL

1. Actually published in April.
2. Produced on Broadway in 1931.
3. "Thanksgiving," never published.

TO Laura Copenhaver
[c. 12 February 1933, Kansas City]

Dear Friend—

You never write to me so I suppose I should punish you by also being silent but I do hear from you, indirectly at the hands of your daughter.

It has been very cold here—as low as 15 below—but today is more moderate—although it is snowing now—and I got the car out and drove Eleanor to Kansas City, Kansas.

Then I went and got pummelled by a man at the YMCA, thinking I would bring her back in perhaps two hours, but she phoned she would have to stay all afternoon and probably dine there.

I got rather dissatisfied with the short story book, feeling it still needed something to give it more distinction, and so I wrote a new short story.[1]

I really took the heart out of the novel I had started—about the people on the cattle farm—and condensed it into the short story—copy of which I am sending you to see. If you want to make any criticisms or suggestions you could make them on this copy & send it back to Eleanor—then I could catch them when I read final proof.

As regards the novel—I felt that the theme I had selected (the land) was not after all my theme. If Mr. Copenhaver were a novelist it would be his—so I am trying to cut into some material I have never used[2] —my own experience among business men in a large advertising agency—such an atmosphere as Nick Carter[3] is in now. I do know that material.

I have definitely decided to keep Ripshin and go live there—now that we are to have roads. If Eleanor marries me we'll make it home. It will be fun to fix it up and perhaps you people will run over now and then for a day or two.

By the expenditure of perhaps $200 I could build a dam on the creek and have a grand swimming pond. We'll plant a real garden this spring.

No definite word yet about the play—3 or 4 managers are considering it.

Morning—Eleanor came back from K.C., Kansas at six and I met her. We went to a hotel to a dinner dance and danced until 9:30. There was a big crowd—a gala night and it was grand fun. Eleanor looked corking.

Love.
S.A.

MS. NL

1. "Brother Death."
2. "Thanksgiving."
3. New York advertising man, whose wife was from Marion and a relative of the Copenhavers.

TO Roger Sergel
[late February 1933, Kansas City]

Dear Roger—

Your letter about the play made me very happy. This is what has happened. A man named Arthur Barton—a pretty good play maker—a theater man—an old vaudeville man—

Singularly cultured and vulgar too. He told me a story of an old vaudeville actor—drunk and sitting on the back of a train—ten years ago—and lecturing the crowd about *Winesburg*.

This man made the synopsis and it set me off. I wrote the whole play—pretty much as it stands—and then he came to Marion and together we put in three weeks of pounding on it.

He went to see Viking[1] and beat them down to 25%. He said they seemed to have it in for me. I suppose, if you've been doing someone dirt for years, you do hate them.

I'll send you a letter I got from him so you'll see where I stand. I'm splitting 50/50 with Barton after the play agent takes off 10%—then Viking 25%—so I won't get rich.

But after I got into it I couldn't think of that side of it.

I am wondering, Roger, that if, the mother having it quite clear in her head—the influence of Doctor Reefy—Dr. Parcival's sarcasm—if all of these things won't say to the boy—and perhaps to the audience—what you say—

Not to want to be some big terrible thing. I hoped so as I wrote—

The implications are, I believe, there—that Reefy had got something—and even poor Elizabeth Willard—

It isn't time even yet perhaps for the drift to turn away from the big in boys like George but it's coming, I'm pretty sure.

I am also made happy by the thought of you & Ruth down at Ripshin this summer. Try to fix it so you can—if you are happy there—stretch it. I'm sure you will love the mountains and the woods and the little streams and the quiet.

I might as well admit that I have a dream in my mind. You know, Roger—I've failed pretty much in relations with women. I'm wondering a little if it couldn't be—partly—what I've been trying to say—and have probably said stupidly—

Not to touch marriage but to help each other broaden it. I think Eleanor and I are afraid of marriage—she to depend too much on me—me upon her.

And I have that place—so lovely really—writing earned it and it's so useless now.

Well we'll see. Anyway you two come.

As for the boys—it would be so easy to fix them. There's a tenant house right near with a great long room where they could all sleep on cots. I think they're rather grand kids and even that kids are rather grand for older people.

I've a new short story—again on the theme of bigness—or success—I'd rather like you to see—but it will be in the new book of short things. If you read nothing else in the book—do read "Brother Death."

S.A.

I will be anxious to hear how the play hits Ruth. Sure keep it until she has time.

I'd be more than glad to take the gamble on the boys—if you & Ruth would.

MS. NL

1. The Huebsch publishing firm, which owned the copyright, had merged with the Viking Press in 1925.

TO Arthur Barton

10 May 1933, [Marion]

Dear Arthur Barton:

I have been very busy since I came home trying to get things arranged a bit at Ripshin and this is the first day I have been able to settle down to try to think a little bit and to write to you. This letter is addressed to both you and Miriam.[1]

In the first place about Ripshin. I have purchased two tents 14 × 16 and have the men over there now putting up the tent floors and the siding. I believe they are going to be charmingly located under the apple trees near the house. I believe I will have beds and chairs, tables, etc. enough for everyone. Tell Miriam that if she has some sheets, towels, etc. to put them in the car when she comes down.

This is the first morning since I came home that I have had time to sit down and actually think of the revision of the play and what must be done with it but immediately [as] I sit down I can see where we can simplify it a good deal and even if anything intensify the drama.

Now as to the matter of money. I believe I could get the money from Burt Emmett but this is what has happened. On the last night when I was in New York I went with Eleanor to dinner at Burt's and as you know afterward went to see a play. It was after that we ran in to say goodbye to you but didn't see Miriam.

As I was coming up from the dining room at Burt's house that night he stopped me on the stairs and talked to me for a few minutes. Burt is rich but like all rich men now is terribly confused, Arthur. He would like to have my friendship and indeed I think he has a good deal of affection for me but when it comes to the money side of life he is like all rich men. He immediately becomes confused.

From time to time I have taken money from him for others. I got money from him to help a painter[2] at Baltimore and also got money to educate a talented mountain boy[3] here. Burt has arthritis and has lost his interest in life. He wants terribly to get it back. When he stopped me on the stairs there was a terrible appeal in his eyes. "Tell me something Sherwood, that will make life taste a little sweet to me," he said.

When I got home I wrote him a long letter trying a little bit to do what he asked but don't know whether I succeeded or not.

Then I wrote him another letter making an appeal to him for the money for your summer but when I sat down to read it I couldn't send it. I didn't want him to say to himself, or think, that I only had friendship for him to get money out of him. This seems to be the way with all rich people. There a wall grows between you and them. They frighten me with the value they place on money. God Almighty if only a play could be written that would tell this story.

It is something of the story I tried to tell in my last book—the story called "Brother Death."

Now I think, Arthur, the sensible thing to do is for you and Miriam to dig around and get up some way a hundred or hundred and fifty dollars so that you can come down here early in June. Then let me loan you another hundred dollars out of my pocket. I think we will feel so much better about this, not trying to get the money out of any rich man. And I also believe that it will give us queerly a better feeling toward each other and toward the work. Write and tell me if you think you can manage this.

I hope you have got over the feeling of defeat that is so damned destructive. I have just begun again to run through the play and I feel sure the stuff is all there and that in two or three weeks of concentrated work we can dig it out.

My love to you both,
Sherwood Anderson

TS. PC (cc)

1. Barton's wife.
2. Charles Bockler.
3. David Greear.

TO Arthur Barton

[4 July 1933], Ripshin Farm

Dear Bart . . .

I am leaving this note for you.[1] It is too hard to say all I feel about what has happened here.[2] I'll probably be back on Thursday evening and I think it would be better for you to go on to New York while I am gone. I think we have done all we can for each other now and that we will both work better separated. As soon as I have the play in type I will send it on for your criticism and suggestion. Give me an address as soon as you have one.

As for the experience here there is but little that can be said. I assumed that you had more background of feeling about life and people that could be worked up into play material than you have now and it is this lack of background, tenderness toward others etc. that has made me afraid to trust the materials of this play in your hands. The whole thing is in no sense personal and if there has been cruelty in it, it is, I want you to know, only the cruelty of the workman at work.

As for yourself, Barton, I want you to know that I feel in you a great sensitiveness and possibility of development as a workman. There is, I guess you know, a great deal of brutality also. As I told you in our talk you will not get at your own possibilities until you get further and further away from Arthur Barton. But all that has been said.

I would like to point it a bit. In your work on this play I have felt that you never at all grasp the real story of the play, the meaning of these lives with which we are working here. What you have got to do, to learn to do, is to feel about the people of whom you are writing as tender as you are now rather in the habit of feeling about yourself. When I have done a really good bit of writing, the reader should never be left feeling that I have been doing good or clever writing. The entire absorption of the reader should be rather in the people written of. I thank God that no one yet has ever thought to call me a smart or clever writer.

Bart, I think Miriam is swell and that little Arthur[3] is a grand kid. Don't take it out on them old dear. Take it out on one Arthur Barton. If it breaks your neck make him get to the place where his absorption, at least a part of the time, is altogether centered in his materials and, for God's sake, every time you write a smart or a clever line be suspicious of it.

I want this letter to say goodbye, for the time, to little Arthur and Miriam too. If you find you need the fifty to help you pull through the next few months, write me. As regards the play remember that it was your idea to do it and that you set it afloat.

Affectionately.

I am writing all this because it is too hard to say it. You and Pete can take the trunk into Troutdale and leave it at Perkins' store with word for Mr. Sprinkle to take it to the N&W station in Marion. If it is not there when you go through, ask the boys in the print shop to attend to shipping it. Bob will attend to things, getting your money from the bank etc.

TS. PC

1. Barton and his family had been visiting at Ripshin Farm. As this letter indicates, Anderson and Barton had not got on well together.

2. Anderson crossed out this sentence that follows: "I am going off for Eleanor and I think that when we come back we will be married." After Anderson picked up Eleanor Copenhaver at a YWCA camp in North Carolina, they were married in Marion on Thursday, 6 July.

3. Barton's son.

TO Roger Sergel

[5 July 1933, Hendersonville, N.C.]

Dear Roger—

I am in a hotel room at Hendersonville, N.C. waiting to hear from Eleanor who is in a camp near here—a camp as isolated from telegrams & phones as we are at Ripshin. After you and Chris[1] left the place was so lonesome and the B.'s had so got on my nerves that I got into the car and went over to Mrs. Copenhaver's—working in her house that day. I wasn't to come here until today—Wednesday—but got up early Tuesday morning, wrote a note to Barton—telling him to pull his freight—and got into a car and came down here. I guess I am too much influenced by atmosphere. Barton got me—the eternal sadness and lack of courage either to really get into the play, walk out or punch my nose. I hadn't the courage to go through another scene with the man begging off, clinging on, even weeping etc.

A lot of things happened the day you left . . .

1st Bob sold his first story[2]—to *American Mercury*—a really good thing—about a cock fight he attended one night in the mountains.

2nd I got $500—a loan—voluntarily sent me by a rich man[3] in N.Y.

3rd a real tragedy—Ferdinand Schevill's wife Clara died June 17th and I didn't know it until a letter came.

Roger—I wonder if you'd mind writing him a note—Duneland Beach—Michigan City, Indiana—urging him to come down here to me. Tell him a little about the place. I want him. I'm a bit afraid for him just now. He and Clara have lived together 25 years. It's as though you lost Ruth. I think he ought to get away. I love the man. It may be vanity in me to think I can help him a little through this but queerly I do.

I went—like a crazy man—and arranged to buy a saddle mare for Eleanor—100 plunks—silly man—but a little beauty.

I almost quarreled with B. that night—Ferdinand on my mind—trying to be nice to B. and play croquet with him—suddenly I decided to boot him out—as gently as I could but effectually.

I got up and drove down here—most of the time at 60—after a sleepless night—got here at noon—fell into bed and slept all afternoon & night. I got up and went through the last scene of *Winesburg*—fresh as a daisy. Now I'll go back over the whole play with a stenographer and without that clam there.

If you have any afterthoughts on the play, shoot them at me, will you. Send me the Green Bay–Ephraim address. I wonder if you and Ruth would mind if, as the revisions come off the machine, I sent them for your two reactions again?

It will be fun thinking of you two working on a play. Do you want to let me see the scenes as you go along?

By the way—as regards any loan to Barton. In the note I left for him, telling him to skeedaddle, I didn't put any money—he has $100 in the bank here—but did tell him I'd send him $50 if he wrote for it. It was mean but there are so many really talented men up against it.

As regards Louis.[4] You see I feel differently about him. I've half promised to try to do this Mississippi River play with him but he understands I must get a real impulse for it. If I don't come through for him he'll be working in any event.

Perhaps this Barton thing has made me wary . . . of Louis. I feel this . . . I'm pretty sure that he is primarily a technician. He talks a bit too much about money & success . . . I know he has written a good deal of cheap music to make money . . . has a lot fine in him etc. I do think,

Roger, that we—if we are each in our own separate ways to tackle the theater—have got to be a bit wary of all technicians. In writing we've both been, at bottom, amateurs (I've never got over being one—as you know)—and I think we ought to keep that. It should lead to the inclination to go to the natural drama of life rather than the built-up technique of the theater . . . you see what I mean.

By the way—if you want me to I'll send you the dismissal note to B. to read.

I feel a queer sort of providential thing about your visit as—more than you perhaps know—you gave me courage to force through the readjustment of the contract and also by little things you said about the play you gave me new courage about my own perhaps natural aptitude for the drama.

On the other hand there was the sad part. As you know I have this rather passionate belief just now that artists, in America, should draw near each other—at almost any cost—and it makes me sick to think of the physical difficulty.

Ruth sent back the big mushroom book. I wrote her to bring it thinking she would come and we'd walk together in the woods and we'd use the book together. There is a handy & good small book—I think called *The Common Mushroom*—with colored illustrations—I think it's Doubleday—nature book series.[5] It has a very effectual scheme for isolating specimens. Don't go to Ephraim without it.

No need my telling you how much I liked Chris. I'm going to pray for a visit from you & Ruth later.

Love,
S.A.

I'm hoping Eleanor and I will do it within the next few days.

What rather stands in the way of the Mississippi River thing is that I am getting a real hunch to try to do the mountaineer play. I even this morning—after going through and revising the last scene of *Winesburg*—wrote an opening scene (rather part of it) for that. It could be rather grand.

I won't forget your suggestion about the book—"I Build My House."[6] Does that strike you as a title.

MS. NL

1. Christopher Sergel, Roger's son.
2. "Chicken-Fight," *American Mercury* 30 (Sept. 1933): 111–15.
3. Burton Emmett.
4. Louis Gruenberg, composer, who visited Ripshin later during the summer in an unsuccessful effort to collaborate with Anderson on an opera about the Mississippi River.

5. Probably William S. Thomas, *Field Book of Common Gilled Mushrooms* (1928), published by Putnam's in its Nature Field Book series.
6. A book of memoirs, never completed.

TO Laura Copenhaver
[26 September 1933, New York]

Dear Friend—

If there is Italian blood in me,[1] making me sometimes bold—there is also something else—occasional long times of unreasonable fear—that I am sure you do not have. This making me rather tremble before life.

We have not yet got our household running as smoothly as we wish—not having yet got a cleaning woman.

However we feel very secure here and it is wonderful, not having to put out a great sum for rent each month.[2]

We get up. We have an electric coffee pot upstairs & start it. Eleanor then runs down to the kitchen and comes up with breakfast on a tray. We eat & have a morning cigarette and then she goes off and I go down and wash the dishes. This about occupies the time she takes getting to her office so we are both at our desks by nine.

On Sunday we drove far over into the East Side—and parked the car. Then we walked in the terribly crowded East Side streets, got down to the East River, watched the boats and looked at people—such hordes, young & old—all the stores open—a fiesta going on in the Italian section, pushcart men, screaming children everywhere underfoot.

Tonight I am taking Eleanor out to dine with a group of my old friends and today, as soon as I have finished this note, I must run uptown to Horace Liveright's funeral. He died suddenly on Sunday.

I am to lunch with Mr. Perkins[3] of Scribner's.

Love to all of you
Sherwood

I thought Bob a little excessively laudatory about the Lincolns[4] but will say nothing.

MS. NL

1. See letter to Hansen, 29 Nov. 1922, n. 4.
2. The Andersons were staying at the Emmetts' residence at Washington Mews.
3. Maxwell Perkins, Scribner's editor, who negotiated with Anderson on affiliating with Scribner's after the bankruptcy of Liveright.
4. John D. and Charles Lincoln had donated 2,000 acres of land near Marion for development as a state park, as prominently reported in the Marion papers, then edited by Robert Anderson.

TO Arthur Barton

21 November 1933, New York

Dear Arthur Barton:

Following up my telephone conversation with you this morning, I might as well tell you how I feel. I presume I should be grateful to you for getting me to work on this *Winesburg* play. You suggested the idea to me and stirred me up to do it. When you sent the first synopsis of the play to me written out on a few sheets of yellow paper—which, by the way, you said you had spent months doing—I saw at once that it violated the whole spirit of the book. But it did stir me up to go to work.

I wrote the entire play—very much as it is in the first draft—and sent it to you scene by scene. Fortunately I kept copies of these scenes as written, and also I showed them to other people.

You came to Marion and we worked together. I was at that time disappointed but very grateful to you for having stirred me up, so said nothing. Afterward when I came to New York I was greatly shocked to find that you had gone around New York talking to everybody as though you had done all the work on the play.

Shortly after this, and although I have thought all along that you were a straight shooter, I came upon something that shocked me. We were walking one day on Broadway and you brought up the subject of copyright, and you said that you had copyrighted the play. "How do you mean?" I asked, and you told me that you had copyrighted the play in both our names.

I was not suspicious at the time, but afterwards, at the advice of a friend,[1] I wrote to the Library of Congress at Washington and got a report from them that you had copyrighted the entire play in your sole name as author. That, if you want to know it, is the reason why I insisted upon your transferring the copyright to me.

You came to Marion this summer and did nothing. I think you must admit that yourself.

When I came back to New York, after working all summer on the play, the play was given to Mr. Thayer.[2] We had a consultation, and if you did not agree with Mr. Thayer's point of view, you said nothing in my presence. I asked you to go to Mr. Thayer with the plans you had for the play and he says you came to him with practically nothing.

Not knowing what else to do I went to work with Mr. Thayer, and have been working practically night and day for two weeks. I have re-written the scenes and as each scene was re-written I have sent it to you. I have waited patiently for any constructive criticism from you and have got nothing until today, when you call up and tell me over the phone—having submitted nothing yourself—that everything Mr. Thayer and I have done is wrong.

Now I am not going to depend on you any more. I depended on you for well over a year and have got little or nothing. I have tried to believe in you but I must say that the business about the copyright gave me a shock. I do not want to send a copy of this letter to Miss Fishbein,[3] but I may do so. I think any human being would be a little shocked at this copyright business.

No Arthur, I don't believe you are a chiseler, but I have already told you what I think about your great ability to think you have done something when you haven't done it, and I will not go into this further at this time. I am very unfortunate in this play. The publishing house is riding me for twenty-five per cent of the royalties as author and you for thirty-five per cent. I expect to go on until I get a good play. I have no particular personal feeling about this whole matter except to feel that I have been rather a chump, and you are not to blame for that.

Sincerely,
Sherwood Anderson

TS. PC (cc)

1. Roger Sergel.
2. Sigourney Thayer, producer of the play.
3. Frieda Fishbein, authors' representative, who negotiated the contract with Theatre Guild.

TO B.G. Braver-Mann[1]

13 January 1934, New York

Dear Braver-Mann:

I am writing this letter to you today to make clear my understanding of your plan for making a moving picture scenario and film from my novel *Poor White*, and to set forth to you my understanding of the way the picture is to be produced, and how the whole matter is to be handled.

In the first place, my understanding is that you are to take charge of this matter, prepare the scenario, subject to my approval, and to go ahead and raise the money necessary to produce the picture. It is also my understanding that the scenario itself is to follow the spirit of the book and that the going ahead with the picture is to depend on my approval of the way this scenario is handled.

If it should happen that the scenario is satisfactory to me and that you are unable to raise the money necessary for the production of the picture, and if it should happen that the scenario is instead sold to a commercial company, a new arrangement is to be made between us, the arrangement to be left open to the arrival of such an emergency. However, the real purpose of this understanding between us is rather that we have no intention of making a typical Hollywood picture.

I understand that you are to get the services of Joseph Houdyma,[2] the Russian camera man, and that we are to go right out into a country town, develop our own actors, and make a picture using actual working people such as are needed in the various scenes. In case it is impossible to find a few of the leading characters necessary for the making of the picture, a few players may be brought in.

It is my own understanding that the entire effort is to do something new and worthwhile in the picture field. No one of us is entering into this project with any idea of making it primarily commercial. The hope is that something so real to American life in the curious situation of America may be produced as to attract attention and achieve its success in that way.

My understanding of the conversations with you in this matter is that I may put up my story *Poor White* and any assistance I may give you in the preparing of the scenario against the money that may be advanced by others to put the project through. We—that is to say myself and those who may put up the money—to share half and half with you and your associates in any profits that may eventuate.

In giving you these rights it is understood that I retain for myself any rights in the novel *Poor White* for stage production. The writer retains the dramatic rights in the story and also is to have the privilege of using any scenes that may be developed in the picture in his own stage production without any question being raised as to his right to do so.

As suggested, the whole purpose of doing this picture and of my giving you these rights is to bring a fresh breath into the production of moving pictures. In talking to you I have liked the whole spirit of your approach to the problem of the American film. Naturally also, it pleases me that you have selected for this experiment my novel *Poor White* as I have long thought that it could make a really significant film.

As you know, the novel is really built about an American town. It might be any town of the American Middle West or of the upper South. The town is the real hero of the story.

As you feel so do I—that is to say that it is possible to do in America what the Russians have done so well—that is to get the people out of the town and out of the fields as players in such a film. With good direction, a good scenario to start with, and a good camera man such as Joseph Houdyma, it should be possible to get a really significant picture. Also it seems to me that we should be able to keep down costs, that the venture does not become too expensive.

It is my understanding that you expect to get the players in the film to work also on an agreement between you and Mr. Houdyma for their mere living expenses, they to share with you in the profits should there be any. All of this, transportation, living expenses of actors, etc., to be taken out of the money to be raised.

The novel *Poor White* has become a kind of classic, as the story of the passing of an agrarian people—out of an agrarian civilization and into an industrial civilization. What happens in the story has happened in thousands of American towns. Since the novel was written some eighteen or twenty years ago, it has become a source to which practically all historians of the period go. It is already used in most of our colleges and universities to tell the story to the present generation of American youth. It is also used to illustrate the destructive influence of present-day uncontrolled industrialism. The film should be tremendously educational.

American scholars have already realized the possibilities of the story but now, I think, it should find a wider public in the film.

I am leaving to you the working out with those who back you in this project the details of who is to handle the money, make any payments necessary in producing the film, etc.

TS. NL (cc)

1. Film director and editor of *Experimental Cinema*, who had proposed a film version of *Poor White* in a letter to Anderson on 22 Dec. 1933. Although they continued to correspond throughout 1934, the plan never materialized.

2. Then living in Detroit.

TO William C. Stewart[1]

24 January 1934, Konnarock, Va.

Dear Bill:

I am sending you the first article on the CCC camps.[2] It runs to about forty-five hundred words I think and I should think would be about the right length. I will be over in the hills the latter part of this week and will strike south at the end of the week.

I would like you to give me more or less leeway on these articles. What I would like to do is to keep an open mind and write about the things in relation to government activities as they come up to me. In drifting along in this way, talking to all kinds of men, it is difficult to tell what will come up.

Of course whenever you fellows have a particular project in mind let me have it and I will try to cover it.

I think some of the articles might very well be just little running stories about the growing differences in feeling in the ordinary man about government under the New Deal. Already I find that almost every man I talk to is beginning to look toward government. I should think a good idea might be to intersperse these groups of little stories with definite set articles on particular phases of life and ideas in the country now.

I will make up my expense account to date in a few days and send it forward to you.

With sincere regards
Sherwood Anderson

TS. NL

1. Managing editor of *Today*, a new pro-Roosevelt magazine to which Anderson had begun contributing articles that were to appear over a two-year period. Many of these were later collected in *Puzzled America*.

2. "Tough Babes in the Woods," *Today* 1 (10 Feb. 1934): 6–7, 22.

TO Roger Sergel

5 April 1934, [New York]

Dear Roger,

After a good deal of fussing and bluffing around, Barton has finally signed the new contract as regards the play. The contract was drawn up for me by the attorney at the Authors' Guild. It gives Barton a cut of twenty-five percent and lets his name remain on the play but he is to have no more part or say of any kind in any rewriting and he surrenders to me all rights as regards making contracts with producers, selecting the cast, etc.

A very amusing thing happened about this matter. I had selected the Authors' Guild and their attorney fixed up the contract for me. The same attorney is also attorney for the Dramatists' Guild. Barton is also a member of the Dramatists' Guild. Barton got himself an attorney and the attorney went over to the Dramatists' Guild and tried to kick up a row about their drawing up the contract. What amused me was that the attorney told them that Barton and I were very happy together until the fellow[1] came along from Chicago and made trouble between us. This I thought was beautiful.

I had simply taken the ground that Barton should sign the new contract or I would withdraw the play altogether and forget it. When he weakened, he demanded that a clause be put into the contract. The clause as he worded it provided that in case any other play was made from the same material, it was not to be called *Winesburg*. I jumped at this. My attorney tells me that his putting this clause in leaves him wide open. I could take the play away from him altogether by simply changing its name. So much for his intelligence. Of course I will not do it but it is amusing.

I have been thinking a good deal about the making of the play from *Dark Laughter*. I haven't worked it out but the idea is to show a contrast between the primitive man—represented by the Negro—and the sophisticated white man. The white man struggling to succeed, to solve the problem of his life, affection, sex, etc. and the primitive man doing the same thing quite simply and giving the sophisticated man the laugh. I thought for a long time, Roger, that no one has adequately worked out the use of sound in the theatre. Why could not sound come from all sides of the audience, from the very walls of the theatre and from the back, the idea being to give a sense of another life going on around the audience and the players in the theatre, sentences coming through, laughter, sounds of people working and fighting.

I do think it might be possible to get at this *Dark Laughter* idea in this way. Perhaps the whole story taking place, say in the living room of the house, the primitive Negro people being the servants in the house. Why couldn't we play the same drama as passing through the lives first of the white people in the house and then the Negroes. I think you will see what I mean. I would like to hear from you about it.

Sherwood

P.S. This letter may come to you when you are moved. You know it doesn't demand an immediate reply. I am only writing it to show you what is going on in my mind, perhaps later to get your mind on it a little.

Love to Ruth.

TS. NL

1. That is, Sergel.

TO Jasper Deeter[1]

6 June 1934, [Ripshin Farm]

Dear Jap:

I got to thinking after I left the other day[2] something in the play I believe should be cut. I haven't the play before me at this moment. It is the scene at Banker White's house between George, Helen and Parcival. Helen tells George about the woman who comes to help with the cleaning and also about the man who comes to trim the grapevines when the cattle pass in the road. I believe the story about the cattle could very well be cut. Don't you think the business about the boy and girl cow is a bit too naive? I believe the point to be made, about Helen's feeling for people, gets over with the first story. If you agree with me cut the second story.

I want you to feel perfectly free to cut any places in the play that you think are redundant or that don't get across.

Again I want to tell you how delighted I am that you are doing the play and with the way you are doing it.

There is another point I want to make although I am sure it will occur to you.

In the last scene, second act, when Tom is making his big speech about the boy and toward the end of the speech Elizabeth begins to laugh. My notion is that she is laughing softly at first so that the audience is aware without Tom's being aware, he being so absorbed in what he is saying that he doesn't notice. His speech is broken by a sudden peal of laughter from her.

I remember sharply where I got this idea, a man I knew, whose domestic life was terrible. He was a repressed man and the only way you felt it was in his laughter, that always startled you because it came as a kind of explosion of pent-up feeling in him.

I want to impress on you, Jap, that you must feel free to make any changes or cuts in the play you feel will improve it. Everything you have done to the play has helped it and I do not want you to feel any restrictions. I was thinking coming home that I would like to do an article about you for some magazine, the article not being necessarily centered on the theater. I would really like to do an article about you as an educator. We will talk about that when I see you.

These are the only ideas that occur to me now but I will be writing you again from time to time as other ideas come to me. My address here until I come down to be with you during the last week before production will be Troutdale, Virginia.

Sincerely yours,

TS. PC (cc)

1. Founder and director of the Hedgerow Theatre in Moylan-Rose Valley, near Media, Pa., which presented *Winesburg* during the summer season.

2. On 3 June, Anderson had attended an all-day rehearsal of *Winesburg* at Hedgerow.

TO George Jean Nathan

[c. 2 July 1934, Paoli, Pa.]

Dear George,

I think, considering his small company, that Jasper Deeter did damn well with the play.[1] It has real moving beauty, George, and the actors love it. I think also that it moved and stirred the audience.

Sherwood Anderson and Jasper Deeter on the *Winesburg* Set
COURTESY OF BOSTON UNIVERSITY LIBRARIES,
HEDGEROW THEATRE COLLECTION

As for the Lee Shuberts[2] and others of that sort who came over to see it, I think it only puzzled them. If it is anything, George—and after seeing it performed I think it beautiful—it is outside the intellectual and emotional range of the average Broadway producer or critic.

I wish, George, that you would see your way clear to go over to Media and see it performed. If it is what I think and what Dreiser and others think, it is as played a new note in the theater and after all, George, that is the sort of thing that you critics are supposed to understand and help.

It has the quality of *Winesburg* itself and even Menck went up creek on that[3]—although he later forgot he did. Boyd[4] didn't.

As always,
Sherwood

MS. Cornell

1. *Winesburg* opened on 30 June 1934.
2. Lee Shubert was an influential Broadway play producer and owner of theaters.
3. Probably a reference to Mencken's highly favorable review of the original *Winesburg* in the magazine that he and Nathan had edited, *Smart Set* 59 (Aug. 1919): 140, 142.
4. Ernest Boyd, critic and, like Nathan and Anderson, an editor of *American Spectator*.

TO Thomas Wolfe

[c. 23 April 1935], Greensboro, N.C.

Dear Thomas Wolfe

As I read it I have a hunger to write you a word about your new novel.[1] It is such a gorgeous achievement.

It makes me a little sad too. Here I've been struggling all these years, trying to write novels, and along you come and show me, very simply & directly, that I'm no novelist. Some things I can write but you—you are a real novelist.

Sincerely
Sherwood Anderson

MS. Harvard

1. *Of Time and the River.*

TO Granville Hicks[1]

[c. 1 June 1935], Marion

Dear Granville Hicks

I just got your letter, about Jack Reed, and am delighted that you are doing the biography. I knew Jack first in the days of the old *Masses*, when he was the friend and comrade of Max Eastman, Floyd Dell, Art Young[2] and the others of that old crowd, but now that I pin myself down, I have to realize that I never did spend much time with him.

I was in Chicago then and Jack was in New York but I used to see him occasionally when I came East and it happens that Jack was the sort of fellow you don't forget . . . that is to say every moment with the man was made very vivid and real by his personality.

I remember one or two walks and talks . . . on winter nights when I was in New York, a breakfast had with him and Louise.[3] He would have been puzzled, laughing, pulling up his pants. There was always the poet in the man and I gathered, Hicks, that the poet in him was often at war with something else, that is to say with the fighter, and I remember that we always did discuss that . . . that is to say whether a man did more by lying low and trying always to get understanding . . . or whatever it is we're after . . . or whether he did more by giving himself altogether to the fight.

Why, Hicks, I do remember a night. We were standing at Fifth Ave. and Ninth Street in New York . . . it was snowing and Jack was without an overcoat and he must have held me there for an hour. "If I could be dead sure I had something on the ball as a poet," he said, and I can still see his big, loosely made figure going away from me after that.

You see I just got this side of him and that's the reason I've never felt competent to write of him. It's largely an impression of a man terribly alive, an essentially laughing man. Out in Chicago, when we were just getting into the war, he one day called me on the phone, saying he wanted to see me, and I went out to the West Side, to a little hall. There was a meeting being held out there. I think it was that crowd Judge Kenesaw Landis got.[4] You'll remember that he gave them each twenty years. Anyway Jack came out of the meeting to me, to where I was standing in the hallway outside and took me off to a water closet down a flight of stairs. "I wanted to show you something," he said and pulled a poem out of his pocket. I wish I knew which one of his verses it was. I have only the impression of something very much alive, in both the verses and the man, and of his standing there in that place, as I read the verses, and looking like a pleased boy because I liked them and him.

And then of his saying, with a gesture, concerning the meeting going on above us in the hall . . . "Hell, Sherwood, they've got to the resolution stage up there."

I think we must have walked up and down for a time after that in a little nearby park and then he left me and went back to the meeting, saying . . . "Well, well, that's enough of this. I guess I'd better get back in there and see what's doing," and I went away and that's the last time I ever saw Jack.

So you see, Granville Hicks, I've just got these impressions of this curiously alive and vital man and no facts at all about him.

And I presume that's why I've never written of him as I'd like to. But I'm glad you are doing it.

Sincerely
Sherwood Anderson

TS. Columbia

1. Then an English professor at Rensselaer Polytechnic Institute and editor of *New Masses*. His book *John Reed: The Making of a Revolutionary* appeared in 1936.
2. All were on the editorial staff of *Masses*; Young was a cartoonist.
3. Louise Bryant, Reed's wife.
4. The 1917 trial in Chicago of the Industrial Workers of the World.

TO Karl Anderson

[c. 20 June 1935, Ripshin Farm]

Dear Karl

When your letter came I had a quick sense of guilt, having so often thought of you and having so often intended to write without doing it. It is largely Eleanor's fault. She has taken care of so much of my correspondence for me this last year that I have got out of the habit of letter writing. I find myself thinking I have written when I haven't.

As for my doings. I got caught up by the fancy to write plays, as you know. Well, as usual there is more to it than appears on the surface. I had been travelling most of the winter. Was here, at Ripshin, for a few weeks in April. Then I went to Jap's. Someone gave me a room there and I ate at the house, along with all the grand little theatre kids. I did that for nearly five weeks, going every day to rehearsals, watching the work on the stage, finding out something of what can now be done with lights on the stage, etc., etc., etc. Incidentally Jap is grand fun . . . a real artist of the theatre.

While I was there Burt Emmett (54 Wash. Mews) died[1] and I ran into New York just the once, to see him buried, hold Mary's hand etc. Poor woman. She was a wreck. I put in a call for you but you were not at home.

I went to Washington. I've got rather fond of Tugwell,[2] Morgenthau[3] and others down there. Then back here.

I got out a new book. Did I send you one . . . called *Puzzled America*. It got a pretty good press. It's the kind of reporting I like doing and may get more of it to do.

I spoke to Mary Emmett about coming down here and bringing you, some time this summer. I think the drive might be fun for you.

It's gorgeous here this year. We'll be here now most of the summer, with a good many interesting guests I hope. Do you remember the log

Sherwood Anderson at Ripshin Creek
COURTESY OF ELEANOR ANDERSON

cabin in which you slept, up the hill. I had it moved down and hidden away, along Laurel Creek, on the same level as the house but across the road and under the hill. I'm in it now. Paul [Rosenfeld] is coming for three weeks early in July. Love to Helen and the son and daughter.

S.A.

TS. NL

1. On 6 May 1935.
2. Rexford Tugwell, undersecretary of agriculture and subject of Anderson's article "Give Rex Tugwell a Chance," *Today* 4 (8 June 1935): 5, 21.
3. Henry Morgenthau, Jr., secretary of the treasury.

TO Laura Copenhaver

[mid-November 1935, Valley Cottage, N.Y.[1]]

Dear Mother . . .

I guess I'll send along this new part of the book,[2] intended to follow immediately the last part sent. Better not give it to the girl until she has finished the rest, so she won't get it mixed, then she can number the pages straight through. But for heaven's sake don't you lose it, Mother.

And I wonder if you will like this. I tried something. There is an Italian girl here, servant in the house, so when I had finished this I called her in and had her read it. It hit her all right. "It's real, all right. That's the way it is, that's about the way I feel," she said. She confided that she was a Catholic and a virgin but that she thought sometimes that wouldn't stop her if she had been a good looker.

I think as soon as any part is finished you'd better send me one copy.

Between ourselves, Mother, E. and I are in a funny time. I can't quite make out whether she wants to quit her job or not. You see, Mary and I have got our proposition pretty definitely worked out. I don't mind telling you, Mother, that I really love novel writing although I have been saying, for the last two years, that I didn't. Frankly it was because I didn't believe I'd ever again have the time to really do the work on a novel I now want to do.

You see I want to advance, not just do the kind of book I've done before, and that might mean say a solid year of work and, at that, even if infinitely fine, it might not sell.

There would remain the kind of thing I did the last two years, something for *New Yorker, Vanity Fair, American Magazine, Today* etc. Not that such work isn't all right. I really haven't any notion that such work is the turning aside of a great writer, literature robbed, any such nonsense, but it is pretty temporary work.

I used to be able, did for fifteen years, work in an advertising place all day and write at night. I can't do that anymore.

And then too, doing a long thing like this, really orchestrating it, demands real absorption.

So Mary and I have come to an agreement. She doesn't know yet just how much Burt left her but she had an annuity that is enough so that she says she can go on in her present way with her life, without in any way cramping her life, and still allow me three thousand a year. She proposes beginning this January first, payments to be made three times a year, a thousand each . . . I think because that is the way her annuity comes.

She has said, in regard to the matter, some pretty fine things I think, for example that I was for years tied to advertising and that the money she has came from advertising. She says also, quite frankly, that association with E. and me is worth more than that to her.

She says . . . "I don't propose to be on your hands . . . will take a good many trips etc., leave you two alone together, but I do want a feeling of something like a family with you." She says . . . "My house is empty. There isn't any real reason for having it. I want a different kind of house, a home in your affections if you will."

I think in spite of all this E. is doubtful. M. has said . . . "We can't do it without her. It wouldn't work." With E. it may be just a natural conservatism . . . she has a good deal of that . . . dread of making decisions, and then again it may be some hurt that she hasn't the privilege herself of giving me this privilege.

I think, in the end, I can make it up to her for I love her more than I ever did.

The plan now is to go to town next week-end. I don't know yet about John's coming. Anyway I may come home ahead of E. and M. They will probably come back here after January 1st while I stay there until I go to Chicago. Then they will drive down, pick me up and go to Chicago with me. We're to go to the Sergels' out there. We'll drive out there, probably M.'s car.

Then I want to go off south, perhaps down to the New Mexico–Old Mexico border, and stay there, where I am less subject to sinus, and finish the novel. M. says she will drive us out there and go on to California, stopping for us when we want to come back.

I wonder if this new section of the novel will shock you a little. I'm trying as you know to show the development of a modern.

Love
S.A.

TS. NL

1. The Emmetts' summer residence on the Hudson River near Nyack, N.Y.
2. *Kit Brandon*.

TO Jasper Deeter

Saturday 16 [November 1935, Valley Cottage, N.Y.]

Dear Jap . . .

I am sending this to Hedgerow, thinking I may miss you on the road. Am still at Mary's farm but will go down to town some time this week. Your letter came and the good news about cash sent home. I was afraid of the other and hope next year you can work out the plan of short trips, under your own management. Business is business and businessmen businessmen.

Jap, I saw a good movie, Dostoyevsky's *Crime and Punishment*, done into a picture by the French[1] . . . some really intelligent acting, particularly by one Henry Baur who did Porfiry, a police officer. The man had real and intelligent use of his hands . . . not to throw flowers but he was the only man on the stage, except a certain little skinny guy I know named Deeter . . . and he wastes himself in a little country theatre training the youth for Broadway . . . Oh great great great white way! The man made his hands say a thousand things. It was grand to see. If you get the chance see it and tell me if you don't agree.

Alas I have to confess I haven't again touched the play. Damn it, Jap, I got really absorbed in this woman, the title lady of this novel . . . I call it *Kit Brandon* . . . and there has been something else.

You see, I have always been a bit suspicious of my novel writing. The short story O.K. but I think that, in the novel, I have been inclined to trust too absolutely to feeling. I have avoided structure and think I know what got me into this. I think it was because, when I came into writing, the prevailing thing was largely structure and little else . . . I mean in America . . .

The plot short story, plot novel etc. . . . O. Henry etc. etc. I think O. Henry got it from de Maupassant and it sure spread out like a disease here. You made your structure very rigid and then goddam your people. You made them go into the structure whether they would or not. It is the basis of most of our bad play writing also and I remember how, time after time in my early theatre going, I had a swell time, say the first two acts of a play, but always went out of the place feeling like a man who has either watched someone masturbate before your eyes or as though you had been doing it.

The possibilities are that, in my own revulsion, I went too far away from structure. I think so. I want to get something of it back. I think, in my longer things, it made me too diffused. Chekhov and Turgenev, to name two masters, managed to give free play to feeling but always, also, to let mind come in and more or less control. Dostoyevsky perhaps went rather the road I have been inclined to take.

All this an interesting technical challenge. I have been walking and thinking more as I worked, going therefore more slowly. It is a full-length portrait I have been trying to do.

Does all of this interest you.

Yes of course. Any problem connected with one art is always also a part of the problem of any other art. I believe that.

There is a marvelous exhibition of Van Goghs here. Say, Jap, you'll be at home until Christmas. My kid John, the young painter, is coming up here, perhaps about two weeks before Christmas, having in mind particularly seeing the Van Goghs. Then he and I plan to drive down to Marion together. Eleanor and Mary will come down later. When I know just when John is to come, I'll write. Then you come over, see the Van Goghs with us, and ride back to Hedgerow with us.

I went and bought . . . Jesus, they cost dollars 22.50 . . . the three volumes of Vincent Van Gogh's letters. God, they are moving. If you get a chance to look into them don't miss it. They should be in Hedgerow library for the whole gang to read. I wonder if I'd ever get big enough to give them up. I doubt it.

Love to the crew . . . in toto.

Sherwood

TS. Boston

1. *Crime et Châtiment* (1935), directed by Pierre Chenal.

TO John Anderson

[c. 20 November 1935, Valley Cottage, N.Y.]

Dear John.

Still in the country, although we are going into town today. The weather has been exquisite although through Oct. it was so dry we didn't find many mushrooms. Bob tells me he has become a really great nimrod. How humble, to be hunting the lowly mushroom.

I wish you would try to tell me a bit more of what you mean by direct painting.[1]

I took a long walk in the late fall woods yesterday. Was thinking . . . my own experience . . . there had been a woman here,[2] a writer . . . also wondering why I have a prejudice against women writers . . . This one, long ago . . . she has forgotten it . . . did me dirt. It was when I first began publishing my short stories and she was a friend of Karl's. There was a great outcry at the time regarding my filthy mind. She joined in it.

She writes a certain kind of books, is now writing one on great seaways, river-ways, land-ways of the world, etc. . . . the kind of work that calls I presume for scholarship and research. Interesting. I walked with her the day before and we spoke of cars. She has never learned to drive, said she had problems enough, didn't want to take the responsibility.

Myself thinking later, as I walked, how all such people do get out of the responsibility of entering into life in their work . . . also that the not taking responsibility in relationships, in life, was a kind of way to death . . . with women what Lawrence called dry ass, anyway dry rot.

I can't help hoping, John, that you will, out of your own desire, return again one of these days to the portraits, of just people. It may be I am only speaking of what I would myself want as a painter. There is an old man here, a thief. He goes about stealing small objects but often goes into the gardens of the rich and steals flowers which he takes to others who have no flowers . . . or even to those who have plenty of their own. He is such a grand old thing, crippled, old, unmoral, a kind of grand inner laughter in him.

I think you may get that too. It is in me a little. Formerly, when I did some of the best of my earlier work, it was almost universally at first called dirty. It hurt like hell but afterwards the laughter came.

Looking forward to your coming.

S.A.

TS. NL (ph)

1. John Anderson was developing a theory of painting dealing with the relationship between an object and the artist's view of it.

2. Madge Jenison, whose book *Roads* was published by Doubleday in 1948.

TO Miriam Phillips[1]

[c. 22 November 1935, New York]

Dear Mims . . .

Woman, do you tempt me? Do you deliberately set out to tempt me from my honest labor, divert, confuse, set me galloping amid stars? This letter of yours has about it that touch . . . the touch that would tempt any American penman to go on and on, whole volumes written.

Pryor[2]

Oscar Ameringer[3]

Letter written from Tonkawa

Huckins Hotel[4]

Wistful soul of America, as in the Pryor, gone alas sour.

Woman be gone. Skidoooo. What, after all, are you, Jap, Katy[5] with her "soul of Bernard Shaw," the whole gang of you . . . strolling players, eh, come into the king's court . . . King Business . . . setting

Sherwood Anderson in New York, Fall 1935
COURTESY OF ELEANOR ANDERSON

yourself up, expecting, why, why, why, why? Did you not know that colleges, universities, theatres, public buildings, yeh even government are subject to that king?

But serioushishishishly Mims . . . it just happens that I yesterday took a walk, alone in a winter wood. I was thinking of all this, very much as set down by your pen. As it happens I have recently had a very moving experience. I bought . . . at a ghastly price . . . the letters of Vincent Van Gogh, the painter, to his brother Theo. Regardless of the price I am going to have them for Hedgerow. They should be there, always at hand, ready for any honorable player who happens to have an hour to pick up a book, the letters so terribly close to all life, sometimes to just what you have all been feeling, so tender often.

Then there came here a simply gorgeous exhibition of the man's work. I have already written Jap of this, fairly commanding him to see it. It must happen to you too. It is at the Modern Museum, on 52nd Street, I think.

As to myself, as I have written Jap, I expect to be here until about Dec. 15th. My youngest son, John, is coming up here, getting here about the 9th, and will stay four or five days. I have already suggested that Jap come over and ride back to Hedgerow with us when we start for Virginia. Why not you and Katy too. It would be wonderful for the whole crowd to see the show. I had planned that John and I would stop for a day with you all on the way down. Eleanor cannot come down to Virginia until later, just a day or two before Christmas.

But let me go back to my walk, thoughts, etc. I have it figured this way Mims. What has happened to all of you happens to everyone who attempts something.

Attempts what?

Why, I should say, an approach to life, to reality, in any art. You speak of your failures, bad night, etc. Of course. You can escape always by attempting less. You see, Jap could have gone on, had success as an actor, acting any material put up to him, not wanting to get down into the material also, had success, even a pleasant enough life . . .

As in writing . . . to keep always on the surface etc. You understand.

Why I do think it is plain . . . this, that if in any art you really attempt to take the responsibility of your art, you have to suffer. Why not. But isn't it also true that the taking of that very responsibility is the only road to life?

I was trying to think what happened to people, and why, during the walk above mentioned. I think it's like this. The hurt affects people in two ways . . . they become silent or resentful . . . this probably from the notion that they and they only have been so hurt . . . or they get what I like to call "inner laughter," and I wonder if that isn't just maturity.

But it is the thing and, Mims, I'll tell you a secret, women get the thing of which I am speaking oftener than men. I don't know why but it seems to me true . . . the thing that is in Jap's mother and in Eleanor's mother.

I suppose, don't you, that it comes to this . . . Work the best you can, don't expect much, don't depend on fellows like Pryor, and if you do depend on them and they sell you down river, grin.

It's all curious enough, God knows. I think this is true, that if you do at all good work, in any art, you begin to disturb people. Closeness to life always hurts. Well, you do not want to hurt but these darts fly out from under your pen wounding people. It takes, I presume, faith that in the long end it won't hurt and may perhaps even heal.

I must quit jabbering and go to work. I know how your gang always heals me, that I get health when I am among you. It is something, by God, to have made a place like that.

Of course I'll see you all sometime during the holiday season.

Sherwood

I feel that my letter was inadequate . . . too highfalutin perhaps. The real point is after all Pryor, what he stands for, what such fellows do. I used to call them, in my own mind, "the little children of the arts." They mess on the floor, do such dirty things like all children.

There is resentment in them too. Let's say such a one has got dimly a look into the land of reality . . . for the imaginative world in which the artist is sometimes permitted to live at least for moments is more real than the real world. I think they don't stick because the test is too hard for them. There isn't strength.

Then, curiously enough, they begin to hate, can't help hating those who do not turn back.

It is curious about these fellows in writing. I've known so many. There are the fellows who go *Sat. Eve. Post* . . . or Hollywood. They are both too humble and too arrogant. They approach you fawning, wanting, through you, to get back something. It can't be had that way, through another. They grow arrogant, hurtful. You have to go away from them, let them alone.

The idea I did try to express is perhaps sound enough, that the protection we must always seek is that inner laughter . . . that is to say, I presume, to try to take it also as a part of the total picture, this damn fascinating thing . . . life.

Jesus, even at its worst, I wish sometimes I could have a thousand years of it . . .

S.A.

TS. NL

1. Hedgerow actress who had written Anderson from Tonkawa, Okla., while the group was on tour in the Southwest.
2. The booking agent who had arranged the tour. Phillips complained that he was preoccupied with profits rather than artistic standards.
3. Oklahoma author and labor leader whom Phillips had met in Oklahoma City.
4. Phillips had written on stationery with the letterhead of this Oklahoma City hotel.
5. Catherine Rieser, Hedgerow actress who had suggested that Anderson read the Shaw–Ellen Terry letters.

TO Roger Sergel

[late November? 1935, New York?]

Roger

I had just written you a note, cursing you because Eleanor came home saying you had written a letter not sent.

First of all about the matter you mentioned—form in the novel. I know this, that if I were a teacher—and I think you are one—I would say always looseness, looseness.

"Keep it loose."

"Keep it loose."

If you tighten too much you let too much of life get away from it.

And this also—take, for example, the portrait painter. He should be trying to find out something about all life in every portrait he does.

I don't believe I ever made it quite clear to you what brought me into writing (are there 1 or 2 t's in that damned word). I think it was because I, as a lad and later, found I had a kind of gift for making people do what I wanted them to.

And it wasn't long, of course, before I found out that I could use this gift to my own advantage. I was so goddam plausible, persistent—doing it to them—doing it to them—

So I got fed up, sick of it—self sick.

I think that's why a lot of what you say in your last letter—me and posterity etc. etc.—becomes just words, without meaning.

Of course they do something to you if you are successful. You have to be on your guard. I doubt if I am in too much danger of that. I should be able to keep ahead of that.

I think that what happened was that I couldn't find out what made me feel dirty all the time so I began to invent or imagine another outside self, and yet a little projection of self, that I could look at.

In other words I wanted the thing to be if possible curative. You'll see what I mean.

And I think I want it yet, the same, and will to the end, and if I can keep it straight what does or does not happen to me, as regards posterity, fame, all that won't matter one good goddam.

I'm sorry, Roger, but I'm pretty sure Julius and Jimmy[1] won't go far. I think I never did take Jimmy very seriously and as for Julius—after the summer in his company—I'd say frankly to you that without losing any affection I did lose respect.

He has thrown up an amazing protection about himself—against wife, children, families—all—

And then there is too much provincialism. There is, must be, something for the thinker as important as for the artist—movements of life, almost outside thought. Seems to me you are yourself essentially much more truly the thinker.

And it may be that it was that—I mean some confusion—between the thinker and the poet—that stopped your writing—for the time.

For example, the layout you make for me—as regards power—is oh so much a theme for you.

God dammit why don't you elaborate on your own. Don't say—"I can't tackle a thing like that with all this other I've got on hand."

Take it this way. "O.K. This goddam Sherwood needs some education. I can think all around him. I'll now and then write him a letter, setting forth some phase of all this."

Or we might get at it together in this way—not thinking of a book first of all but, if we could, thinking of helping each other. You tell me what you think of this.

There [is] something on with John, something he's trying to say about what he calls Direct Painting. I'll try to keep his brief notes on it together. I might want, one of these days, to turn your mind loose on him.

As regards E.—do you really think (I'm a pig I know) that she will feel more valuable, filled, giving her mind—and body for that matter—to YWCA or anything of the sort than the help she can give me.

If you'll remind me I'd really like to tell you what I think about most of all that—as it goes on just now—

I mean political thinking.

It may be pretty near Frank Knight's[2] point of view.

MS. NL

1. Julius Friend and James Feibleman, New Orleans friends, later the co-authors of *The Unlimited Community: A Study of the Possibility of Science* (London: G. Allen and Unwin, 1936). Friend had visited the Andersons at Ripshin Farm during the previous summer.

2. University of Chicago economics professor and author of *The Ethics of Competition* (New York: Harper, 1935).

TO Miriam Phillips

[late December? 1935, Marion?]

Dear Mims

Jap is such a poor letter writer that I shall have to depend on you to keep me in touch with Hedgerow, what is going [on], what new plays you work on, changes in personnel (as they say in the YWCA) etc., for I do feel that I am in some way a part of it all . . . sort of one of the family, away from home, etc.

I had an impulse to write Jap about something but it is perhaps a writer's idea. It might however also do for painters. I myself find that I cannot start a day's work without writing at least one letter. It seems to do something, take me away from myself and my own annoyances and worries. The idea is to try to establish a kind of circle of people, all workers, who will be personal with one another and not too personal. I do think that you people there . . . it may be a privilege only of theatre people . . that you have an advantage. I can sit there, having a grand violent quarrel with Cele,[1] regarding the South, aristocracy etc. We can even get half angry but the next morning we meet, at breakfast, look at each other, grin and it's gone.

What I have in mind I may have already written to Jap. I often put ideas down in letters and forget who I wrote to—my own impulse being selfish—often just to use another personality to shoot at, to get something clear in my mind if I can.

Anyway there was my son John. He was tremendously tempted by Hedgerow, something he felt there, so that he spoke a good deal . . . for him . . . about the isolation of painters. The truth is that most of the men you meet in America seem so tired . . . I don't quite know why. As soon as ideas are brought up, fought over perhaps, they run to cover . . . or to the *Saturday Evening Post*, as though to say . . . "God protect me in my childhood. Do not disturb it," etc. etc. . . . the curious refusal to take thoughts . . . is it peculiar to America? The idea to break this up. John said, regarding Hedgerow . . . "God, but it's all theatre isn't it?" . . . this however in admiration but also with a feeling that he wanted something of the sort for painters.

What I wonder is, have always a little wondered about, is this . . . does Jap, there, with all you others about, also get this feeling of isolation. He must get it for example when he is among N.Y. theatre people. He must have felt deeply the loss of men, say like Eugene O'Neill, when he felt that O'Neill had more or less given himself to the N.Y. thing.

Does he feel the loss and the need of others or can he live on what he gets there.

These are impertinent questions but they are asked because I do have a feeling that it is time for working artists here to begin to try to work closer together. They do it and have done it in Europe. It may be it cannot be done here . . . physically I mean. After all, in France for example, real things are done by men who work together but Paris is France. Certainly N.Y. is not America. Do you see what I am driving at? Is an attempt at some sort of communication, constantly kept up between say twelve or fifteen men, worth making?

I would be interested in hearing what Jap might say to this. He is one of the really vital men.

Last night for the first time, after I began to feel I must do this novel[2] and after I had written a good chapter the day before, my fancy went back to the theatre . . . this after going to bed . . . and I began to see how I could finish the unfinished play.

As always
Sherwood

TS. NL

1. Cele McLaughlin, actress at Hedgerow.
2. *Kit Brandon*.

TO Jasper Deeter

15 January [1936], Marion

Dear Jap

I wish to god and hell I had your natural toughness. I might possibly get a little work done. I'm always being floored just when I'm going good.

I guess Mims [Phillips] told you that I gave up the idea of sending the Dreiser letter.[1] It wasn't that you talked me out of it. I think I realized later that it was nonsense . . . the sort of thing you do naturally if you wish and that you don't do because someone suggests it.

I have just read Hemingway's *Green Hills of Africa* and am wondering. He is presumed to represent, be, more than any other, the voice of the after-the-war generation . . . you know, Jap, the far-famed lost generation—and I am wondering what, say, Sol, David, Bud[2] would think of him. I wish one or all of them would write and tell me how they feel.

You know, Jap, he went in for a kind of super-realism. The imaginative world, as I understood it, was to be more or less chucked but it seems to me that in trying for this he has only got into a kind of romanticization of the so-called real . . . a kind of ecstasy over elephant dung, killing, death, etc., etc.

And then too he talks about writing the perfect sentence—something of that sort. Isn't that rot? Isn't it what you would call in the theatre "point making"? It seems to me that, with most of us, the struggle is first of all to get others out from between ourselves and the canvas . . . that is to say nature. Usually you have to kick some woman out from between you and it.

And then . . . Christ . . . the hardest of all . . . to kick yourself out.

It seems to me that the theatre for example is and . . . as a Civil War statesman would say . . . "by rights ought to be" . . . a thing in itself, that you can't emphasize reality too much because the reality of the theatre is as real as what they call REALITY . . . etc. etc. Am I talking nonsense?

Hope you aren't all too much fed up on the bus, the road, the work, the broken sleep, the hard work. After all, it is something, perhaps not to old birds like you and Harry,[3] but to the others . . . to see so much of America . . . you know, having this look-see.

I'm leaving here tomorrow and will send you an address when I get to a country where the sun shines and I don't have a lousy snotty nose most of the time.

E.'s chucked—at least temporarily—her YW job and is going with me, wherever I happen to go, and we are going to be citizens of the vast unknown. That sounds pretty swell to me.

God rest your digestive organs.

S.A.

TS. Boston

1. Acting on the idea suggested to Miriam Phillips in the immediately preceding letter, Anderson had written to Theodore Dreiser proposing a network of correspondence among American writers and artists. As he explains, though, he decided not to mail the letter—a copy of which appears in *The Portable Sherwood Anderson*, ed. Horace Gregory (New York: Viking, 1949), 606–12.

2. Sol Jacobson, David Metcalf, and Walter ("Bud") Williams, all actors who had appeared in the Hedgerow production of *Winesburg*.

3. Harry Sheppard, also an actor in the Hedgerow *Winesburg*.

TO Karl Anderson

[16 February 1936, Tucson, Ariz.]

Dear Karl

You see where we have landed. Is it bitterly cold and disagreeable there? Here it is warm . . . a town of say 20,000 at the edge of the desert . . . Mexicans . . . a good many Negroes, cowboys, real and the stage sort . . . ten gallon hats . . . red, blue, green and purple shirts . . . I am getting one of each . . . great wide and really splendid sun-washed spaces . . . giant cactus . . . absolutely everything outdoors is prickly

. . . mud houses, some quite splendid . . . old Spanish churches, often standing quite alone in the desert, beside some dry stream . . . a kind of rare sweet air that makes you feel like assaulting passing females . . .

I could go like this for hours. I'll stop.

We came out through Chicago, E., Mary Emmett and me . . . I spoke there,[1] very very badly . . . then more ice, more snow . . . often not ten miles an hour made. Illinois, Missouri, a corner of Kansas, Oklahoma . . . still snow . . . still ice . . . the panhandle of Texas . . . New Mexico . . . Mabel Dodge,[2] Indian pueblos, then at last the warm and inviting desert.

There are such strange towns, strange places. I really think sometimes I shall travel always. Even the worst of hotel life is so good compared with family life . . . so impersonal, nice, free. We landed here and I think, if Mary hadn't already made arrangements to go on to California, she would also have been here yet. I think we will stay until March 15th and then to New Orleans, where Eleanor has to do some lifting of the proletariat. I'll bet we'll linger there or thereabouts until all the reports of snow, ice and zero get quieter.

I'm about finishing off my novel . . . of prohibition days . . . funny no one else has done that and I am reading daily for my Civil War.[3] It's going to be such a grand impossible thing to tackle.

Love, Karl, and do plan, right from now, to come to us next summer. We want you so much.

Give all my best to Helen and Melissa[4] . . . and of course to that wonder of wonders, Ray[5] . . . if you see him.

Write and say how things go with you.

TS. NL

1. Anderson addressed The Friends of American Authors on 23 Jan.
2. Mabel Dodge Luhan, author and prominent literary figure, living in Taos, N.M.
3. Anderson was projecting a four-volume history of the Civil War, with emphasis on the implications of the war for the beginnings of industrialism.
4. Melissa Anderson, daughter of Karl and Helen.
5. Raymond Anderson, younger brother of Karl and Sherwood.

TO Laura Copenhaver

Sunday [23 February 1936, Tucson, Ariz.]

Dear Mother

The weather here remains grand . . . very warm, so that I am wearing white pants etc. We went yesterday to the rodeo, some of it rather brutal and dangerous but on the other hand some of it . . . the calf and steer roping etc. . . . very exciting. The calf, or steer, half wild things, are turned loose and, at a signal, the cowboy on his pony comes tearing out of a chute. The rope is whirled about his head, the frightened calf bolts, the trained cow pony . . . they are wonderfully intelligent . . . tears after him and the rope is thrown.

It settles about the steer's head, at the base of the horns, and the pony settles back on its haunches, bringing the flying steer to a sudden stop. He is usually thrown clear off his feet and when the pony has stopped, the cowboy, at the same instant, leaps. He rushes over and ties together the feet of the calf so that it is helpless.

In the beginning, in these contests, the calf or steer is given an eighty-yard start and when I tell you that the record for roping, throwing and tying is something like ten seconds you will realize with what wonderful speed and technical beauty the thing is done, a technical beauty in which the pony shares as well as the man, for, when the calf or steer is thrown, the pony constantly keeps him helpless until tied by backing away and keeping him off his feet.

The wonderful thing however is the setting, the grandstand, the colorful crowd, the Indians, Mexicans, and then the grey sand of the desert going away in front and always, in the distance, the fantastic mountains.

You do realize after a time why it is that certain tribes of Indians and certain of the pioneers grew to love this country, so big, so essentially lonely, for we also find ourselves more and more inclined to go away from people out here, get into our little truck and run away to the desert. It becomes itself a kind of companion.

I think E. is really very well. She works every day, sometimes on her own work, sometimes at the typewriter typing my notes on the Civil War.

And in the meantime *Kit* advances toward the finish.

You should have been with us the other day. We were up in the mountains, on a little mountain road, and had stopped at the base of one of the highest peaks near here. I sat down by the car to read in the reminiscences of Davis[1] and presently saw E. climbing up the mountain. There was a twisted path and she went up, kicking to one side mountain lions, wildcats and rattlesnakes, and presently stood upright on the peak, like Balboa (I trust that's the fellow) on his peak in Darien. She looked like a very proud little fly up there and the next day was pretty stiff but very very proud.

We have friends here, at least all we need, best of all a little black Irishman,[2] with a charming wife, very well read and intelligent but not literary, and when we want someone to play about with we play with them.

Anyway your honorable daughter seems very well and is growing more and more saucy. I constantly catch her flirting with handsome men, chiefly cowboys of course, but dare say I'll manage to bring her home.

We are going down into Mexico by a new road this afternoon.

Love
S.A.

TS. NL

1. Probably Jefferson Davis's *The Rise and Fall of the Confederate Government* (1881).
2. Padraic Walsh, a mathematics professor at the University of Arizona.

TO Laura Copenhaver

Saturday [21 March 1936, New Orleans]

Dear Mother . . .

Here we are, after a wonderful trip. It was really gaudy. God what a country.

And Texas. It's so huge, Mother. We had over nine hundred miles of just Texas. We were in the high mountains, on grand upland plains, in deserts, in cattle country, sheep country, the vast plains, plowing going on.

E. told you of our going to the graveyard where your ancestors are buried.[1] I took several pictures. It is no longer used by the town, except that in one end they bury Negroes, but it has real dignity. E. will tell you more about it.

It seems a little German community and I went into a saloon to get beer and there found an old man. He was very old and buttoned his collar at the back so I asked him about the Scherers. "Yes, sir." He took me about, to the house where you were born[2] . . . he said so . . . I of course told him what a distinguished woman you were. "I remember her as a very beautiful little child," he said. The man reminded me strangely of my own father. He said your father was a wonderful preacher. He said . . . "You see before you a man saved from God knows what life of sin by that simple good man's words," so I took him back to the saloon and bought him two large beers. I was sure he was a man, as one might say, wedded from youth to truth. His name he said was Goddard. He had, I thought, a curiously virginal look.

E. didn't see him as she had gone off to the graveyard to copy inscriptions. I took her afterwards to the house of your birth and she thought it quite as good as my own at Camden, Ohio.

Get well quick Mother. Lots of love.

Sherwood

TS. NL

1. In Columbus, Tex., where Laura Copenhaver's father, uncle, and grandfather had settled in the 1850s. Her father, John Jacob Scherer, had been pastor of a Lutheran church and president of Colorado College there before moving to Marion, Va., in 1871.

2. Anderson's anecdote is probably a fabrication intended to please his mother-in-law. According to Eleanor Anderson, he arbitrarily designated a house as the one in which Laura Copenhaver had been born.

TO Maxwell Perkins

29 June 1936, [Ripshin Farm]

Dear Max:

I got the first batch of proofs of the book and your nice letter. I am glad you like the idea of the Rudolph book. In my mind I have already changed the title of it to "Cousin Rudolph."[1] I have been at it almost every day. There is certainly a world of rich material. In fact, there is such a richness of material that it may well turn out that you will have as much trouble with it as you do with a book by Tom Wolfe.

By the way I wrote you a note about doing an article on Tom Wolfe's town. I notice Ham Basso has done something in *New Republic*.[2] If this would stand in the way of the magazine wanting something of the kind, I know you fellows will say so. I can't think of any magazine to do it for other than *Scribner's*. What I had in mind would be quite unlike the Basso article.

I am being very busy, not only working on the Rudolph book but finishing off the last of the one-act plays.[3] When I am clear of them and I am now on the last one, I expect to devote the summer to Rudolph's adventures.

By the way I have a very glowing letter from Jasper Deeter at Hedgerow Theatre near Media, Penna., in regard to the *Winesburg* play. I am going to enclose a copy of the letter. They have made a new setting for the play and I wish sometime you could run out there and see it. I have asked Deeter to send you the schedule showing when it is to be done. It is a repertory theatre. It is about a three-hours drive from New York. You go through the Holland Tunnel and follow number 1 to Media and there is a nice inn on the way within a quarter of mile from the theatre. I may run up there myself for a weekend in July or August and perhaps you could come over and meet me. I will write you about this when I know about my own going. If you want I could pick you off the train in Philadelphia.

I had a day with Basso who said he was about ready with his novel.[4] He didn't speak of it and I didn't ask questions. I didn't feel him too cheerful. I don't know why.

About *Kit*—I wish, as you read it, you would feel free to mark all of it that seems to you useless repetition—also any places in the novel that do not seem to carry the story forward or that seem to you to hurt it. As you suggest, the repetitions are sometimes intended to catch a kind of prose rhythm but in doing this a man is likely to fall into too many repetitions. As I suggested, I will be very grateful to you for any help you can give me as I have a belief that this novel has a pretty good chance of catching a rather wide public. It seems to me much more objective than most of my novels.

I am enjoying the Whitman book.[5] I see it is not a Scribner's book and I am afraid it is out of your personal library and I will therefore return it to you as soon as I have finished reading it and taking some notes.

Sincerely yours,
Sherwood Anderson

TS. Princeton

1. An autobiographical work, not completed, earlier called "Rudolph's Book of Days."
2. Hamilton Basso published "Thomas Wolfe: A Portrait" in *New Republic* 87 (24 June 1936): 199–202.
3. Anderson was planning an evening of one-act plays, consisting of "Triumph of the Egg," "They Married Later," and the one he was completing, "Tobacco Market."
4. *Courthouse Square* (1936). Anderson visited Basso in Brevard, N.C., on 24 June.
5. *Walt Whitman and the Civil War*, ed. Charles I. Glicksberg (1933).

TO Laura Copenhaver
[25 July 1936, Ripshin Farm]

Dear Mother—

I haven't written you for a long time. It's odd that, when I do see you, we so often get into some discussion, like that the other night . . . "God or no God, etc., etc.," my real love of you, surely as strong as I could have for my own mother, or a sister, never coming out.

You & E.—how really precious you are to me.

And Mr. C. too and also Miss May.[1]

I don't know why I want to tell you this, in words, this particular morning.

I am deep in the "Cousin Rudolph"—such fun, Mother. I am writing these last ten days with a kind of gaiety I never knew before. Except when I wrote *A Story Teller's Story*. It seems to me a kind of joyousness like I feel sometimes in dead leaves dancing along a dirty town street in the fall—

As though nature itself were speaking in me—joyousness, even in death.

Absurdity and splendor of human aspirations.

I do, Mother, feel a new kind of—what shall I call it—"maturity," I guess.

Something too—you and your house have brought me.

S.A.

MS. NL

1. May Scherer, long-time dean of Marion College and sister of Laura Copenhaver, lived with the Copenhavers.

TO Ferdinand Schevill

Thursday [24 September 1936, Marion]

Dear Ferdinand—

Excuse pencil. I am sitting on Mother Copenhaver's front porch. It's raining. Have got the flu licked I think. If I keep feeling stronger and better will go to New York next week.

I keep thinking about the *Florence*[1]—its real beauty. It has given me a kind of new horizon, the past pointing down into the present, the present into the past . . . a kind of continual flow of life out of the old into the new.

Also, I think, dear man, a new light on what scholarship really means.

I think I did have a little fear of something—so many long years of class room, fear perhaps that something of the class room would get in. It's so clear of all that, the flow going on so naturally, like a great river.

I have been through something that will perhaps amuse you. It concerns Mrs. Emmett, wife of a friend who died a year and a half ago. He was a nice fellow, art patron, left her a million more or less.

She rather dropped herself on us, was lonely. She proposed giving me an income, $3000.00 a year. It was rather suggested as a kind of memorial to her dead husband, etc. I never actually took any of it.

I presume, Ferdinand, there will always be some fear left in me.

For a good many years I worked, as you know, as an advertising writer out there, in Chicago.

I would get a few hundred ahead, go off, write something like *Poor White, Winesburg, A Story Teller's Story*, etc., and then back into that filth of word use—advertising.

I tried to be cheerful about it, not to belly ache, but I never did make any real money.

Sometimes I wake up in the night yet, a kind of dread on me. "Will I yet, someday, have to go back to that?" It's silly, just an old fear. It has been hard sometimes to shake it off.

I don't think the other temptation to go cheap, the movies, etc., has ever touched me much.

I suppose I thought of the offer of Mary's as perhaps lifting, finally, that old fear.

It hasn't worked out. Something happened. Even though no money had been passed actually I became, in a more and more distinct way, the poor, lonely, rich old woman's private property.

It got worse when I was ill. When I got some better, Eleanor had to go off to New York, to her job. Mary, who was here, stayed on.

She became more and more assertive, dogmatic, rather terrible. Being ill, I couldn't escape her.

At last I thought of something. I got up a cock and bull story that the doctor has told me I must go away, get new scenes etc. and got, still very weak, on a train. I went over to Knoxville and stayed in a hotel sending back word I was going on, to Chicago, Minneapolis etc. Just a plain case of cowardly running away I guess, but I was just too weak to tell her to get the hell out.

I couldn't be rude to the damn lonely old tyrant.

So she went off to New York and now I'm writing her, telling her the stuff, about the money, etc., is off. As soon as she was gone I began to get well.

Am I a damned rotter, or what?

Dear man—I don't see any reason why you should not think of Ripshin for summers as though it belonged to you. We want you so much, both of us. You must know it.

And after all—where will you find another such a croquet opponent.

We love you.

S.A.

MS. NL

1. Schevill's book, *History of Florence from the Founding of the City through the Renaissance* (New York: Harcourt, Brace, 1936).

TO Laura Copenhaver

[9 November 1936, New York]

Dear Mother.

It was good to get your grand letter. We'll probably leave here Thursday, spend Thursday night at Mazie's,[1] Friday in Washington and home Saturday evening.

Yes Mother, I know about Ham Basso.[2] Let it go. It's so mixed up —feelings having nothing to do with me, his own right to live not earned—inordinate ambitions.

It is the very force of *Kit* that raises all this. I believe that. If it were really second-rate in conception, in execution, it would be easier for such men.

It is a bit silly, my making the comparison, but you know, Mother, how hate was poured over Roosevelt.

Why—

Because he had a conception of government. I believe that.

And I also have a conception of art—a real one. I know that. It hurts and reproaches men who haven't. All I have to do, to make all such men happy, is to die.

I won't.

They feel me, sometimes, being honest where they have been dishonest. They fear and even hate, not me, but honesty in work—which makes such demands.

It has happened whenever a really significant book of mine has been published. It used to be a great sickness for me. It isn't any more.

Lots of times I think it is because I have Eleanor—

And you too.

Yes—it would be nice if you would invite Mary for a few days, at the Christmas time.

Love,
S.A.

Drove out to Karl's, with Mary, E. and John Emerson yesterday. Karl gave a big party—very very nice. We had a grand time.

MS. NL

1. May ("Mazie") Copenhaver Wilson of Baltimore, a younger sister of Eleanor Anderson.

2. Mrs. Copenhaver had asked if some spite had motivated Basso's largely negative review of *Kit Brandon* in *New Republic* 88 (21 Oct. 1936): 318.

TO Roger Sergel

[23 December 1936, Marion]

Dear Roger . . .

I guess this will not reach you until after Christmas but, anyway, greeting to Ruth and the boys.

Have been rather in a jam here. Jap Deeter and Ferd Nofer[1] and Miss Phillips, the three most responsible for everything about the tone of things at Hedgerow, suddenly appeared at the hotel here. The theater is closed while everyone takes a Christmas vacation and they wanted to talk, make plans for the coming year, thresh out problems, etc. You see it is rather like a big family and, like a family also, puzzling personal problems appear and, I guess, they felt that, as I had been about the place so much and rather knew everyone there personally, and was, at the same time, an outsider, it would be well to have me in on the discussions.

And so we have been sitting, hour after hour, day after day, and until after midnight, talking and talking, and it has been on the whole good . . .

Especially for me now. As to whether I was able to help in their problems, that is a matter about which I have my doubts. But, as for myself, I have been, or was, until they came, in one of the worst glooms I've been in for years.

I don't just know why, except that it has been dominated by a terrible feeling of futility. It often happens after the publication of a book. You must know the feeling . . . that you have anyway poured all you have into something and then that it has been rather like a child and, taking it in your arms, you have gone and dropped it down a deep hole and walked away.

And what did you want? I swear, Roger, I don't know but do know that it has been good to have all this whirlpool of thoughts in self quieted and to be thinking, even a little, of the problems of others.

While they were here we took several long drives, one to Ripshin in deep snow and another to the tobacco market, so, I guess, they had a good time and did not sense the beast, lying in wait, to jump on my shoulders again as soon as they left.

John, who expected to be here at Christmas, has gone instead to Michigan City, Indiana, just, as you know, out of Chicago. His mother has been ill. Do have him in for an evening. He can be reached c/o Mrs. Cornelia Anderson . . . 227 East 10th Street, Michigan City.

There are a thousand things I'd like to talk over with you. I should write pages. I probably won't. As for work I write and write, day after day, and throw away. All seems bad. I do very much wish that the *Winesburg* thing out there[2] may come off and, I think, chiefly because it might lead to seeing you. It is likely that Jap's company may go for a week in Boston, and he tells me that one of the plays asked for there is *Winesburg*. He is also playing with the idea of taking the company for a week in some New York theater and, if he does, will try doing *Winesburg* there.

In the meantime I sit here by a window in Mother's house, still and in spite of this feeling I have, now writing and writing what will presently go out the window. Aint it hell, what we are, both and all of us?

Anyway . . . love to all in your house. E. will be here tomorrow and will, perhaps, shake me out of it.

S.A.

TS. NL

1. Actor who played Tom Willard in the first Hedgerow production of *Winesburg*.
2. The Federal Theatre Project was considering a production of *Winesburg* in Chicago.

TO Mary Emmett

Monday[22 February 1937], Corpus Christi, Texas

Dear Mary.

So this is the 1st letter I've written by my own hand since coming from the hospital Saturday. I was really a sick lad, this time.[1] I have an idea myself that there has been a low infection, from the sinus, poisoning a little the stomach & intestines.

So I caught flu & it hit me there, as my weak point. For a week nothing would stay down. Such vomiting. Oh, how sick I was.

The doctor,[2] a Jew, much more the surgeon than physician. It's a wonder he didn't insist on an operation. He laughed later & told me he had been tempted. Think he rather took a liking to me.

Now I am out. I eat, walk about, sleep, eat again. The great weakness goes away.

And how good you have been. Well I'll not speak more of gratitude.

Even there, while so ill, in hospital something interesting. I kept talking to other patients, getting their stories. There was an oil well driller,[3] young and handsome, who had been operated. I found out from him 1000 things about his trade. Others too.

Mary, my love, I will write more when I'm stronger. It will come fast—the good clear sunshiny days have come.

Sherwood

MS. NL

1. Anderson was taken ill while vacationing in Corpus Christi.
2. Dr. Jerome Nast.
3. Rush Weatherby, with whom Anderson shared the hospital room.

TO Thomas Wolfe

27 July [1937, Boulder, Colo.]

Dear Tom

I was glad to get your note. It came to me out here, where they do seem to have a mighty vivid memory of you.[1]

Am afraid this writers' conference will have a bad effect on me. I'll

Sherwood and Eleanor Anderson at Writers' Conference in Boulder, Colorado
COURTESY OF ELEANOR ANDERSON

become a moralist. When I meet a woman who thinks she wants to write, I feel like saying—"What t'ell for?"

I imagine I'll do about as I fancy you did. I'll look at the country and the people, get my wife to read the manuscripts, and do a fair amount of drinking.

They all seem decent enough people. Why do decent people want to write. That should be left to us bastards.

We'll head out of here August 11th. I drove my car to Chicago and I'll pick it up there. Hope to be home, in my own shack and tending to my own business, about August 15th. You might drift down that way. We'll be there until well into September.

O.K.?

Sherwood Anderson

MS. Harvard

1. Wolfe had attended the Writers' Conference at the University of Colorado in 1935.

TO Mary Emmett

Thursday 9 September [1937, Ripshin Farm]

Dear Mary

"The piece of paper"[1] came and many many thanks. It happens that I will have to reroof the house before I leave this fall. The old shingles are giving way and there are a good many leaks. I am afraid that if I let it go the plaster will be ruined. I am going to put on the green prepared shingles.

The flowers are still lovely and we have had an abundance for the house. Nothing is nicer than the bright blue petunias. They are still blooming away.

Paul Rosenfeld is here, for a week and, yesterday, Tom Wolfe came for a day. He is six feet six, a giant of a man, big in every way . . . a great boy. He spreads out like his books. There wasn't a bed in the house long enough for him. What a flood of talk and, Mary, you should see him eat. Ruby[2] made corn cakes for breakfast and he got behind a dozen of them.

Paul brought us some beautiful phonograph records and so we have had some evening concerts.

John is making an application for the Guggenheim. He has been doing some mighty good work.

And that is about all our news. Ethel[3] wrote E. about our coming to 54. I think E. answered her.

And how gorgeous your trip sounds. It was the thing to do. I was sure it would be great for Alice.[4]

I have been plugging away at the novel.[5] Can't tell yet what it will amount to but it is different from anything I've done. I sit and write and giggle.

It will be swell to see you again. Don't run off with a French count or a German baron.

Lots of love.

Sherwood

TS. NL

1. That is, a check.
2. Ruby Sullivan, who was working at Ripshin as housekeeper.
3. Ethel Miller, a Washington Mews friend of Mary Emmett and the Andersons.
4. Alice Wolf, a friend of Mary Emmett.
5. "How Green the Grass," not published.

TO Thomas Wolfe

29 September 1937, [Marion]

Dear Tom

Your letter was like you, warm and alive. It had the surge of the life in you. There are some men you know, by their work, before you ever see them. They become, in advance, your friend. You trust them, believe in them. You are one.

I just can't believe, Tom, that you will, in the end, have any real trouble in getting published.[1] Every man of force and originality has some trouble. My own *Winesburg* went begging a long time and you know the story of Dreiser's *Sister Carrie*.

I don't know, Tom. Lots of times, since you were here, I have walked about thinking of you and your problem. I keep wondering if it is not personal, often a too great surge toward other people and things. You are very strong and you want to take life into your fists and shake it into order. I guess we all feel that vast order, just there, a bit always just beyond the horizon. We rush at it and it recedes.

I keep thinking. I've lived a long time now in the country. There is something beautiful even fine here . . . in men I mean. You see them year after year, often on poor farms. Such terrible things happen, crop failures, droughts, floods, but next year you will see them again. When spring comes. They are again plowing.

I went yesterday to see some men threshing grain. There was a field, a steep hillside field, that had been planted to rye. It was tough plowing in the spring, I'll tell you. There were two acres. It didn't turn out. The straw was long but the grain heads small. It only threshed out eighteen acres [bushels?] but the man didn't start tearing any trees out of the ground, didn't make a bonfire of his fences. I saw him laughing and joking about it with the others.

I guess, by God, Tom, we need a hell of a lot of this patience. I guess we need to know that, if it's there, it will come out into the light. There was a French firm took the rights to a book of mine and didn't publish for five years.[2] I was in Paris and went to see them.

"Is it a good book?" he said.

"You're damn right it is," I said.

"Well, then, if it's good, it will still be good when we do publish it."

I had to laugh at that.

Anyway, Tom, all I care is that nothing wears you out, checks the flood of you. I don't want you to wear yourself out. There are too many niggardly men. Maybe, Tom, you'd better go live in Texas. There's a state with size and sweep to it. They'd like you and you'd like them, down there.

I love your guts, Tom. You are one who is O.K. Don't know when I'll be in New York. I may go out to Chicago for a month first. I've got a sudden feel for Chicago. Just now I've got to stay here and reroof the house.

Sherwood

TS. Harvard

1. Wolfe had decided to leave his publisher, Scribner's.

2. Gaston Gallimard actually took seven years before publishing in 1927 the French translation of *Winesburg*.

TO Charles H. Funk

[23 October 1937, New York]

Dear Andy

The last few times I have been with you I have been, I have realized, a bit on edge, sometimes perhaps rude. You often laugh about the idea of such fellows as me speaking of work. Also you sometimes speak of the books you intend to write. I wish you would write one. I'd like you to tackle a long story, many people involved, the effort to get inside them, get a little at their thoughts and actions, be compelled to hold the balance of something of the sort, likely, at any moment, to explode into nothingness, under your hand. I doubt if you would laugh at the idea that it is work, after that.

I think that in our relations there are certain things we'd better let alone. Of course, on certain subjects, I know you are joking but sometimes the jokes hit on old sore places in my life you can know nothing about and I fly off the handle, am not myself. I value your friendship too much to want to spoil it some day, by saying things that might hurt you.

The truth is that, at bottom, I guess I'm not a kidder. I'm not so young any more and, most of the time, I'm in a hurry to do things I'll probably never get done.

Anyway I want you to know that, in spite of all this, I realize the essential allrightness in you.

Thank you. Step aside.

S.A.

TS. NL

TO Laura Copenhaver

Thursday [11 November 1937, New York]

Dear Mother—

I am leaving here, this P.M.—for Philadelphia and Eleanor will join me there tomorrow—Bellevue-Stratford. We will drive down to Baltimore on Saturday morning and leave there that night—Eleanor for Chicago and me for Charleston.[1]

We had a cocktail party last night—Dreiser, Paul [Rosenfeld], Joe & Ann,[2] Maud Fangel,[3] Joe Taulane—Joe is the boy who did George Willard in *Winesburg*. He is now a New York actor.

Yesterday I was called to the Algonquin Hotel. Bill Faulkner had been there, on a big drunk, for a week. The poor chap is an alcoholic. He had been so for two weeks. A friend[4] had been sticking to him and trying to straighten him out. The friend was exhausted. Bill had been wandering—nude—about the hotel corridors.

We got Dr. Joe up there and he gave Bill something to make him sleep. We got a nurse in. They hope to get him off for home—Oxford, Miss.—today.

Dreiser seemed very well.

Mary will be in some time late today but I'll be gone.

A woman, named Mayorga[5]—one of our Colorado friends—came in and I went off with her to see the play—*Susan and God*.[6] E. wouldn't go—claimed she had to pack—had a headache etc.

Well, the play gave me a headache. It is a play on the Oxford movement—pretty shallow & second rate, I think.

It is pretty hard to work here—too much ringing of the phone—the door bell, etc. When I come back I'm going to get a work room outside. Will drop you a card, giving Charleston address.

Love
Sherwood

Also love to Aunt May.

MS. NL

1. Anderson spoke at a meeting of the Poetry Society of South Carolina on 16 Nov.
2. Joseph and Ann Girsdansky, New York physician and his wife.
3. New York socialite and friend of Karl Anderson.
4. Eric J. Devine, who had written Anderson asking for help in getting Faulkner back to Mississippi.
5. Margaret Mayorga, whom the Andersons had met at the Writers' Conference in Boulder, Colo., the previous summer.
6. Written by Rachel Crothers.

TO Miriam Phillips

Wednesday [8 December 1937, New York]

Dear Mims . . .

It was good to get your letter. We have been expecting Jap, or some of the rest of you, to be in town. We are still at Mary's, 54 Washington Mews, although I do not work there. I have got a room, in an old hotel, below 8th street, on Broadway, called the Broadway Central, and am there every day, from about nine in the morning and until two or three in the afternoon. The phone at Mary's is Gramercy 7-4373 and here, at my work place, it is Spring 7-2600. You ask for room 465.

As for this weekend. We are free Saturday night. On Sunday, 5 to 7, a man named Charles Studin,[1] at 12 East 10th Street, is giving a cocktail party for me and my brother Karl. If either you or Jap are in town please do come to it. On Monday night we are asked to dinner at Dr. Joe Girsdansky's, 16 East 9th Street, and he would be mightily pleased to have either one or both of you. If you can be there drop me a line so I can tell him you are coming.

And by the way, there is a comfortable bed at this very very Jewish hotel that I do not use at night. It is a really wonderful place, Mims, with old bearded men in the elevators and a kosher restaurant upstairs. Think of a place where the hotel clerk begins to talk with you about one of your stories and where the manager comes shyly to you and asks you if he may send his son to have a conversation with you. I got into it by accident. While looking for some such place to work that didn't cost too much, I happened to meet, on the street, a Jewish poet who brought me here. I am quite in love with the place.

As for the trip home. Eleanor has to work until about the 22nd or 23rd and I guess it will be a rush down for the Christmas celebration.

I want to see you, and Jap. I hope you do come soon.

Lots of love.

Sherwood

TS. NL

1. New York attorney who frequently gave parties for writers, artists, and musicians.

TO Laura Copenhaver

Tuesday [15 February 1938], San Antonio, Texas

Dear Mother . . .

As I write you are still on the train[1] and, as you see, we are still here. We have turned over R.'s place to Mary and the woman Winona[2] . . . whose coming is, I assure you, going to be a great help and we stayed on a day longer than expected to let E. clean up the last of her work and because Mary seems enamored of R.'s place.

What a gal! The Mrs. Allen has a tale to tell of the drive down, Mary getting in one of her curious contrary hard-headed moods, insisting on driving from Marion to New Orleans in one day etc. She, that is Mrs. Allen, was on the point of just getting out of the car and going back home but stuck it out. I made Mary take the car to a repair man yesterday and he said that the front axle was bent and the two front wheels all out of gear. "How anyone ever got here alive with that car I don't know," he said. She will manage to kill herself on one of these drives alone yet and the joke is that she thinks of herself as a good driver.

It seems that, for some reason, I am the only one who can make her behave. She was terribly afraid Mrs. A. would tell me of her bad behavior coming down and made her swear to keep it secret, a promise that Mrs. A. of course promptly broke.

And it is well she did, as M., to cover up the fact that she had almost smashed the car three times on the trip, would have gone on with it as it was.

All of this mixed up with a curious generosity, wanting really to give Mrs. A. a fine trip etc. etc. She is and will be as gentle as a lamb now. But I swear that neither you nor E. shall ever take a trip with her.

Great swarms of planes in the air yesterday, flying in formation, at one time almost a hundred machines up, the whole thing curiously and strangely impressive. They are so like great monstrous insects, of some new terrible sort.

We have got our entrance cards into Mex. and will, I presume, be off in the morning. E. is just giving the address Gen. Delivery, Mexico City at present. She is well and in fine spirits and I am still writing busily. I am as you perhaps know ashamed of my own outbreak in the car, apropos of K.,[3] but what is done is done. There is in me a thing from which I will never recover, a kind of inner shrinking when people talk of aristocracy, giving the word the meaning it has got and a basic feeling also that all of this, the attempt to bolster oneself up thus, notion of self superiority thus built up, has been one of the very great evils of life, always defeating any real democratic give and take and adding to the separateness that makes all of life at times so terrible.

Lots of love to you and to all there. Do you not think it possible that when a word, such as the one spoken of above, has been abused long enough it comes to lose all value and had better be entirely discarded?

Love again
S.A.

TS. NL

1. Laura Copenhaver was returning to Marion after having come with the Andersons to San Antonio to visit her son, Randolph Copenhaver, an air force physician.
2. Mary Emmett and a friend, Winona Allen, arrived on 13 Feb.
3. Katharine Van Meier, Eleanor Anderson's sister, living in Stillwater, Minn.

TO Roger Sergel

30 March 1938, [Brownsville, Tex.]

Dear Roger . . .

As you will see we are out of Mexico but, as Eleanor does not have to get back to her job until the 15th, we have stopped here, at the mouth of the Rio Grande, about as far south as we can be and still be in the USA. We came on out of Mexico for two reasons . . . first that I wanted some time alone with E. and second that, just now, I do not believe that the feeling toward Americans is any too cordial.

Not that anything happened to spoil our good time there but there is this jam, the government at war with the American and British oil companies, the people very much for their President . . . Cárdenas[1] . . . the general feeling that the country has been too long exploited by outsiders and this more or less reflected in the whole attitude toward all Americans.

God, what a country, Roger. In these northern states, just south of the USA, you feel some of our influence but, further south, when you get below Monterrey, say a hundred miles below the border, you certainly get into something new, often strangely attractive, certainly sometimes pretty savage.

And then the whole history of the country. Exploitation and more and more of it for so long. The living conditions of most of the people . . . Indians . . . so brutally primitive. Nevertheless a something you feel in the people. It's hard to name it. It is a kind of rhythm, a dancing laughter underneath, a refusal to accept our northern idea of what a civilization should be. It is as though they were so used to poverty that they can stand anything but, with all of this, a feeling that they have their own determined point of view.

I really think that we might well be fooled by this people, that it is possible that they may slowly get a kind of civilization unique and that they may be able to do it by an ability to go through hardships for it that we are now too soft to stand. Lord, how I wish that you and Ruth and, more particularly, the boys could have been through this whole experience down here. I mean just the seeing. It may be that we . . . meaning myself, you, Ruth, Eleanor etc. are in the wrong generation to get it. You get the feeling that this people may possibly get at some real kind of socialism by a new technique, by the ability to go without, a thing we older ones talk about a lot but seem unable to do.

It's pretty strange. In spite of our living conditions, at least a dozen generations ahead of these Indians, we seem, comparatively, so tense, so essentially unhappy about it while these people can still dance, sing, get into their bodies some kind of earth rhythm we miss.

I think of ____, so tense about his Trotskyism, compared to one of these Indian boys we perhaps pick up along the road . . . he riding on the running board of our car . . . the kind of laughing thing you feel in him.

And, underneath, I'm sure, just as determined.

Can it be because they have been licked and licked, so often and for so long, so that they do not have to make the great decision . . . to be successful or not successful . . . they having no chance at that, so that they can relax to life.

It is something puzzling and certainly educational.

And do tell the Perrys[2] how grateful we are for giving us the names of their two friends in Mexico City . . . very very swell gals indeed.

I told a man, met at Acapulco, to call you and taunt you a bit for not coming. Acapulco was so grand.

As for the Barton matter, I am leaving it more or less up to the Authors' League to get me out of it, by compromise or any other way. I was the fool who got into it. I presume I ought to pay for being a fool.

Lots of love to you all. We will be back in Marion at least by the 15th.

S.A.

[P.S. in Eleanor Anderson's hand] Did you see Craven in *Scribner's* (April)[3]—it certainly makes your idea seem better.

TS. Va.

1. Lázaro Cárdenas, president of Mexico from 1934 to 1940, who had just expropriated all foreign-owned oil companies.
2. University of Chicago professor and his wife, who had suggested to the Andersons that they go to Mexico and referred them to two friends there, Lena Strackbein and Betty Kirk.
3. Thomas Craven, "Double-Dealers in Art," *Scribner's* 103 (Apr. 1938): 9–15, on the exploitive practices of unscrupulous art dealers.

TO Karl Anderson

Thursday [June 1938], Ripshin Farm

Dear Karl

It was mighty good to get your letter but sad to hear of the loss of your good friend.[1] We are, both of us, I presume, getting there, to where our friends drop off about us. As you know I never knew Hal well. It is strange how early memories stick. I remember sharply a day . . . I must have been a small boy and Hal perhaps a student in college. He came home and joined others who were skating up on Waterworks Pond, in Clyde. I stood by a small fire the boys had built and he asked me to hold his overcoat, afterwards paying me for my trouble, and I still remember what seemed to me the extraordinary fineness of the cloth and the lining of the coat and with what sharp pleasure I caressed the fabric so that I think that forever afterwards Hal has remained in my mind in connection with the incident and with the whole idea of elegance.[2]

I had an offer to do a ten thousand word story for one of the more popular magazines,[3] for which I was to be well paid, and sent an outline which they liked and so started but, immediately, the people of the tale got out of hand, got completely away, I am afraid, from both the outline and from the demands of such magazines but, having got into it, it has got into me so that I shall perhaps have a novel out of it.[4]

Do come to us, Karl, when you can. We must go west from July 1 to about the 15th but, after that, will be here all summer. It may be we can catch a sight of you on the way west as we plan to go by way of Cleveland to deliver there a friend of Eleanor's.[5] I'll write before we set out on the trip and anyway we'll be counting on you later.

Sherwood

Mary Emmett asked me to ask you to drop in on her occasionally when you are in New York. She will come here later.

TS. NL (ph)

1. Hal Ginn, whose friendship with Karl Anderson is described in *Memoirs*, 101.
2. Anderson refers to this brief incident in *Tar*, 278, and in his *Memoirs*, 519–20.
3. *Redbook* had offered $1,500 for a "romance."
4. "A Late Spring," never published.
5. Annetta M. Dieckmann, Chicago YWCA executive. The Andersons left her in Cincinnati, rather than Cleveland, on 3 July and went on to a YWCA conference in Milford, Iowa.

TO Charles H. Funk

Wednesday [29 June 1938], Ripshin Farm

Dear Andy . . .

I am at work on a long story[1] about a country boy, of a very poor family, who became a lawyer and finally a judge. It is not a very large part of my story but, the other evening, when you were talking by the fire, telling of the different approaches to the study of the law, giving some account of the professors, the different branches of law studied etc., I wished I could take notes. I fancy my young fellow going to just such a school, in just such surroundings as the one you attended. To be sure, in using any such material I would change it about, to be unrecognizable, but I wonder if you would mind writing me a letter, telling me just about what you told me the other evening, as a kind of basis, the different branches of law to be studied, a bit about each, something about the professors, anything you know of their past, a short description of one of the moot trials, books read and studied, what you said about the great principle of law to which there were so many exceptions, what that law is etc.

I can promise you that I will not use the material in any way that will embarrass you. My idea is that you might dictate such a letter, very much as you talked and any touches you might add.

It was ungentlemanly of me to show you up as such a sap at croquet but I won't tell anyone. I know you must be suffering a terrible humiliation as it is.

As always
S.A.

TS. NL

1. "A Late Spring."

TO Lewis and Nancy Galantière

[c. 30 August 1938, Ripshin Farm]

Dear Lewis and Nancy

It was very very lonely here after you two left. Major[1] and I took the cot back to the green house, he at one end and me at the other. We sang "Nearer My God to Thee" and "I Am So Glad Salvation's Free." The garden seemed empty, the house empty. Our songs didn't in the least cheer us up. I really don't think that Ruby and Charlotte[2] have put on clean aprons since you left. They must have taken some sort of vow.

There has been a circus in Troutdale. Bob has got himself elected president of the state Young Democrats. Mary built a place for next year's flowers, to raise young plants. She hired Major and his brother. She went to the woods and got leaf mould, got sand, got manure, got lime, got black earth, brown, red, grey earth. She sifted all through a screen. She stood over the two men. She was magnificent.

"Now a shovel of this. Now a half shovel of that."

I have to confess something to you, Lewis. You will remember the two big poison mushrooms I brought from the woods. I had in mind feeding them to you and Eleanor. I thought of stealing Mary's station wagon, loading Nancy in it. "Away to where the blue begins." There was something of that sort in my mind. I weakened. I was afraid to mention the matter to her. I may do it later.

You were the damnedest nicest guests we ever had. We love you.

Sherwood

TS. Columbia

1. Major Sullivan, son of Ripshin Farm caretaker, John Sullivan.
2. Ruby and Charlotte Sullivan, daughters of John Sullivan.

TO Roger Sergel

[c. 6 September 1938, Ripshin Farm]

Dear Roger,

It seems a long long time since I have heard from you. We have had a very happy summer. As for work, not too much done. I wrote 40,000 words of a novel.[1] Dissatisfied. Started again. 30,000 words. Still dissatisfied. I was seeking a form that would bring me a feeling of looseness and ease. In the meantime I wrote some pretty good short stories.

Suddenly I decided to go back to the *Winesburg* form. That is really a novel. It is a form in which I feel at ease. I invented it. It was mine. "Why not use it," I told myself.

Lewis Galantière and Laura Copenhaver at Ripshin Farm
COURTESY OF ELEANOR ANDERSON

Since then I have been happier and have been doing work I feel I can send to the stenographer. What I now hate most is the thought that summer will soon end. We have to go to New York Oct. 1st. Eleanor has been made head of the whole industrial department.[2] She felt she had to take the job. More and more I become a country man loving more and more this place. I can't stay here alone. I should have two wives.

We have had good company, although we did feel cheated about you & Ruth. Schevill and Lovett[3] are coming at the end of this week.

God knows when I shall see you all. I am making a rogues gallery[4]—of men loved and admired. I'm sure I wrote you about it. I want your own photograph. Don't put it off.

Love to all,
Sherwood

MS. NL

1. "A Late Spring."

2. Eleanor Anderson became Industrial Secretary of the YWCA, a position she held until 1947.

3. Robert Morss Lovett, English professor at the University of Chicago.

4. After securing a large number of photographs from friends, Anderson hung most of them on the walls of a bedroom at Ripshin.

TO Mary Emmett

Monday [31 October 1938, New York]

Dear Mary . . .

I have been looking through the book . . *The Left Bank*.[1] It is all right but I think it does tend to give to the life of the artist some of the same false glamour that I was speaking about in my letter to Andy. It is doing the same thing to the artist as was done to the American cowboy. It too much separates the life of the artist from the ordinary life of the ordinary man. I remember being in Paris at about the time this man is writing about and used to go to both the Rotonde and the Dome. At that time Paul, having suddenly inherited some money from an aunt he had forgotten, decided to ask me to go to France with him and spend it.[2] We met most of the poets and painters. I think there is a kind of falseness here, in this book.

You see, Mary, if it were true that the life of the artist were so much separated from the life of others his art would mean nothing. They did just this sort of thing to Gauguin and to Van Gogh after they died. They put this false glamour on it all. It is only as he feels everything others feel, meets the same discouragements, has the same disillusionments, eats the same food, makes a fool of himself like others, does mean and generous things like others that the artist can work at all. If there is a separation it lies in the ability to occasionally go more out of himself, away from self and into others . . . just as you sometimes speak of your own feeling when acting, the painter surrendering to something in nature, the musician to sounds, the writer to his characters. There are times when self is thus thrown away and, as we all want to escape from self, we envy him in doing it.

But we shouldn't so completely separate him from ourselves. We do him a wrong thus. We falsify. I am sure you see what I mean.

And I don't think, really, we should be too sorry for the artist who happens to be let alone, not recognized. Recognition has its terrible side too and starvation isn't the worse fate man has to endure.

This is the Left Bank letter I didn't give you.[3]

TS. NL

1. Probably the English translation, published by Liveright in 1931, of *Les Montparnos* (1924) by Michel Georges-Michel.
2. See letter to Paul Rosenfeld, 23 Jan. 1921.
3. Anderson added this note after neglecting to mail the letter. See letter of 3 Nov. 1938, p. 225.

TO Roger Sergel

Tuesday [1 November 1938, New York]

Dear Roger . . .

I have not heard from you for a long time. We are in New York, have been here for two weeks. Eleanor came on ahead and I drove up. We are leaving tonight or in the morning for Niagara Falls, where E. is attending one of her conferences. We hope to make the trip up there a kind of delayed honeymoon.

I didn't much fancy coming to the city but I have made no money this year and so E. must work. I have been through a rather longer than usual depressed time. It may be allergy . . . allergic to Hitler, to the ugly thing going on so rapidly, apparently growing. I keep clinging to the idea that men will not stand for it but who knows? Historically such times have sometimes lasted a long time. I have been trying to get back to something. It is so obvious that the individual man can do nothing and, when I am most healthy, my inclination has been to avoid the illusion that I can think or feel nationally or internationally. I have been trying again to get back to entire absorption in some individual life, some little girl, or man, struggling along in life. Lately, for the last week or two I have been a little succeeding in this. It has helped.

I keep thinking of it as I walk about in the streets here. There are these crowds, masses of people. How can anyone think of them in the mass.

When you begin, with your eye, to pick out individuals, wonder about them, it gets a little better.

It was very beautiful in the country before we left and it may be that I have grown more and more a countryman.

But enough of me. How are you and how are you taking life just now? I would like to hear from you. Mary came down before we left the country and did some wonderful work with our garden and hedge. She has grown more mellow. She seems to have adopted us and we her. We are here in her house now, at 54 Washington Mews, and I have here a quarter of the house, quite isolated, so that if I do no work it is my own fault.

Lots of love to all in your house.

Sherwood A.

TS. NL

TO Mary Emmett

[3 November 1938], Niagara Falls, N.Y.

Mary

I know now that I shall probably never make much money. I missed my chance. I had the one successful book, *Dark Laughter*, that built my house and, had I been wise, should have pushed success. It is the way it is done. I should have played literary politics, having written a book that sold, I should have written another in the same tone, should have quit experimenting.

I didn't. I couldn't. Because I couldn't I missed the great opportunity. It is too late now. I have gone too far on another road, can only try and keep trying to find something better, more honest, more real. I can't now do the glamorous thing they want. As far as all of that is concerned I guess I'm sunk.

To tell the truth though I am quite cheerful about it at that.

You'd better practice stacking the cards while we are gone. Remember you are six behind.

TS. NL

TO Mary Emmett

Thursday [3 November 1938, Niagara Falls, N.Y.]

Dear Mary

I hated leaving you there alone. I hope you got someone to stay. I am afraid that, being alone, you may get back into the glooms. Having had them so hard I hate to think of you in them.

I drove clear up, getting here at six thirty and as I had not slept the night before, dropped right into bed. I hardly heard E. come in and did not hear her leave in the morning.

The place here, just now, is as I imagine one of the southern places is in the summer, a resort place in the dead season, the hotel dining room as empty as a church on a week day, nothing in but two waitresses, both with bow legs, the American and English flags crossed on the wall at the end of the room and me, breakfasting in solemn splendor. The bow-legged waitress took me for a traveling salesman and an Irishman. It was because of the Irish homespun. I think the hotel must be quite old as there is a picture of Lincoln outside the door of this room and a placard under it saying he and wife stopped here in 1857. I had the bell boy bring me a table to write on . . . a folding card table is just the right height for a typewriter but this one he brought had legs as long as Tom Wolfe's. Then he brought another and it was broken. I guess they had the same furniture when Lincoln was here.

However the drive up was wonderful and the weather here is beautiful. The window of the room looks out on the roaring rapids below the falls. I kept wishing you were along on the way up.

I had written you a letter about *The Left Bank*[1] but forgot to give it to you. I'll enclose it. I don't know whether or not it says just what I meant. I wrote another about your helping me, decided not to give it to you and then got a jolt.

I had got saved up about $900 and thought first I would live that up but, on the evening before I left, I got a letter from Cornelia, who is, as you know, the mother of the children. It concerned Mimi.

As you know, Mary, after Burt gave me the start on the papers down there and after I had got them about clear of debt, I made them over to the three children, Bob buying them and agreeing to pay John and Mimi five thousand each. I did it because I felt I should give them a start in life and because it was a tough time for kids.

But I did think it freed me and, as a matter of fact, it turned out fine for both John and Bob. Mimi had married a man named Russell Spear, a New Englander, and they took M.'s money, or a part of it, and made the first payment on the paper in North Carolina.[2] However before this, Russell being out of work, they had lived up about two thousand so they had to go in debt some when they bought the paper. There is nine hundred, the last payment, due at the end of November and Russell has been ill for nearly a year. They hadn't any money and stood to lose the paper so Cornelia wrote she would pay half of the nine hundred if I would pay the rest.

I felt I had to do it and have sent it, that is to say half of the sum. When Cornelia divorced me, because she thought I was a little crazy, trying to write etc., she was square, never asked any money from me. She has worked hard as a school teacher ever since. The money must mean a lot to her. I couldn't do less than she did. She thinks that, with the debt cleared and Mimi running the paper, they can get along and at least make a living.

So there is that tale of woe, of which you, poor Mary, hear so many and I guess I have to say I must go on taking your help. The only reason I don't like it is that it seems sometimes that everyone is after you for something. I hate to be one of the pack barking at your heels.

E. can leave here on next Wednesday morning. There isn't much exciting here but why don't you come up early next week, have a day or two here and drive down with us. Do it, Mary. Let me know. Address Cataract Hotel, Niagara Falls, N.Y.

S.A.

TS. NL

1. That is, the letter of 31 Oct.
2. The Spears had bought *The Messenger* in Madison, N.C.

TO Hedgerow Theatre

[3 January 1939, Marion]

Dear Hedgerowers

Eleanor and I went down into North Carolina over the New Year's and when we got back here E.'s father said that someone had called. He said it was at four A.M. from a theatre so I knew there must have been a real party at Hedgerow and wished I had been there. Eleanor had some sort of meeting, with industrial girls, at Greensboro, N.C., so I went over and spent an evening and night with Paul Green.[1]

We are both leaving here in the morning, E. to return to New York by train and I to go out to a place called Olivet College, in Michigan, to spend the month of January out there. Just why they want me or what they want me to do I don't know.[2] It is to be a decoration I guess. I have to do it because it is so long since I have earned any money that I am growing ashamed. I wish it were Swarthmore instead of this Michigan place.

More and more, as I think of Hedgerow, it comes to mean more and more to me and often I wonder if it is not about the nearest thing we have in America to a healthy place to live and work. I presume, however, that a man has to be out in the world a long time and see a lot of other ways before he can fully realize how near it comes.

To be able to work and live with others . . . what else is there? Almost every place you go, with high hopes, disillusions you so completely.

It has been a very fine thing, in my own life, that you have, in a way, included me as you have. It makes me at times a bit afraid. "Don't go there too often," I tell myself, the fear in me being that you may possibly get onto me and that I may lose something of the fine welcome you have always given me.

A grand good year to you all.

With my sincere love
Sherwood A.

TS. Boston

1. Playwright living in Chapel Hill, N.C.
2. Anderson's position at Olivet was Resident Lecturer in Creative Literature.

TO Charles H. Funk
7 January 1939, [Battle Creek, Mich.]

Dear Andy . . .

I have had a quite adventurous trip. I went to Parkersburg, W. Va., where I met a man[1] who wanted me to run a newspaper in a town called Front Royal, Va. He had written me a letter. There is to be a big rayon plant established in the town and it will suddenly grow from some three thousand to ten or fifteen thousand. The man to whom I talked is a C.I.O. man. They have a contract with the company. They want however a country newspaper that will be, on the whole, sympathetic to labor. You have often said you want to change your profession. These people will put up the money to start the paper. Do you want the job? I think I might get it for you. I have written Bob about this. Talk to him if interested. However keep the project confidential. I doubt you will want it.[2]

I went to see a woman[3] who is doing her college thesis on me. She is quite beautiful and I had made up my mind I would try having a flirtation with her but when I saw her didn't. I found that she thought of me as a great man, above such foolishness . . . a great mistake on her part, but a real handicap to my own evil purposes. I let it ride. To have someone think you are a great man may be as valuable as to be one . . . what?

I went to Springfield, Ohio. I went there to college for a year to a small college that later conferred on me a doctor's degree. However I didn't go there. When I was there I worked to pay my way in a big boarding house. There I met a woman school teacher[4] who became my friend. We used to walk about together. She was older than I was but, because we were much together, there were whispers of scandals about us . . . all unfounded. She was a great woman to me and the one who first introduced me to fine literature. I had heard she was dying of cancer and went there to see her, finding that what I had heard was true. It was a shaking experience. She is a big bodied German woman of strong character but has got a kind of wistful cheerfulness that is very moving. It must be very strange to have inevitable death right at your shoulder every day. I wonder how well we would stand up to it.

I went to the town where I spent my boyhood and there spent an evening with my best boyhood friend.[5] He belongs to a family that has run a grocery store in the same building in the town for 110 years and now he runs it. I like him as well as I did when we were boys.

Now I am here and going up to the college town. Olivet, at Olivet, Michigan. Write me there.

S.A.

TS. NL

1. Kenneth Douty, representative for the Textile Workers Organizing Committee of the CIO.
2. Funk replied that he assumed Anderson was joking about the offer.
3. Mary Helen Dinsmoor, who completed her thesis, "An Inquiry into the Life of Sherwood Anderson as Reflected in His Literary Works," at Ohio University in 1939.
4. Trillena White. She died on 8 May 1941.
5. Herman Hurd.

TO Charles H. Funk

Tuesday [31] January 1939, [Yellow Springs, Ohio]

Dear Andy . . .

Here I am, as you see, still being a college professor.[1] I was three weeks at the Michigan college and am to spend three days here. At the Michigan place I delivered four long talks but only have to do one here. Most of the work consists of talks with students, giving them bits of wisdom. In reality what I am doing is learning a damn sight more from them than anything they can learn from me. They are pretty swell kids, a good deal more disillusioned than we were as kids. For one thing they have been pretty disillusioned about all the *LAND OF OPPORTUNITY* thing . . . *WORK HARD AND YOU ARE BOUND TO SUCCEED* etc. etc. They are a bit more hard boiled, wised up than we ever were. You see I am putting you in my generation. It is because of your grey hair.

Anyway Andy, sitting and talking with some of these kids and, at the same time, thinking of the terrible fits of the blues into which we both occasionally fall, I wonder if they aren't getting a better start. Anyway they don't seem to indulge quite so much in impossible dreams of some kind of good life, always just around the corner and always in some way missed.

I'll be through here on Wednesday evening and am to meet Eleanor in Philadelphia on Friday and wish you were here to drive with me. I have been wondering how you have been cutting it and whether or not you have escaped some of the worst fits. Write me at 54 Washington Mews, New York.

My best to the good wife.

S.A.

TS. NL

1. Anderson was at Antioch College following his stay at Olivet.

TO ————[1]

Sunday [9 April 1939], Marion

I think that when I got your first letter I had rather a notion of what might be coming. I don't know why and, now that I have read it, I don't know what to say. It isn't that I had any impression from the time I saw you. It must have been something in your first letter or perhaps just the feeling that what you are up against is about the toughest problem an individual in our society has to face.

You frighten me a little when you speak of the drinking and of promiscuity. I have had some friends in the past who have gone down that road and it has ended in a kind of degradation that is terrible. We have recently had such a case here, in this town. But you know all about that. I don't have to tell you.

Naturally I think of your father. Would it not be infinitely better if he knew. Couldn't you bring yourself to talk it over with him. Is there any friend there who might do it for you. Surely, if I lived there I would, if you wished, try to make him understand. It seems to me that might clear up a good deal.

What about the psychoanalysts—do they, can they help?

In a few cases I have known fellows who in trying to escape the horrible misunderstanding that is the constant danger have married women but it has been ghastly unfair to the women and hasn't helped.

There is one thing, ——— , I think you should know. You go through quite horrible fits of depression, even desperation. I think you should know that this is not all due to the so-called perversion.

(I presume it is perversion. It does of course strike at the source of life. That is the reason, no doubt, that what we call the Normal man reacts to it in such an ugly way.)

To get back to the point. It happens that, for some peculiar reason, due I presume to something in my work, there is a constant flow of letters to me. They come from both young men and women and just now they all seem to be passing through these terrible times of depression. There is a curious feeling of impotence abroad and sometimes I am a little amused that each when he writes seems to think he [is] the one and the greatest sufferer. I know also many men who are presumably successful, in the arts writers say like Faulkner, Wolfe, Dreiser, etc., and all of these go through these same black times.

I have myself just come out of one and last week, a man I know, a very successful lawyer, told me that during the last winter he one night went out of his house naked and stood for a long time so in his back yard in the darkness and in a snow storm, not wanting to suicide but hoping he would get pneumonia and die.

I tell you these things, ———, only to suggest to you that you are not really so separated from other men as you must often think.

God save me from preaching but really I know of no way out for you but to find some work that may absorb you. Many people do lead terribly lonely lives. There is a note in your letter that tells me there is love in you. Love can be poured out into work too. God knows how to find the work. That is your problem all right.

This you may be sure of, that whatever you tell me will be down the well. I do think that probably you should get out of the small town. Certainly you should work at something, even if it bores you, while you are seeking.

Lord God, what wouldn't I give for the golden key I could pass on to you.

I wonder. Do you think it possible you might get some relief by trying to put down the story of your experience, when realization first came, etc., the whole thing, to keep you occupied, something to keep your mind busy. I don't know.

Sincerely
Sherwood Anderson

I am sorry I am so inadequate.

TS. NL

1. The name of the homosexual correspondent was deleted from the letter by the Newberry Library at the request of the donor.

TO Henry Van Meier[1]

Friday [21 April 1939, Marion]

Dear Henry . . .

I guess that if the repetition of the same story, sometimes twenty or thirty times, drives you nuts, as it does me, Mary E. would get your goat. She is so damned decent in many ways and so essentially kind but she will repeat and repeat. It may have made my flu worse.

Anyway, Henry, you are constantly occupied. The writer has these long dead times. I guess, at such times, he's a good deal like a woman going about carrying a child. There isn't any damned way for the child to come before its time, or at least not much before. Something must be pitched just right in a man to enable him to write at all effectively and the times don't always come when he wants them to and he goes half crazy. At such times the life of a busy doctor seems pretty swell to him.

However the thing you speak of must be pretty universal. Sometimes, Henry, in spite of your backhand slaps at the horse and buggy age, I think the whole mechanical age has ended in guns and little else. It's certainly a time of pretty gloomy outlook for the young. My mails are full of it these days.

Last week and the week before I had a job. I was chauffeur for E. one week in North Carolina and the next in Tennessee. She went off alone this week to Nashville but will be home this P.M. We start to drive back to N.Y. on Sunday.

You shouldn't have sent the books, Henry, but, now that you have, I'll take them with me and send them back from New York. Your letter gave me pretty much what I wanted to know.

Mother is pretty well, and busy as usual, people tramping in and out of the house here. If a man could write the story of this house it would be something.

Lots of love to Katharine and many thanks for the letter and books.

Sherwood

TS. PC

1. Physician and husband of Eleanor Anderson's sister, Katharine.

TO E.E. Cummings

[3 May 1939, New York]

Dear Cummings

I went to the shindig last night[1] because I thought you might be there. I should have known better. Ford looked better. I think he must have put on a corset. His pants were buttoned and also his vest.

Williams said that your driving impulse was economic. I asked him what the hell he meant and he began to try to bite his own nose. It was a ghastly party really. Jesus Christ, we writers are a mess. We have no morals. The implication seemed to be that you loved beautiful women. "What a strange man," I thought. I don't think it was exactly said . . . in spite of Besssie Breuer's[2] report to your wife later . . . but the idea seemed to be that you only got beautiful women by buying them in the market and that therefore everything was economic. Hell, I hope I got it all wrong. I was annoyed and sore and a little drunk. The wine wasn't much good but I drank my own and everyone else's I could reach. A man has to have some comfort. There was a beautiful woman sitting next to me I'd never seen before and I began trying to annoy and, if possible, insult her to relieve my feelings.

Your wife will tell you that we came, the Breuer and me, to try to find you afterwards. What I had in mind was to fix it up that you two come down to us this summer, anyway for a week or ten days. In our minds we have rather been building our idea of a decent summer around you two and that Galantière couple we like so much.

Your wife said you were going away, a bit tired and maybe sore at the world, but I hope you will be back before the end of the month. We'll be here at least that long. Let's fix up this summer thing.

Sherwood Anderson

TS. Harvard

1. The occasion was a dinner in honor of Cummings given by the Friends of William Carlos Williams, a literary group formed by Ford Madox Ford.

2. Writer of short stories, novels, and drama.

TO Roger Sergel

Saturday [13 May 1939, New York]

Dear Roger . . .

New York is all right until they find you out. It is like Washington. I was told when I stopped there on my way up here that there are seven hundred dinner parties in Washington every night. Here it's cocktail parties. Eleanor and Mary had one the other night and I'm not over it yet. It looked like a hundred people and some of them stayed right through a pickup dinner and until one A.M. Great God.

I went up to Wells College . . . a mistake . . . I'd promised an artist friend[1] I'd come and speak. I didn't prepare. I was rotten.

There's a little book, called *Sunday Is the Day You Rest*, by John Terrell, I think is fine. A woman named Katherine Anne Porter has written some good stories, a book called *Pale Horse, Pale Rider*.

Too many people get me down. It may be because I want to know too much about too many people. If you lived here and went about much you'd have to get so you could take them casually.

I'm temporarily off all thoughts of international matters. My mind has quit functioning in that field if it ever did. I'm trying again . . . a man has to begin over and over . . . to try to think and feel only in a very limited field, the house, the street, the man at the corner drug store.

Lots of love to all the Sergels.

Sherwood Anderson

TS. NL

1. J.J. Lankes.

TO Laura Copenhaver

Friday [4? August 1939, Ripshin Farm]

Dear Mother . . .

I am sorry that I do not see you every day during your illness and keep hoping it will not last. I think of you all the time.

Just now I seem to be writing well. I think, Mother, that the determination not to work on a novel but to devote myself to short stories has given me a new rush of what people are fond of calling inspiration.

And also Eleanor has been very very lovely this summer. She seems to grow more and more lovely to me.

It may be that this hunch to go to the short story now is also a part of the times and the situation into which life everywhere seems to have got. I find myself dissatisfied not only with my own attempts at the novel but also with the attempts of others.

It seems to me best therefore to keep on these shorter things, crowd into them all of the life I can. At any rate I am just now very happy with my work.

You must get well soon. We all love you very much.

S.A.

TS. NL

TO Carl Van Vechten[1]

6 September 1939, Ripshin Farm

Dear Carl:

The new photograph came and Mrs. Anderson is full of gratitude and admiration. You know how it is, Carl: when a man has reached a certain age he loves to think of himself as a boyish figure running lightly over hills.

Photos are more realistic.

If I could only look at them without thinking of self.

I am sure they are fine but you will know how to forgive me that I want still to be a beautiful youth. Many thanks for your fine generosity.

Sincerely
Sherwood Anderson

TS. NL (cc)

1. Music critic, novelist, and photographer.

TO David Virgrin

5 October 1939, Marion

Dear David Virgrin:

Your letter[1] came to me some time ago and I read it with genuine interest and I presume, if you have the feeling that you can see through what is going on now in the big world, where the masses of men move, or are moved—and can understand something of what it is all about, if you or anyone can find a way to move and direct men without losing your sense of individuals and becoming all self, then hurrah to you.

Just the same I am puzzled.

"Why do you have to leave Elkhart?" I ask myself. "Why go to New York? There is such a noise of words there." However I presume you have to make your life by your own pattern.

I hadn't any idea that what I had to say in that little piece would change anyone but just the same if the large doesn't grow out of the small it will never really be large.

I used to go to Elkhart years ago, walk in the streets there at night. At that time I wasn't doing what I wanted to do and was very unhappy. I walked about in Elkhart in dark streets past dark houses. I was very unhappy as I dare say you often are.

Sincerely yours
Sherwood Anderson

TS. NL (cc)

1. While this letter, from Elkhart, Ind., has apparently not survived, Anderson seems to have used the gist of it and his reply in an article which he sent off on 6 Oct. to *This Week*, where it appeared as "From Little Things," 11 Feb. 1940, p. 2. It was later reprinted as the first section of *Home Town*.

Sherwood Anderson by Carl Van Vechten

COURTESY OF ELEANOR ANDERSON

TO Roger Sergel

Tuesday [17 October 1939, New York]

Dear Roger . . .

What a long time since I have heard from you. We closed the house nearly a month ago. Eleanor came on here and I went for a week to the Grand Circuit trotting meeting at Lexington, Ky. Had an assignment to write it up for a magazine[1] and took it because I so love the trotters. It was a grand spree.

We will be leaving here day after tomorrow. In connection with her work Eleanor has to go to the Pacific Coast and I am going along as chauffeur. We are going to Denver, San Francisco, Fresno, Los Angeles, Tucson, San Antonio and Houston and expect to get home about Christmas.

It should be a grand trip.

Are you going off on any expedition this winter?

I keep working on short things, as it seems impossible now, the state of the world being the state of the world, to stay on any long thing but have been doing rather well with the short things. Got $1500.00 for one and $800.00 for another recently. That will carry me quite a while.

I keep hoping that Hitler has put his foot in it, in the Russian matter. It looks a bit as though he might have. But isn't it a war. The good part of the whole mess being that there seems a real passion here to stay out. You get it in the theatre and everywhere, also the feeling that Franklin D. is again gaining in favor. That's a lucky guy. Perhaps, after all, it's better to be lucky than smart. I've long suspected it.

Write me at Marion. Any letter sent there will forwarded.

Love to all in the house.

Sherwood

TS. NL

1. "Here They Come," *Esquire* 13 (Mar. 1940): 80–81.

TO Lewis and Nancy Galantière

Monday 20 [November 1939], Fresno, California

Dear Lewis and Nancy

We got Nancy's letter here but our chances of getting to her mother's[1] seem rather thin. The trouble seems to be with Eleanor's appointments . . . she being, alas, a creature of affairs, every day occupied with interviews etc., meeting, God knows what, while I, bird-like, flit from limb to limb of this California tree. As you see, if you know your California, we had to come down here, from San Francisco, in the valley east of the coast range to get to this place. It seems your mother is on the other road, by the sea.

Well, it's our loss if we don't make it.

The trip has been, for me, quite marvelous, the great long stretches of desert country, the strangeness, the high mountains to be driven over, deserted mining towns, sunshine, people. I like these Californians, particularly the San Francisco ones, the hills of that town, the good restaurants, the tall beautiful women (Nancy a true Californian all right), a kind of aliveness in the people in the streets. They don't seem quite so tired and that's good.

I went out for a day with John Steinbeck, the *Grapes of Wrath* man, although I haven't read the book.[2] He heard I was in S.F. and insisted. He lives on a ranch in the high hills, about thirty miles out of S.F., a big man, giving rather the impression of a truck driver on his day off. Haven't quite figured him out yet.

It seems I've become a kind of Papa. "Reading you is what started me writing," etc. etc., so I sit like a wise owl.

I'm sure of this, having gone to take in several of these labor camps, that what goes on in them is in no way different from what is going on all over the country and am convinced also that one of the reasons for the great popularity of the book is that it localizes a situation that is universal. It seems we have got back about the same standard of production we had in '29 and have a million and a half more men out of work. That looks like a more or less permanent situation, not just a California one.

I've been doing some short stories, having a pretty good time at that.

Have been wondering how much all of this rapidly changing thing in Europe will disturb Lewis in his work. Damn, I hope he will get at something that will make things a bit clearer to all of us. I keep quoting him, often, I'm afraid, passing off his shrewd sayings as my own, thinking him, as I do, about the brainiest man I know.

Much love to you both, from both of us. Lordy we do value your friendship.

Sherwood

TS. Columbia

1. At Santa Barbara.
2. Anderson visited Steinbeck near Los Gatos, Cal., on 14 Nov.

TO Roger Sergel

Wednesday [3 January 1940, Marion]

Dear Roger . . .

We have been having a bust time. For one thing I have suddenly got to writing again at a great rate and that has kept me busy to the point of exhaustion every day.

Then deep snow and extraordinarily cold weather for us. It has all been very Christmasy.

And now, in a day or two, we will be off to New York, stopping a few days at Washington on the way. We will not be at Mary's but at Hotel Royalton, 44 West 44th Street, as I find it too disturbing to live in a house belonging to another.

And then, besides, I adore hotel life. There is a grand freedom to it. I find that, when a man works intensely, as I always must to work at all, he is likely to be irritable, and even nasty, until he recovers. You simply pick up the phone in your room and tell the girl at the switch board that you are out, for 2, 3, 4 hours as you choose. Then you read, walk up and down, take a drink, do whatever you can to try to make yourself human again.

A happy new year to all the Sergels.

But what the hell? There is no happiness. Good health then.

Sherwood

TS. NL

TO August Derleth[1]

4 January 1940, [Marion]

Dear August Derleth

Answering your letter of the 29 December I can say that, when it came, two points of view in the criticism of my work completely disconcerted me. I don't believe I took the matter as very personal. It seemed to me rather that this kind of criticism was a spreading of dirt over the people of whom I wrote.

The people did not seem hopeless to me. They were just such people as I saw about me everywhere. To be sure, Derleth, as you well know, most people are defeated. That's life, isn't it. What a splendid dream back of the whole idea of the modern industrial development of life, for example, and now it seems at times that it is only ending in greater and greater efficiency in the art of killing.

Indeed you are quite right. I think with all of us now the effort is, as you say, to see life a bit more completely. It is the one way that will create understanding, isn't it? Do you remember the story of the philosopher who seeing a man passing in the street said, "I hate that man." "Why," someone asked. "Because I do not know him."

Yes it is all foolishness.

There was that point of view and the other that we were dirty-minded because we realized the terrific effect of the sex urge on people. There was, for a long time, a lot of that, so much in fact that for a long time I was puzzled. It is hard now to believe that some of these earlier tales of people should have aroused such talk. It was so prevalent for a time that they have had me convinced that I was guilty, that there must be something wrong with me.

But the satisfactory thing to a man now is the thought that perhaps the very boldness in looking at life brought about a chance, enabling other men to go ahead. The whole point of view of the Mrs. Herrons seems pretty silly, doesn't it? If they think life is so giddy let them take a look at Europe now.

Sincerely
Sherwood Anderson

TS. SHSW

1. Wisconsin educator and author, who had asked Anderson for his reaction to being termed "disillusioned and pessimistic" by Ima H. Herron in *The Small Town in American Literature* (Durham, N.C.: Duke Univ. Press, 1939), 353.

TO August Derleth

17 January 1940, New York

Dear August:

It is hard for me to tell you how right I think you are in everything you say,[1] but I wonder if they will listen to you.

The truth is, Derleth, that I am not terribly concerned. If a man is to work and to live now, with the state the world is in, it seems to me that he has to do it pretty much under the guns.

A little opening here and there. A man says his say—lays stones along a path—makes a mark upon a wall.

"This way" he said, "go along this way."

"Into what?" "Into the sunlight." A man always hopes that.

You see, Derleth, a woman like that one down at Duke University[2]—well the chances are a hundred to one that no man ever took her for a walk on a summer night, kissed and hugged her under a tree or under a wall.

We all get so serious. We want to be so big. Maybe it is because of the terrible bigness of the country, modern inventions, the radio, and so forth. "Here I am speaking to these thousands."

If we could only learn to be very small, walking quietly and not asking much.

For example, a man like me. I will have no quarrel with what they have done to me. Let them bandage their own sores.

Many fine men and women have been my friends. I have always thought of myself as one of the lucky ones. I have always had health, good digestion, a liking for people, for fields, for food. It is true that the critics are pretty lousy. Most of them have too much to do. They have to read too many books, see too many pictures, go too often to the theater or to the movies. They haven't time to go slow, look around. Wait, look, and listen.

And then too, there is this passion for success abroad. I think that all the impulses that so confuse us now, like the passion for success, power, and so forth, are really diseases that eat away people's lives but they do not know it.

I would like to suggest, Derleth, that you tell your kids in your class to try to be small, take it easy, to enjoy their life, to taste what they eat, to listen to what they hear. Let them try to make all their senses more alive. Tell them never mind whether or not they are successful in life. Tell them to skate on the ice, roll in the snow, love, and live.

So, you see, Derleth, I am not quarreling with my own critics, at Duke University, or anywhere else. People are people.

On the whole I have been treated well enough. There are always you and others like you.

And then too, there has always been a kind of respect paid to me even by those who have panned my best efforts. I have been able to eat, to sleep in fairly warm beds, to get along. It is enough.

You see, I keep thinking of the thousands who haven't had my own rare privilege of doing pretty much what I have wanted to do, the point being that I don't want you to think of me as kicking at the pricks.

Go after them, Derleth, give them hell, but do remember what they are up against. Don't blame them too much. We have all been fed the poison.

Sincerely,
Sherwood Anderson

Student stenographer.

TS. SHSW

1. Derleth had complained of the over-influence of bad criticism.

2. Herron's book was published by the Duke University Press; she was an English professor at Southern Methodist University.

TO Charles H. Funk

Saturday [20 January 1940], New York

Dear Andy . . .

Watch your step. I had a friend out in Chicago.[1] He used to tell me many fine stories that I immediately put down and sold. I fairly lived on the guy for a long time then my conscience got to hurting me. "Look here," I said, "why don't you write these stories yourself?" He had been a fairly prosperous man, a highly paid advertising writer but set about being a writer. It is a tragic tale. He has been at it ever since. I dare say that, at this moment, he is somewhere in a cold garret, slowly starving to death. Watch your step.

In this country there must be innumerable young men I educated. They were given my stories to read when in college. Now they are here, in New York. They have got jobs on magazines. What counts is a virtuous youth. Now they all want to throw money at me. "You made me what I am today. I hope you're satisfied," they sing.

I tell you this because I am as likely as not to get a swell story out of that last letter you wrote me.[2] Did you keep a copy of the letter? If you have a copy and being a lawyer you can probably some day sue me for plagiarism. Sometimes I think I have stolen everything I ever did from someone. Not in vain have I cultivated your friendship all of these years.

However read over again the first paragraph of this letter.

S.A.

TS. NL

1. George Daugherty, an advertising writer at Critchfield and Company, whom Anderson called a "feeder" to him of story material. See *Memoirs*, 376–81.

2. Funk had written Anderson a long letter about his boyhood memories of life in the village of Wheel, near Shelbyville, Tenn.

TO August Derleth

30 January 1940, New York

Dear August Derleth:

I hardly know how to answer your letter of January 22. You suggest that my recent letter to you has stirred up thoughts in you and certainly your letter does this to me.

I do think that some of us should at least try to keep the faith. Hardly any of us succeed fully. As you know the real sin against the Holy Ghost is the artist's, man or woman, lies in betraying the imagination of others.

We have for example a Huxley writing a book making very clever fun of Hollywood life,[1] while at the same time he is employed out there at a salary of $1500 a week doing the same thing for which he is condemning others. This goes on all the time and until we can accept the responsibilities of our craft, we are the ones who should be blamed.

I think you are quite right in your suggestion that it is this sort of corruption of the imagination of others that lays the foundations for Fascism and Communism.

I sincerely appreciate your letter.

Sincerely,
Sherwood Anderson

TS. SHSW

1. Aldous Huxley published *After Many a Summer Dies the Swan* in 1939.

TO Laura Copenhaver

[31 January 1940, New York]

Dear Mother,

Signed two contracts yesterday for 2 small books—the book—half pictures, of present day life in small towns[1]—about 20,000 words.

The story of a mountain childhood[2]—about 30,000. This is the one I hope John can make the drawings for.

I got a total of $1150.00 advance on the two books. I think they will be quite simple to do. They should be fun.

Have really turned out a lot of work here and am sure now that the determination not to go back to Mary's was the right one. It is so peaceful and quiet here.[3] After all, Mother, it may well be that we humans, often with the best intentions in the world, do manage sometimes to do terrible things to each other.

I lunched with Chambrun.[4] He tells me that, among the editors now, there is a great desire for short editorial essays about life.

I suspect it is the old desire you have, to find the answer, put it in a phrase, a paragraph, an editorial.

I have tried my hand at two or three.

I have got a secretary, a Miss [Jean] Black—a student but very good. There was your question, when E. got her, about her coming here to work, in this hotel room. She is a tall long-legged girl. Some of the things I am doing now are rather intimate revelations of men and women. I said to her—"How about this. Some of the things I will be wanting to dictate are pretty intimate. You may be shocked."

She grinned. "I'm from Iowa," she said. She seemed to think that would explain.

"I know you are a realistic writer. I have read your stories. You do not need to be afraid of shocking me."

These modern kids are grand. It saves me a lot if I can just scribble, as I am doing here, then dictate, editing as I dictate.

Eleanor seems in fine form but, just now, we are going out too much, seeing too many people. It seems unavoidable.

Love to R.[5]
S.A.

MS. NL

1. *Home Town*, published in Oct. 1940 by Alliance Book Corporation.
2. Anderson did not carry out this project. The contract was with Harcourt, Brace.
3. The Andersons were staying at the Hotel Royalton.
4. Jacques Chambrun, Anderson's literary agent.
5. Randolph Copenhaver, visiting on leave from the air force.

TO Jacques Chambrun

13 February 1940, New York

Dear Chambrun:

After my conversation with you this morning on the telephone I thought it might be well to give you a brief outline of one of the editorials about which you spoke.

One of the editorials I had in mind and which I have written but about which I am not yet entirely satisfied, wanting to simplify it and make it clearer, is on the use of big words and how the use of words like "The Masses," "The Proletariat," "The Capitalist," and so forth and so forth, affects the minds of people who get into the habit of using such words.

The idea that I want to develop is that when people begin using such words they begin to think in such terms and lose all sense of the infinite variety of life.

Life itself, with all its coloring, strangeness, gets lost in a haze of words. In my mind it is one of the causes of human loneliness.

This is a brief outline of what I have in mind but it may be sufficient for you to suggest the idea to the editor of *This Week*.[1] I think the idea might appeal to him and to their readers and I am quite sure the editor will see the possibility in the development of this theme.

Sincerely
Sherwood Anderson

Dictated but not signed.

TS. NL (cc)

1. Anderson's essay, "Oh, the Big Words!" was published in *This Week*, 31 Mar. 1940, p. 2.

TO Roy E. Stryker[1]

28 March 1940, New York

Dear Roy Stryker:

As you may know I am at work on the American small town book for the Alliance people. When I was in Washington about a month ago I tried to get in touch with you but you were out of town. I had however a nice visit with Mr. Rosskam[2] and met Miss Post.[3] I was told that Miss Post was going up into New England and I was glad to hear that as we would like to get some shots of winter scenes for the book.

I thought also that you might be interested in having Miss Post get some shots about a county seat town down in my country.[4] We could certainly use some of these. I hope it will be possible to get some good shots in a small town courthouse with a typical country jury and a lawyer pleading with them. Also some shots of a country justice of the peace. I wrote a note to Mr. Rosskam giving the date of the April term of court and I think there is also another term of court in June, when I will be down there myself. However my son is running the local newspaper down there and if Miss Post or some other photographer goes, he will be glad to help her out. When I was at home recently I spoke to the trial justice and to several other people. My son has a photographer employed for the newspaper who will also be glad to be of assistance to your photographer. As regards a good shot of a jury I have written a circuit judge but haven't heard from him.

Before the coming of the movies, every town had its opera house where road companies used to come. There must be some of these in existence and I would like a shot of the front of one.

I want to bring out how the radio and the movies have changed life in the towns. It has pretty much broken up the little assembly of citizens that used to gather at the back of the drug store, the hardware store, the harness shop, or some other place. These would be country lawyers, doctors, and so forth discussing national politics. I would like such a shot.

In some of the towns the jail is a miserable place. All sorts of people jammed into a small space, the jail terribly unsanitary. We should be able to find and shoot such a jail, then we should find and shoot a more modern and sanitary jail.

I would like a scene in a small town bowling alley and if possible in a roller-skating rink.

A scene of a square dance.

A scene in a typical country doctor's office with patients waiting about, a shot in a country lawyer's office with perhaps a client consulting the lawyer and law books on the shelf behind him.

A couple getting a marriage license in a county clerk's office. I have spoken to the county clerk down at home and he thinks there will be no trouble about getting the above scene.

If possible I would like a birth scene, the mother in bed, a neighbor woman perhaps holding the new born babe, a country doctor and the father in the scene. I do not know whether we can get such a scene as this but the country doctors down there are friendly to me and it may be possible.

We should have a strike scene at the gate of a factory.

By all means we should have a picture of the old swimming hole, with kids diving and swimming.

We should have a picnic scene, a family picnicking at the edge of a small town perhaps beside a stream.

Recently in a good many of our states there are new, so-called state parks built with government aid, often with charming artificial lakes. There is a beauty down at Marion where I live.[5]

It would be nice to have a shot of several small town young men in an old Ford, without a top, with sentences scrawled all over it.

Nowadays there is quite a movement of theatrical people to small towns where summer theaters have been established. There is one at Abingdon near Marion.[6]

A shot of working men from farms unloading out of an old car at a factory gate in the early morning. I am making the above suggestions hoping that they will fit in with the work of your department. I think also that when your photographer is in that section of the country it would be possible to get some good shots of mountain people, their homes, and so forth, if you haven't already plenty of these.

Naturally I would like it very much if these shots could be taken when I am down there in June but I am not certain as to just when the Alliance people want to bring out the book.

With most sincere regards and thanking you very much for the assistance we are getting from your department.

Very truly yours,
Sherwood Anderson

TS. NL (cc)

1. Chief of the Historical Section, Division of Information of the Farm Security Administration, which supplied the photographs for *Home Town*.

2. Edwin Rosskam, editor of *Home Town* and other books in an Alliance Book Company series, *The Face of America*.

3. Marion Post, Farm Security photographer.

4. Although many of Post's photographs were included in *Home Town*, Anderson's suggestions in this letter were not acted upon.

5. Hungry Mother State Park.

6. The Barter Theatre.

TO Roger Sergel

Tuesday [2 July 1940], Ripshin Farm

Dear Roger—

We have just come back from a week at Eleanor's camp of industrial girls.[1] We have a guest this year, in the green house, across the creek. Augusto Centeno, a Spaniard, a Princeton professor, has come there to live with his wife for the summer months.

They are charming people. I was at Princeton in the fall to make an address and we became friends. He had translated one of my books into Spanish[2] but I had never met him.

I do hope you have heard from Chris & Hope.[3] How strange it seems that these boys, like my own, have now become men, married and setting out upon their own adventures, and in such a strange and rather terrifying world.

Even here, in these hills, we hear constantly the distant roar of airplanes, often above the clouds.

The bees are swarming. We are to become, not individuals, but simply a part of the swarm.

All hail the state, eh?

Sometimes it makes you a bit ill to think of how recklessly we have slung our seeds, to make this new life.

Well, we shall cling to the old. The old desire to be again young is gone. A man is simply glad that he has lived out most of his life, not in the new but in the old times.

Love,
S.A.

MS. NL

1. At Lake Toxaway, near Brevard, N.C.
2. *La Risa Negra,* a translation of *Dark Laughter,* published in Madrid in 1931.
3. Christopher Sergel and his wife.

TO Robert Sherwood[1]

21 November 1940, [New York]

Dear Robert Sherwood:

I am turning over to you some correspondence that came to me by mistake.

I certainly think it very nice the way you and Maxwell Anderson[2] continually work away to build up my reputation. People persistently refer to my authorship of *Abraham Lincoln*, and whenever I am thrown

Sherwood and Eleanor Anderson at Ripshin Farm
COURTESY OF ELEANOR ANDERSON

into the company of a good-looking blonde who thinks I am Maxwell Anderson, I tell her that I am writing a wonderful part into a play for her, and to come and see me. I do this to try to help Mr. Maxwell Anderson's pleasure in life.

Sincerely yours,
Sherwood Anderson

TS. NL (cc)

1. Dramatist, whose play *Abe Lincoln in Illinois* appeared in 1938.
2. Verse dramatist.

TO Roy E. Stryker
21 November 1940, [New York]

Dear Roy Stryker:

Is there any chance of your being in New York soon? I think I have a rather good idea for further use of the grand photographs your photographers are constantly taking. I want to talk it over with you.

What I have in mind—although please do not speak of it to any publisher or anyone connected with a publishing house until I see you—is a high-grade child book.[1]

As you know, Roy, in the average modern home the child has no way of knowing where the food he eats comes from, where the clothes he wears come from, how the very house in which he lives is made. Nowadays the child knows only that his mother goes to the store. Almost all the products of the farm come to the house in cans.

What I want to do is to make a book showing the child in simple, direct prose, and in pictures, the drama back of the production of almost everything that makes the child's life comfortable. I believe such a book could be made absorbingly interesting to a child, and at the same time tremendously educational.

I would like to talk this over with you before proposing it to a publisher, and therefore look forward eagerly to seeing you at the first opportunity.

I speak of your not saying anything about it to anyone else because I do not want someone else to jump in and steal the idea from me, as it is a job I would myself love to do.

Sincerely yours,
Sherwood Anderson

TS. NL

1. Anderson did not undertake this project.

TO William O. Player, Jr.
30 November 1940, New York

Dear Player:

You sure put me on the spot when you gave my address in the nice piece you wrote for the *Post*,[1] in fact you fairly dumped New York into my lap. They were in my room; they were at the door; they were in the hallway leading to the door. They had poems that they hoped I could help them get published; they had it in their heads that I was a rich man and wanted to interest me in inventions. They were playwrights just about to be produced by the Shuberts but for the moment broke and wanting $10.

However, I forgive you. The young boy who had a swell chance to get a job and needed 64 cents to get his hair cut and his suit pressed was worth all the bother. And then there was the delightful old workman, an engineer from somewhere over in New Jersey, who made a special trip over to New York to tell me a story that he thought I might be able to handle. It was a good story at that, and he didn't want a cent.

If the advertisers in the *Post* get such results from your newspaper, I don't see how you have any room for anything but advertising.

Sincerely,
Sherwood Anderson

TS. NL

1. "Sherwood Anderson Hopes—and Wonders," New York *Post*, 27 Nov. 1940, p. 15.

TO Charles H. Funk
Saturday [30 November 1940], New York

Dear Andy . . .

I have been a long time writing to you. I have been pretty busy, have been in one of my most sustained writing moods. You often laugh at the idea of me at work but I tell you, Andy, that it is work. There is a kind of concentration required, to get through a short story or the chapter of a book, that in a queer way takes it out of you.

And then there is something else. When I am in Marion I have few personal friends but here I have a good many. You go about with them, go to see them and they come to see you. People take something out of you. There are very few who have anything to give. You know how it is between us. Sometimes we get on each other's nerves. We poison each other. I guess any friendship is like that. Marriage is like that. A man is dissatisfied with himself (that is, I'm sure, at the bottom of it) and takes it out on someone else, a friend, a wife, if a woman a husband. It's the way we are made.

I do not really like New York. As a matter of fact, as an American writer, I have always been treated pretty well, better perhaps than I deserve, but just the same, in the world of writers, as in politics or business, there are all sorts of petty jealousies, meannesses. You make, say a casual remark, perhaps in fun, about someone, as though I should say, after some act of yours in which I didn't agree with you . . . "Oh, Andy's a damn fool."

Well we are friends. You know we wouldn't be friends if I thought you a damn fool but someone who heard the remark builds it up.

I dare say you have such experiences oftener than I do as you are habitually more violent in your remarks than I am.

I am just saying how people take it out of you sometimes, that's all. I have no particular thing in mind.

I have had pretty good success, selling things, getting what money I need, have even had two or three temptations to get more into the big money which I have turned down. It may be foolish but I have had, for a good many years, the conviction that, to do any decent work, a man had better avoid trying to become any kind of a public figure. You know how we are in America; we build someone up and then knock him down. It's better to live rather under the rose, be just a guy going along.

Well, enough of philosophy. I hear that the hunting hasn't been so good which is bad for you. I depend upon the hunting to wear off a part of that paunch you are getting.

I expect we will be coming to Marion at the end of next week, to stay until about January 5th. I think that, in the middle of January, we may go off to South America. A scheme of that kind is in the wind. I rather think I may get one of the magazines[1] to at least pay a part of the expenses of the trip. I think we may go to Chile. I have friends down there and am in negotiation with a publisher there.[2] Have been putting in about two hours a day on Spanish and have been having a teacher come in to teach me several times a week. Must say I am not very eloquent in it yet, wouldn't be much good before a Spanish jury if they should find me out down there.

Will be seeing you.

Sherwood A.

TS. NL

1. *Reader's Digest.*

2. Anderson refers to Carlos Davila and his wife, of Santiago, Chile. Davila was director of Editors Press Service in New York, which had put Anderson in touch with Chilean publisher Empresa Zig Zag.

TO Maxwell Perkins

30 November 1940, New York

Dear Max:

I am writing this letter both for you and as an answer to the fine letter I received from Mr. Charlie Scribner. As I told you the other day on the telephone I have been half ill, I think because this whole matter has upset me so much. It seems, Max, that changing publishers is a good deal like getting a divorce, and I have decided to change.

I think, Max, that if the three of us had had the talk we had the other day in our office two or three years ago, all would have been different. But as it is I have the feeling of having forced the issue, which leaves me with a curious feeling of self consciousness about it all.

I hope you will understand that this in no way changes my personal feelings about you. I think you are really a great editor. I do, perhaps, feel a little that you are happier with younger writers, so many of whom need and profit by [that] which you can give them so abundantly.

Anyway, after going through a little kind of private hell of my own, I have decided to go to Harcourt Brace.

Although this may sound to you like taking the whole matter too seriously, I dare say it is more important to me than to the house of Scribner.

Please, Max, let us continue the friendship we have begun and that means a lot to me.

Sincerely yours,
Sherwood Anderson

TS. Princeton

TO Ilse Dusoir[1]

14 December 1940, [New York]

Dear Ilse Dusoir

I am sorry for two things—that my typewriter is being repaired, forcing you to try to read my script—that your letter just caught up to me.

I am delighted that you are making this study of the *Seven Arts* but am sure that Mr. Waldo Frank, Mr. James Oppenheim or Mr. Van Wyck Brooks could help you more than I can. I was never an editor, only a contributor and a friend of the editors.

I shall try to answer your questions as you ask them.

I first learned of the existence of *Seven Arts* through Miss Edna Kenton.[2] I was then living in Chicago and was invited one evening to Miss

Kenton's sister's house. There was a discussion of the possibilities of the magazine, its purposes etc. in a room of the house but I was not invited to take part in it. I however understood that Miss Kenton had come to Chicago to interest middlewestern writers. I was not invited into the conference because, no doubt, Miss Kenton did not know I was writing.

2. A short time later, however, I heard from Mr. Waldo Frank. I believe he wrote of my work in the first issue.[3] My employment took me on a visit to New York and I met him.

3. At the time I believe I had published a few things in the *Little Review*—started in Chicago by Margaret Anderson—not a relative—and in the old *Masses*. Floyd Dell had gone from Chicago to New York to be one of the *Masses* editors. The piece about my work in the first number of *Seven Arts* was one of the very first appreciations of what I was trying to do.

4. I never did feel any great restraint on my expressing myself although of course the popular magazines did not print my stories. I didn't expect them to. Yes, the *Seven Arts* was a great help.

5. I thought, when I began to see it, that it was doing a fine, bold, intelligent job.

6. I certainly think it was a very important instrument toward greater freedom of expression.

7. I became acquainted with the entire group. I respected them all, was fond of them all. It may be because he died so young and was such a brilliant man that I remember Randolph Bourne[4] as being to me, at the time, the most vivid figure.

8. I was deeply in accord with the magazine's anti-war policy.

9. Really I do not remember what they paid me for any stories of mine they published. I was simply glad to see them in print.

10. I have no way of knowing how the magazine was received by the general [public]. Perhaps it never reached the general public.

———

I think it was a time of general awakening. There was something growing that the World War pretty much killed. There was a turning toward actual life as we lived it here in the U.S.A. It seems to me that the *Seven Arts* was a roadway along which we could march. I still look back to the effort made and to the men who made it with most sincere respect.

Sherwood Anderson

MS. NYU

1. Graduate student and later English professor at New York University, who was then writing a thesis on the *Seven Arts*.

2. Chicago writer who had moved to New York.

3. "Emerging Greatness," *Seven Arts* 1 (Nov. 1916): 73–78.

4. An editor of *New Republic* and *Dial* and contributor to *Seven Arts*. Bourne died in 1918 at the age of thirty-two.

TO Juan Adolfo Vazquez[1]
15 December 1940, New York

Dear Juan Vazquez:

In writing you as I did about the feeling in the United States for South America, I have to confess that this may possibly not be a true expression of the political viewpoint of my own country, although I sincerely hope it is. This, however, I am pretty sure, is the way the common man in the street feels.

I do, however, feel, as I know you do, that it is too bad that the common man, in your own and other South American countries, and the common man in my own country do not know each other better and I sincerely believe that if this knowledge is to grow it will have to be through the efforts of the artists of the north and south.

My own trip in South America is not yet definitely decided upon, but I rather think that I will start for South America about the middle of January[2] and just now I am putting in two or three hours a day trying desperately to acquire at least a speaking knowledge of Spanish. The truth is that I am not a rich man and my going will partly depend on one of our magazines at least partially bearing the expenses of my trip, but I have great hopes that this will come about.

Because I have friends there I believe I shall first go via steamer through the Panama Canal and down the west coast, perhaps to Chile. I would really like to get out of one of the bigger cities and into a town of five or ten thousand and perhaps stay in such a town for some months. My own work has always been a reflection of the every day life of the every day man for the most part in the small towns of my own country, and this had led me to want very much to know something of the same kind of life in South America.

I do, however, promise myself that I will come overland to Argentina and I sincerely hope I may see you.

As suggested by your letter I will let the matter of the publication of my book by Mr. Losada[3] go until later. I have hopes that I may be able to talk personally about it when I am down there.

Sincerely yours,
Sherwood Anderson

TS. NL (cc)

1. A young writer, translator and teacher in Buenos Aires, who had written Anderson about the possibility of publishing his works in Argentina.
2. The departure was delayed until 28 Feb.
3. Gonzalo Losada, head of Editorial Losada, a Buenos Aires publisher.

TO Karl and Helen Anderson

Saturday [21 December 1940], Marion

Dear Karl & Helen.

Eleanor and I left New York suddenly on Wednesday. On that morning when the maid went up to take Mother Copenhaver's breakfast she found her dead in her bed.

It has been an intense and rather grand family life these people have had and they have been wonderfully gracious in taking me wholly into it. As for Mother Copenhaver—well you know, Karl, our own mother died when we were all so young—she has been certainly a second mother to me—that and a kind of sister too. The woman had a lot the spirit and the feeling of an artist and a wonderfully keen critical mind. It's a terrific blow.

I want particularly to see you, Karl, when I get back to New York. We'll write to you.

Sherwood

MS. NL

TO John Anderson

day before Christmas [24 December 1940], Marion

Dear John—

Your letter, about simple things—the tin cans etc.[1]—is here and it cheers me that you have taken hold again, after the depressed time.

I guess what a man has to learn is just to live the day—as far as possible no past, no future. Anyway that would be ideal. The other, to look too much forward or backwards, gives too horrible a feeling of futility.

All you say in the letter today sounds so right. It is especially so now, when everything outside the little, the near seems so futile.

It is pretty strange in the house here, with Mother gone, but the woman was so filled with life that she seems to have left the sense of her still alive and no sense of death at all.

Just a kind of queer disappointment that she doesn't suddenly walk through the door.

Love to all yours
S.A.

MS. NL (ph)

1. John Anderson had written of his recent interest in painting "simple objects like a tin can or a shell or a log of wood."

TO Herman Hurd[1]

7 January 1941, New York

Dear Herman:

I recently received from a Miss Helen Dinsmoor a copy of her thesis she had prepared for the purpose of taking her degree in some college. In the thesis she speaks of having visited Clyde and of interviews she had with you, Barley Mann,[2] and others. Among other stories she tells in her thesis is one concerning a librarian in the Clyde public library.

According to this story, there was an old-maid librarian there who burned up my books as fast as they were received, I dare say, thinking them too profane. I wonder if this story is true.

She also says in her thesis that later the Clyde library wrote and asked me for copies of all of my books to put on their library shelves and that I answered by writing a rather impertinent letter telling them that if they wanted my books they should buy them. I wonder, Herman, if this story is also true as I have entirely forgotten the incident.

I would like particularly to know because if the library there in my home town really wants my books I would be glad to arrange to have them presented to the Clyde library.

Do you mind investigating this matter for me and writing me about it at the above address? If they still want the books, find out which ones they have, so that I can check up and furnish the books they have not got.[3]

I hope you and all your family are well, and that you all have a happy and successful year in 1941.

From your old friend,
Sherwood Anderson

TS. NL (cc)

1. Close friend of Anderson's during their boyhood in Clyde, who later became a grocer there.

2. A Clyde barber, also a boyhood friend, who had joined the army with Anderson.

3. The library owned only four of Anderson's books, two of which needed replacement. Eleanor Anderson filled out the collection in the months following her husband's death on 8 Mar. 1941.

Index

SHERWOOD ANDERSON: SELECTED LETTERS

has been composed on the Mergenthaler Variable Input Phototypesetter in ten point Bembo with one point of line spacing. Bembo Italic was used as display. The book was designed by Frank O. Williams, typeset by Computer Composition, Inc., printed by McNaughton & Gunn Lithographers, and bound by John H. Dekker & Sons. The acid-free paper on which the book is printed is S. D. Warren's Olde Style Wove, designed for an effective life of at least three hundred years.

The University of Tennessee Press
Knoxville